# GREAT FOOD STARTS FRESH

SIMPLE, INNOVATIVE CUISINE FEATURING FRESH, SEASONAL INGREDIENTS

# GREAT FOOD STARTS FRESH

SIMPLE, INNOVATIVE CUISINE FEATURING FRESH, SEASONAL INGREDIENTS

## NATHAN LYON

Great Food Starts Fresh
Published by Nathan Lyon

Nathan Lyon
www.chefnathanlyon.com

ISBN 978-0-578-09762-6

Book and Cover Design: Chris Davies and Paul Soady
Photography: Nathan Lyon
Cover Photo of Nathan Lyon: Sarah Forman

Printed in Canada
FIRST EDITION

*For my parents, Dorcas and Robert Lyon, who have supported me through*

*all of my many endeavors. Thank you for teaching me never to let*

*fear stand in my way, always to follow my dreams, and to live life to the fullest.*

*I love you more than you will ever know.*

# CONTENTS

# RECIPE LIST

continued on next page »

## ENTRÉES

# ACKNOWLEDGEMENTS

It took many, many years to create this cookbook, and thanks to the support of my family, friends, farmers, neighbors, and fellow chefs, it's finally complete. You all went above and beyond what I could have ever hoped for, and traveled alongside me throughout this 5-year culinary journey to completion. I am eternally grateful to you for your feedback, suggestions, encouragement, company, time, and loving support.

Thanks to my grandparents, parents, and brothers who taught me how food, when prepared and shared together, is truly an experience of love—and a delicious one at that.

To my dream team of close friends and family who selflessly took my words, sculpted them, and distilled them into something clear and concise: my mom, Scott Albright, Sarah Forman, and Shannon Russell. Without you, this book may have never come to fruition. I love you guys.

To Paul Soady and Chris Davies for designing exactly what I've always wanted in a cookbook: a clean, easy-to-read book that flows effortlessly. I couldn't be happier.

Special thanks to Sarah Forman (my sous-chef and right-hand woman) who not only took my photograph for the cover of this book and streamlined my cookbook by organizing my countless recipe files and photographs into one concise document, but also single-handedly tested over 135 of my recipes during the final five-month push to the printers—no small task. Your efforts made it possible to approach my recipes with new eyes and I will be forever thankful for your endless support.

To my final line of editorial defense: the one, the only, Dave Lieberman, ladies and gentlemen! Those last grammatical tweaks (albeit 350 pages of tweaks) made all the difference in the world, Dave. Thank you. Also, to Bobby Bognar for first introducing me to Dave during an evening filled with amazing food and drink—thank you, brother.

To my entertainment lawyer and legal eagle, Judith Karfiol, who has taken on the role of my lawyer, agent, and manager. I promise, Judith, I'll get an agent soon! And to Sarah Spitz, who invited me to her wonderful birthday party six years ago and introduced me to Judith.

Thank you both.

A huge thanks to Ken Lee of Ken's Top Notch Produce who, 14 years ago, welcomed me to the world of farming and Los Angeles farmers markets.

To the chefs from the culinary school I attended, who continue to inspire me. Thank you for your guidance and friendship, Chef Richetti, Chef Coker, Chef Novo, and Chef Cone.

To Suzanne Goin for welcoming me into her kitchen at Lucques restaurant right out of culinary school and sharing with me the true meaning of farm-to-table cuisine: respecting fresh, seasonal ingredients and allowing their flavors to speak for themselves.

To Donald Thoms, my twin, mentor, and executive producer of *A Lyon in the Kitchen*. Thank you for your humor, friendship, and guidance over the years. I love you, buddy.

To all the DJs at KCRW who, over many years, kept me inspired as I cooked and tested recipes by playing the best music on earth.

Thank you to everyone around the country who tested my recipes over the years in their own kitchens and kindly offered suggestions as to how better to design my recipes for the home cook.

To my entire Facebook community of friends who took the time out of their days to share their honest opinions with me about how to best organize and word my recipes, in addition to keeping a smile on my face—at all hours of the day and night. (Looks like I'll finally be getting some sleep, now!) Thanks to each and every one of you.

To those of you I have yet the honor to meet and share a place in your kitchen, cooking along side your families and friends—it might be my book, but I wrote it for you.

THANK YOU TO ALL OF THE FARMERS WHO HAVE SHARED THEIR KNOWLEDGE AND PASSION FOR DELICIOUS SEASONAL PRODUCE WITH ME OVER THE YEARS—
IT'S BEEN THE BEST EDUCATION A CHEF COULD EVER HOPE FOR.

THANKS TO EVERYONE WHO WORKS AT THE BOURGEOIS PIG AND COUNTERPOINT RECORDS AND BOOKS IN LOS ANGELES' FRANKLIN VILLAGE WHO ENCOURAGED ME AND GAVE ME HONEST AND CONSTRUCTIVE FEEDBACK AS I CREATED AND TESTED MEAL AFTER MEAL.

# INTRODUCTION

### FRESH FOOD IS LIFE

I was five years old when I began walking by myself to my grandparents' house. They lived just five houses away and I happily skipped over to help my grandmother cook, can, and freeze the vegetables that my grandfather and I grew together in their humble backyard garden. My grandfather was the master grower in the family and coaxed the most magnificent produce from that little patch of land. I clearly remember my grandfather and me, out there in the garden, dressed in our shorts and white t-shirts, sitting on a two-by-four piece of wood so as to not compact the dirt, and more importantly, so as not to track dirt back into the house.

"It's not dirt," he would say. "It's soil."

Armed with a scraggly branch, we picked large chunks of clay into smaller, more manageable pieces, and then smaller pieces still, until eventually the whole thing began to resemble a gardening plot. It was our own private playpen, and it was a beauty. Over the next several days we shoveled under compost, topsoil, peat moss and eggshells— a small mountain of eggshells saved from weeks of my grandmother's mouth-watering cakes, brownies, and cookies. After days of picking and shoveling, the soil looked healthy; rich and dark with nutrients, smelling ripe with potential. My grandfather looked pleased.

With his hand on my shoulder, he smiled. "All right, Nathan, let's go get the seeds."

From days of roller-skating endless circles in my grandparents' tiny basement, I knew exactly where the seeds were kept: in large Mason jars on the windowsill, just to the left of the washer and dryer, approximately four hopscotch jumps past the old Victrola.

Those heavy Mason jars, backlit by the light against the window, stood tall and strong. Their contents held the power to create an almost endless supply of garden delights.

Like a freshly tapped oil well, nature's bounty burst forth from the earth.

All summer long, I, like a lone worker ant, hauled bag after bag of freshly picked produce back to my family. It was an almost unbearable weight of produce for a young Lyon to carry. My mother then magically turned that bounty into the most delicious tomato and cucumber salads, tasty greens, and hearty vegetable casseroles.

As the summer sun began to set into the autumn sky, I stood proudly at my grandfather's side as we watched the beans continue to climb and the tomatoes continue to grow. Amazing. In spite of the passing months and inevitable cooling weather, the harvest just kept on coming.

"Well isn't that something?" my grandfather mused.

You know what? It really was something.

It really is something.

Food is life.

From birthdays to holidays, from weddings to anniversaries, food plays an important role in all of life's celebrations. It brings us together as a family, a community, and a country, and I'm thankful that food has now brought us together, to cook, laugh, share, and give thanks.

Together.

## FRESH FOOD IS EASY

The best part about preparing seasonal meals is that Mother Nature gives us the perfect ingredients to cook with throughout the year. Think about it: during the summer months, when it's hot, she keeps us cool by offering refreshing fruits and vegetables, like tomatoes, peaches, and cucumbers. During the winter months when it's cold, she keeps us warm by providing produce perfectly suited for rustic winter stews, like kale, sweet potatoes, and other root vegetables.

To make things easier, seasonal flavors complement each other naturally: morel mushrooms with peas in spring, tomatoes and basil in summer, apples and cabbage in autumn, and in winter, Brussels sprouts paired with my favorite winter vegetable... bacon! As if that weren't enough, seasonal foods are the most nutritious (because they're the freshest), the most flavorful (because they're picked at the peak of their flavor), and more often than not, the least expensive (because they are growing locally in abundance).

I guess it's true what they say, "Mother knows best."

Thanks, Mom!

## FRESH FOOD IS FAMILY

I have received a great number of emails from parents asking how to get their kids involved in the process of shopping for, preparing, and eating fresh, seasonal foods. Now, as I don't have children of my own, I only have a limited amount of experience here, but I've found that kids love responsibility. Give them some responsibility, and they will rise to the occasion.

When I visit with my nephew Parrish or my niece Mason, they know that at some point in time we will be going to a farmers market. We'll grab our cloth market bags, load up the car, unroll the windows, crank the tunes, and sing our guts out all the way there. Once we arrive, we huddle and go over the Lyon family strategy: each kid gets to choose three items. They don't have to choose three, rather, they get to choose three. "Take your time," I tell them. "It's a big market. Ask questions. Speak with the farmers, and taste everything." I then set them loose, and off they run. With coffee in hand, I float behind them and watch as they zig-zag through the market, sampling as they go, carefully narrowing down their selections to just three, all while learning the names of the farmers, and how to best pick out the best seasonal produce available.

En route back home, giddy with excitement over their selections, they never fail to ask me what we're going to cook with their items—the items that they picked out on their own. "Uncle Nathan? What are we going to make? When? Can we cook it today for lunch? Tonight for dinner?"

Note the word "we," as in "us," together, cooking.

Listen, we're all adults here, right? "Grown-ass people," as my buddy Scott would say. Scott's right. We are grown-ass people, all of us. All of us, except kids. Kids are not adults and, because they look to their parents for guidance on lifestyle choices, it's up to us to teach them what's best. So let's invite our kids to help plan the family meals, shop with us at our local farmers market, and, ultimately, cook with us in our kitchens. It is, after all, our responsibility to set them up for a lifestyle that promotes health, not one that condemns it.

If we don't teach them, then who will?

## FRESH FOOD IS MEMORIES

On December 29, 2010, a close friend of mine, Tracie, invited me over for an impromptu crab feast at her house not far from where I live in Hollywood. Tracie's uncle had lovingly shipped her a bushel of Maryland blue crabs as a New Year's gift, and Tracie, in turn, wanted to share this special gift with some of her friends who were still in town for the holidays. So I did exactly what any right-minded person would do: I immediately stopped washing the dishes, threw on a decent shirt, and drove to her house as quickly as possible. Moments later, I arrived to a glorious scene: a dining room table covered in layers of fresh newspaper, a bushel of steaming crabs piled high, the sound of wooden mallets cracking open claws, a smile on every face, and fingers meticulously picking through shells for small pieces of succulent crab meat.

Armed with a clean paper towel and cold beer at my side, I rolled up my sleeves, and dove into my first blue crab of the evening.

The fresh crab meat had barely touched my lips when I was instantly transported back in time to when I was seven years old, to my grandparents' cottage in Kenwood Beach, Maryland, seated a few hundred feet from the edge of the Calvert Cliffs on the Chesapeake Bay. In the mornings, long before the sun even broke the horizon, seagulls soaring high above, I helped my grandfather launch his tiny metal boat into the calm waters of the bay. Our crab traps were stacked and baited with a mixture of frozen fish heads and chicken bones. A seemingly endless supply of blue crabs poured onto our boat, which later made their way into our pots to be seasoned, steamed and finally, piled high on our table. One bite that evening in Hollywood brought back the huge mounds of empty shells, the crispy fried crab cakes, the sweet, slow burn of Old Bay Seasoning, and the warm, soft washcloth my grandmother used to clean my face.

It was a virtual Polaroid of childhood memories, as real as the day they happened, all from a single bite of freshly steamed Maryland blue crab enjoyed among friends some 3,000 miles and thirty-five years later.

Such is the power of fresh food.

Since most memories are born from our sense of smell and the majority of taste comes from our sense of smell, I wish for you and your loved ones to experience fully this great pleasure in life—food memories based on fresh food: the smells, images, and textures leading back to emotions experienced, to times past, to places loved.

I hope that perhaps a recipe or two from this book, shared with family and friends, will plant the seeds for future memories—fun, sweet, delicious memories; memories that will last a lifetime.

## FRESH FOOD IS HEALTH

"Let food be thy medicine and medicine be thy food." Smart man, that Hippocrates.

Healthy eating is synonymous with preventive medicine, plain and simple. Now, add to that equation some regular exercise and you're well on your way to dealing with stress more effectively, having a better night's sleep, and maybe even enjoying a more vibrant love life. Whoa! Nothing wrong with that, right?

Exercise and a diet of fresh, seasonal food is key to maintaining a healthy, sustainable lifestyle. In fact, if you're looking to lose weight, fresh food and exercise can do that, too.

Don't get me wrong. I don't advocate rejecting the tasty treats that life has to offer, far from it. Chocolate, butter, and wine happen to be very good friends of mine. I do, however, advocate limiting the volume of food consumed, in addition to raising one's metabolism by means of exercise. In other words, when it comes to food, don't go without; go with less.

Many people have approached me at farmers markets, sharing stories of losing 30, 80, upwards to 150 pounds. Awesome. Over the years, I have noticed that these stories always include two main ingredients: exercise and cooking fresh, seasonal dishes. Truly, a recipe for success. It's inspiring to hear how these people have transformed their lives by replacing old habits with new, healthier ones, like shopping at their local farmers market and cooking at home more often.

If you're looking to embrace a healthier lifestyle, fresh, seasonal foods paired with regular exercise seems like a great place to start.

Others have done it, and so can you.

You can.

Really.

You can.

## FRESH FOOD IS REAL FOOD

There are so many advertisements these days that tout caramel-coated, double-chocolate, low-carb, vitamin- and antioxidant-enriched weight-loss bars, drinks or frozen dinners. I'm sorry, but if you see an advertisement for a food product, chances are it's not that good for you, because real food isn't packed with chemicals that are hard to pronounce. Do you know how much high-fructose corn syrup is in fresh, seasonal produce? None. What about added artificial colors, sweeteners, flavors, hydrogenated fats, or sodium? Exactly. None, again.

Fresh food is naturally delicious.

It doesn't have to be processed to make it delicious, because it already is. Do you know what this means? It means that any person with the desire and respect for great food can combine fresh, flavorful ingredients to create a culinary masterpiece. How fun!

So, let's pass on the processed food and instead, enjoy what our great-grandparents would have eaten when they were growing up—food we should all be enjoying and can enjoy each and every day.

Real food.

Wholesome food.

Fresh, seasonal, local food.

I guarantee it will be delicious.

## A RECIPE FOR SUCCESS

To set you on the road to culinary success, I have compiled this "Great Food Starts Fresh" list to be applied to every recipe.

**Whenever possible, use:**

- Seasonal, organic produce from local farmers markets.
- Large, free-range, organic eggs.
- Organic dairy products.
- Organic meat.
- Fish and seafood that is sustainably fished or farmed. It can be hard to remember which is which; there's a printable guide ("Seafood Watch") at the Monterey Bay Aquarium's website (montereybayaquarium.org).
- Homemade stock.
- Kosher salt.
- Freshly ground black pepper from whole peppercorns.
- Extra-virgin olive oil.

**Always:**

- Prepare all ingredients before you begin each recipe.
- Whisk flour to aerate before measuring.
- Keep your knives sharp!

**You're going to love these tasty food sources:**

- Bel Gioioso Cheese, Inc. ricotta cheese (belgioioso.com)
- Lucini Italia olive oils and vinegars (lucini.com)
- My Spice Sage spices (myspicesage.com)
- Nueske's bacon (nueskes.com)
- TCHO chocolate (tcho.com)

# KITCHEN TOOLS

Before I began shooting *A Lyon in the Kitchen*, I was asked to write up a list of cooking items I would need for the show. My answer? A pasta pot, some sauté and sauce pans, an immersion blender with attachments, a mixer, a sheet pan, and a good chef's knife. The basics. Don't get me wrong—I still salivate when walking into those high-end, glossy kitchen supply stores, but I don't actually need any of those things in order to cook successfully; I only want them. Yet, because everything's so darn shiny and professional looking, it's easy to imagine that I would somehow cook better meals with a $250 chef's knife. My $34 chef's knife cuts like a dream, and spending $34 sounds better than $250, don't you think?

So, where to begin?

Before I purchase any new cooking items for my kitchen, I do two things. First, I go to the Consumer Reports website and do a little research, because more often than not, the most expensive item is rarely the best. Second, I look for secondhand deals: at yard sales, swap meets, on eBay, Craigslist, or in my local newspaper—the ultimate form of recycling. You just never know; a couple may have received one too many stand mixers, food processors, or immersion hand blenders as wedding gifts and may be selling them cheaply or giving them away for free.

While you don't need drawers crammed full of fancy tools to be able to cook well, the proper equipment can make cooking a lot easier. Therefore, I've compiled a list of tools that I feel are well worth the kitchen space.

## OVEN DIAL THERMOMETER

Keep an old fashioned, oven-safe, dial thermometer in your oven at all times, no matter how new or expensive your oven might be. Why? Because the calibration of even the newest of ovens can be off. Thank goodness oven dial thermometers only cost around seven bucks, so even if your oven's 350°F is actually 325°F, at least you'll know. A small investment for huge peace of mind.

## DIGITAL THERMOMETER / TIMER

I cannot stress enough the importance of having a digital thermometer. Go out and get one of these. The initial $25 investment will more than make up for itself by saving your pork loin, roast chicken, Thanksgiving turkey, and leg of lamb from overcooking, or for that matter, undercooking. They double as a timer and have saved many a meal from burning in my temperamental oven. Go out and get yourself a digital thermometer, or better yet, ask for one as a present. Isn't your birthday coming up soon?

## IMMERSION BLENDER, PLUS ATTACHMENTS

This little gem is among my favorite kitchen tools and is perfect for those smaller jobs. I use my immersion blender mostly for blending soups, which saves me from having to use—and then clean—my blender. The whisk attachment effectively whips cream or egg whites for smaller jobs without my having to lug out the larger stand mixer. Finally, the food processor-like blade attachment makes fast work of homemade bread crumbs, a fresh batch of pesto, or even salsa without schlepping out the food processor. Get one. Seriously. You'll be glad you did.

## KNIVES

The most important tool in the kitchen is your knife. Your knife should fit in your hand comfortably and be kept razor sharp.

If your knife's handle is too small for your hand, your hand will get cramped. If the handle is too large, the knife will feel clumsy and be difficult to control. You would never buy a pair of shoes without at least trying them on, would you? Well, the same goes for knives. Now, to keep them in top condition, you will need a honing steel, which looks like a steel rod with a handle and is often confused with a knife sharpener. A honing steel will not sharpen a dull knife, but it can keep a sharp knife sharp. Honing steels realign the blade of your knife. As you swipe the blade across the honing steel, any little pieces of misaligned metal come off your knife's blade and stick to the steel (which is magnetic). Of course, you could purchase a knife sharpener, call your local hardware store to inquire whether they sharpen knives, or better yet, ask your friendly butcher where they sharpen their knives. Sometimes they'll even sharpen them for you. Whatever you choose, just keep that blade sharp.

The knife I use 95% of the time is my eight-inch Victorinox Swiss Army chef's knife that I bought for $34. It's my pride and joy. It has a thick wooden handle that fits my hand perfectly. This brings up another question: how many knives does one really need? Not the 24-piece, serrated, swiveling knife-block set, that's for sure. Three knives will cover most of your culinary needs in the kitchen: a chef's knife like my eight-inch knife, a paring knife for smaller cutting jobs, and a serrated bread knife for slicing bread or fresh tomatoes. Only three? Yes; three knives. That's all.

Lastly, none of your good knives should ever go into the dishwasher. The high temperatures and abrasive detergents used in dishwashers will dull your knives beyond the reparative power of the honing steel, so it's always best to wash them right away, by hand.

## MANDOLINE

A mandoline can slice food quickly like nobody's business. Most mandolines have interchangeable inserts that allow you to cut the food into long strips of differing sizes and widths. I prefer a mandoline with a V-shaped blade because I find it cuts with less resistance. Go online, and with the click of a button you can have a mandoline delivered right to your door.

## MICROPLANE GRATER

This is one of the best advances in kitchen technology. Microplane graters are super sharp, inexpensive, and perfectly designed for zesting citrus, grating hard cheeses, and even shaving chocolate. Trust me on this; you'll love it.

## MIXER

Now, whether it be an old-school mixer like my mom's (the original ceramic bowl broke, so she now uses a metal bowl that she physically holds in place), a dual-beater hand-mixer with the cool ejector button like the one my grandmother used, or a newer stand-mixer, this is one kitchen tool that is definitely good to have. There's no need to spend a fortune, either. All you need is a quality mixer that works well.

## POTS AND PANS

More often than not we get into the habit of keeping our old pots and pans even after we purchase new ones. What is the outcome? Cupboards stuffed to the gills with items you never use. Every pot and pan you own should conduct heat evenly, be comfortable to work with, and have a function. That said, if you are in the market for new pots and pans, the rule of thumb is to hold them to see if they're comfortable. Much like purchasing a new dress or suit, you need to try them on first and see if they fit properly. Are they comfortable to hold? Are they something you might use every day, or do they just look good? For pots and pans, comfort over style is always the way to go.

## SPICE GRINDER

If you enjoy freshly ground coffee, chances are you'll love freshly ground spices, too. The premise is exactly the same. You use freshly roasted and ground coffee beans to make the best cup of coffee, just as you would use freshly toasted and ground spices to make the most flavorful dish—and the fragrance? Intoxicating!

# KITCHEN STAPLES

Every restaurant kitchen I have ever walked into has certain basic food items necessary to facilitate great food any time of the year, and there's no reason why we all can't have those items at our disposal too. In this chapter, I have listed what I feel every kitchen should have in its culinary Rolodex: ingredients that work with every season.

## BLACK PEPPER

Sometimes when I visit a friend's place for the first time I will bring a small pepper grinder filled with fresh peppercorns, just in case the pepper they use is from a massive, red, family heirloom tin of "ground pepper" from the 1950s—you know the one. Keep in mind, the delicious flavor of pepper comes from the oils found in the peppercorn, and once ground, the oils break down quickly, taking the flavor with them. You wouldn't brew your fresh morning coffee with stale, ten-year-old coffee grounds, would you? No thanks. The same is true with pepper: fresh is best. Purchase whole peppercorns and store them in a cool, dark place.

## BREAD

I love to have fresh bread on hand at all times; if I don't buy it from my farmers market or local bakery, I'll make it at home by pulling out my seventeen-year-old bread machine, adding the ingredients, and simply pressing the start button. It doesn't get much easier than that. By always hav-

ing bread on hand, I can make fresh bread crumbs, croutons, or bread pudding. Any excess bread can be sliced, wrapped tightly in plastic wrap, sealed in a zip-top bag, and frozen. Need some toast on the quick? Simply remove a few slices from the freezer and put them into the toaster. Bingo! You've got toast.

## BUTTER

Using unsalted butter gives you more control over the final dish; you can always add salt to a dish if you think it needs it, but once the salt is in there, it can never be taken out. Keep in mind that butter tends to take on the flavors of things around it, so be conscious not to store your butter next to, say, chopped onions. Store any excess butter in its original wrapper, wrapped tightly in foil, then stored in a plastic zip-top bag. If there's an amazing sale on butter, grab as much as you can afford, and store any excess in the freezer in the same manner as above for up to one year. When your supply starts running low, thaw it overnight in the refrigerator.

## CAPERS

Capers are the flower buds of a particular bush cultivated mainly around the Mediterranean that are picked, dried, and pickled in a vinegar brine or packed in salt before they have the chance to flower. Before use, simply give the capers a quick rinse to remove any excess salt, and you're ready to go. Store any remaining capers in their brine, in the original container, in the refrigerator.

## CHEESE

I recommend having a nice piece of aged cheese such as Parmigiano-Reggiano or Pecorino Romano on hand at all times. Aged cheeses have more flavor than younger cheeses which means you use less cheese, not more. Aged cheeses, when stored properly, also last a very long time. Keep your cheese cold and wrapped tightly in plastic film, then sealed in a zip-top bag. In addition to aged cheeses, keep at least one soft cheese, like goat (chèvre) or ricotta, on hand to enjoy with eggs, pasta, or paired with dessert. Sure, you can purchase a huge block of neon orange, waxy, shelf-stable "cheese product," but why? Cheese product isn't really cheese, just as orange drink isn't really orange juice. Get the good stuff; you're worth it.

## CORNMEAL (POLENTA)

Once thought of only as a peasant food, polenta has made an impressive comeback. If I'm preparing an authentic, rustic Northern Italian polenta dish, I'll reach for the coarse stone-milled cornmeal. More times than not, if I am tight on time, instant polenta it is! Store cornmeal in a cool, dark place.

## EGGS

There are three main parts to an egg: the yolk, the thick white, and the thin white (which spreads outward from the thick white). As the egg ages, the thin white will get thinner,

and therefore, is the best visual indicator for the approximate age of the egg. For example, a really fresh egg, when cracked into a pan, will have a beautiful, perky, bright orange yolk that sits up nice and high. You know... perky. The yolk is surrounded by the thick white, which should be resilient and firm, and then by the thin white, which shouldn't run all over the pan, but should stay fairly close to the thick white. When eggs stick to the bottom of the egg carton, unless the egg is cracked, it's probably because the egg is so old that the thin white has seeped through tiny pores in the shell. In fact, I have been told that some grocery store eggs can be upwards of three months old, if not older. Whoa! So, when it comes to presentation, like with a poached egg, or a beautiful sunny-side up egg, the fresher the egg, the better, and the freshest eggs are usually found at your local farmers market.

## FLOUR

Unbleached all-purpose (AP) flour is another heavy hitter in my kitchen. With it, you can make pizza, cookies, crêpes, molten chocolate cake, bread, pancakes—you name it. Before measuring flour for any recipe, gently whisk the flour (still in the bag) to save yourself from having to sift the flour later. Store AP flour in a cool, dark place.

## FRESH HERBS

Fresh herbs are like the talented supporting actors in your favorite movie or the back-up singers for your favorite band. In truth, much like the main actor or singer, a successful dish is made great by its supporting flavors. Cue music,

cue lights... enter herbs, and the crowd goes crazy. Fresh herbs are best kept wrapped in a barely dampened paper towel and sealed in a plastic bag in the refrigerator, for up to two weeks. If you get a bunch of freshly cut herbs from your own garden or farmers market, simply snip off the bottom inch of the stems, place them into a glass with water, and pop them into the fridge, except for basil; basil hates the cold. Instead, treat basil like fresh flowers: cut off the bottom inch of the stems, and place them in a glass of water. Easy-peasy.

## GRAINS

Lentils, quinoa, pearl barley, and spelt are among the many grains and legumes that you can use to make delicious salads, soups, and risottos. Grains are highly nutritious, simple to cook, inexpensive to buy, and have a wonderful rustic flavor that gives real structure to a meal. What's not to like? Store grains in an airtight container in a cool, dark place.

## OIL

Now you're talking my language. Olive oil, to be exact; extra-virgin. The first important thing to know is that the main difference between extra-virgin olive oil and virgin olive oil is the acidity, or pH, of the oil. Both extra-virgin and virgin olive oils are made by physically pressing the olives without heat or chemical means. I don't enjoy the flavor of so-called "pure" or "light" olive oil, so I don't use them. In fact, anything other than "virgin" or "extra-virgin" olive oil, in my opinion, is less than amazing.

I've witnessed people spending upwards of $4 for a chocolate frappy-seven-pump-latte, but then freak out at the notion of spending three times that for a quality bottle of olive oil. Something's not quite right about that. The sugar-laden coffee beverage will only last you a few minutes; a bottle of good-quality olive oil will bless many a family meal.

So where to begin? When shopping for olive oil, politely ask your grocery store sales person for a taste. I have, and you can too. Sampling olive oils is how I came across my all-time favorite extra-virgin olive oil: Lucini Italia. It is by far the best bang for the buck because it tastes like fresh olives: full-bodied with a fruity, spicy, clean finish. It would seem finding an olive oil that tastes like itself would be a simple task, right? Not so. Ask yourself this question, "Would I dip fresh bread in this oil?" Would you dip fresh bread in canola oil and eat it? Try it and see. If you don't enjoy the flavor of the oil you're using in your kitchen by itself, how on earth is that going to translate into better tasting meals?

A second, equally healthy, neutral-tasting oil to consider having on hand is grapeseed oil. Grapeseed oil works great for a quick high-temperature stir-fry or for a flavor-specific salad dressing or mayonnaise, where the flavor of olive oil would overpower the delicate flavor of the salad ingredients.

A rule of thumb for storage of oils: if you don't use your oils everyday, or perhaps have a few nut oils on hand, such as sesame, almond, or hazelnut oil that are prone to spoilage, store them in the refrigerator to ensure a much longer shelf life.

## PASTA

From orzo to lasagna to capellini, dried pasta is both versatile and everlasting in your pantry. That said, let's discuss how best to prepare pasta. First, bring a small pot of water to a rolling boil. Next, add 2 tablespoons of salt. It may seem like a lot of salt, but this is actually your only real opportunity to season the pasta itself. Add the pasta to the boiling water and cook until *al dente* (almost done, or "to the tooth"). Once done, drain without rinsing, then immediately toss with your favorite sauce or olive oil. The sauce will stick due to the residual starch on the surface of the pasta. Please note, there's no need to add olive oil to the boiling pasta water. Rather, to prevent pasta from sticking, simply stir occasionally during cooking. *Buon appetito!*

## RICE

I like to have three different types of rice on hand in my kitchen: real aged basmati from the foothills of the Himalayas, arborio, and any variety of brown rice. Most varieties of rice keep best in an airtight container stored in a cool, dark place. For brown rice, which is unrefined, store in an airtight container in the refrigerator.

## SALT

I mainly use one type of salt: kosher salt. It tastes like —you know, salt. It has a consistently clean finish, plus it's inexpensive. To make cooking easier for myself, I keep a small dish filled with kosher salt within arm's reach of my stove at all times. This one action saves me from having to constantly open the box of salt as I cook. I do have iodized table salt in my pantry, but I use it for one thing, and one thing only: to gargle with in case of a sore throat. I don't use it in my food. Also, keep in mind, a single flake of kosher salt is at least twice the size of a grain of table salt, so if you are using table salt in a recipe that calls for kosher salt, you are actually using twice the amount of sodium by volume, and it's likely the dish will taste too salty. When I dine out, if I feel my meal needs more seasoning, I will politely ask for a small dish of kosher salt. Why not? If the chef cooked my entire meal with kosher salt, why would I use iodized at the table? One last thing, when seasoning any dish, let me share a chef's tip with you: season from high above the food so that you can ensure that the salt is evenly dispersed over the dish.

## SPICES

When purchasing spices, consider buying in bulk. I buy my spices in bulk online because I find them to be of higher quality, and far less expensive than the little glass containers at my local grocery store. You can even go in on buying spices with friends, therefore splitting the cost and dividing up the bulk spices according to your specific culinary needs. Purchase enough for the next nine months to a year, then store spices in a cool, dark place. I recommend having on hand cumin seed, bay leaf, fennel seed, coriander seed, red chili flakes, yellow curry powder, ground cayenne powder, nutmeg, cloves, ground ginger, and cinnamon. Well—and black pepper, of course. From these twelve spices, an amazing number of flavor combinations can be achieved. (For toasting spices, see page 43.)

## SWEETENERS

There are some, close to my heart, who don't just have one sweet tooth, they have many—an entire mouthful, really. I do keep sweeteners on hand, but I only use those sweeteners that my great-grandmother, Mema Hattie, would have had in her family kitchen when she was young, like local honey from the farmers market, molasses, real maple syrup, brown sugar, and even (granulated) table sugar. What's not fair game: high fructose corn syrup (HFCS), a sweetener found in just about anything and everything processed. I mean, c'mon, with orange blossom honey or real maple syrup on hand, even the sweetest of teeth will be more than satisfied.

## VANILLA BEANS AND PURE VANILLA EXTRACT

Why, oh, why are vanilla beans so expensive? Well, for one, they are the only thing edible produced from one of thousands of varieties of orchids. They must be pollinated by hand during an excruciatingly small window of time. Then, after nine (nine!) months, the pods are picked and left out to dry during the day, then rolled up in cloth at night to sweat, for almost a week. If I had to do all of that, I would be charging at least fifty dollars per vanilla bean. Of course, a cheaper alternative to using vanilla beans is to use pure vanilla extract. Read the label, though; even some "pure" vanilla extracts have corn syrup in them. How is that still called "pure" vanilla extract? I have no idea.

Or, you could just make your own vanilla extract.

Simply grab a small eight-ounce glass container with a lid, slice one fresh vanilla bean in half, both lengthwise and

widthwise, scrape out the seeds, then add the seeds and the pod to the container. Then, fill that container with vodka (yes—vodka), seal, and shake every few weeks for six months. I promise, you will have the most amazing vanilla extract. In fact, as I type this very sentence, I have a 750ml bottle of vodka with eight freshly scraped vanilla beans in it; vanilla beans that I got for free when ordering $25 worth of fresh spices online; vanilla beans that were shipped for free! How about vanilla sugar? Oh, yeah, I got a recipe for that, too. (See page 44.)

## VINEGAR

A quick splash of vinegar can accentuate existing flavors in a dish, add depth and complexity, and really make a meal pop. If you had to choose only three vinegars, go for a good quality balsamic, red wine and white wine vinegar. I try to keep six varieties of vinegars on hand: aged balsamic, red wine, white wine, rice wine, apple cider and sherry. Now, that may seem like a lot of vinegars to invest in. Each of these vinegars, however, will ultimately last you many months, if not years. For pennies per splash, it's totally worth it.

## WINE

It's always a good idea to keep a few bottles of wine around for when unexpected guests stop by. Personally, I don't buy wine that needs aging, I buy wine that needs drinking. In my apartment, wine works double duty; not just as a tasty libation on its own, but also as an ingredient that adds depth and flavor to stews, risottos, and sauces. I don't cook with any wine that I wouldn't want to drink on its own. With so many wonderful, inexpensive wines out there, why would I?

Wines should be stored on their side, away from both heat and direct sunlight. When serving wine, I recommend serving red wine slightly cooler than room temperature—65°F is best—and white wines slightly warmer than refrigerator temperature, between 42 and 50°F. Only Champagne (from Champagne, France) and sparkling wine (from everywhere else) should be served very cold.

# TIME TO SHOP

## GROCERY STORES

Eating healthy is easy when we have access to farmers markets, right? During the winter months, though, this is not an option for much of the country and we must, therefore, purchase food from supermarkets. Not a problem. Given that the floor plan of every grocery store is generally the same, the healthiest way to shop in the grocery store is called "perimeter shopping." Take my hand, and let's go for a stroll.

As we walk around the grocery store we'll do our best to stay clear of the aisles, where most of the processed food can be found. Rather, we'll remain mainly on the outside, or "perimeter," of the grocery store as we shop. It's there in the perimeter where we will find the fresh fruits, vegetables, eggs, dairy products, fish, seafood, meats, whole grains, and breads. Sure, there are always exceptions to this rule: extra-virgin olive oil, dried pasta, dried beans, plus frozen and/or canned vegetables are found in the aisles, but by and large, mainly processed foods which are low in nutritional value lurk in the middle of the store. True, processed foods are convenient, but given the amounts of high-fructose corn syrup, sodium, and artificial ingredients found in them, eating food that may ultimately bring harm to your health doesn't really sound all that appetizing, does it? No, sirree. Stay on the perimeter and stick with the fresh stuff.

Finally, when you find yourself in the produce section of the grocery store, keep this helpful tip in mind: if you want to know what's in season, look for the "Grown in the USA" label. Not only is this your clue as to what is in season, but these items will be fresher than, let's say, something grown and shipped in from halfway around the world. So, when you do shop in the grocery store, consider "USA" your local food source!

Now, with all that in mind, are you ready to shop? Great! Grab a cart, take one loop around the store, and we're done.

## FARMERS MARKETS

Got a farmers market nearby? Go.

Get to know your farmers and don't be afraid to ask them questions like, "Where do you farm? Are people welcome to visit the farm? What do you spray with, if anything?" Asking specific questions is how I learned about sustainable farming practices, what it means to farm organically, and also how to pick out the best seasonal produce. So much knowledge, all for free! Also, while you're at your local market, really pay attention to the food samples that the farmers are offering, because the answer to picking out the best seasonal produce is always in the samples.

Let me repeat that. The answer to picking out the best seasonal produce is always in the samples.

Don't just grab a sample and eat it. Really look at it. If the skin of that super sweet nectarine sample you just ate

was dull in appearance with lots of spots on it, then purchase those! Don't grab the pretty, shiny nectarines because those aren't going to be as tasty as the dull spotted ones—if they were, the farmer would be sampling those instead.

I buy from local food sources for many reasons: I'm supporting my local community and its farmers financially, all while keeping my carbon footprint as small as possible. In addition, my experience is that buying from local family farmers is safer. It's far easier for a small-volume farmer to walk through and check up on his or her chickens, cattle, or hogs than it is for some guy making minimum wage to check up on a building packed from floor to ceiling with thousands of chickens owned by some faceless corporation. It's easier, too, to care for chickens that are allowed to range free in the open air and peck at bugs, as chickens were

intended to do. Smaller, family-owned farms know their animals. They know when their animals look or act ill and they can respond quickly to remedy the situation.

Come to think of it, after working at Los Angeles farmers markets four times per week for over a decade, no farmer I know has ever recalled any of their products—not one egg, not one ounce of beef, not even one tomato, or single leaf of spinach. In fact, I've never heard of anyone ever getting sick from anything they've ever consumed from a farmers market. Anywhere. Ever.

Now, do I always get my chicken, beef, eggs, and produce from the farmers market? No, not always, but I certainly try and do the best I can. Supporting my local farmer or small business owner is a simple yet effective action that keeps my local mom and pop businesses from going under. I invite you to join me in doing the same.

Every dollar we spend on food counts as a vote: for farming and fishing practices that respect our earth; for American farmers and fishermen who farm and fish sustainably; for those who do not use synthetic sprays, fertilizers, antibiotics or growth hormones. If you want to support American mom and pop food purveyors, local businesses, small family-owned farmers, and fishermen, then seek them out and do exactly that: support them with your dollar, with your vote.

To all of the farmers and fishermen, not only do you make a chef's job very easy, but you also nourish and sustain us all by providing us with the freshest, healthiest, and tastiest products possible. Thank you.

# TIME TO COOK

The oven I have in my apartment is an inexpensive "back of the rack" floor model, and the temperature is off by as many as 80 degrees at any given time. 80 degrees! That's a huge (insert expletive of choice here) difference! It has four gas burners that are not the most impressive things to cook on, but they do get hot enough to boil water—barely. If you are fortunate enough to have a sleek, cutting-edge oven with convection abilities and buttons that light up when you push them, then please invite me over, because I would love to cook in your kitchen! What I'm trying to say is: if I can cook impressive, quick, delicious meals using only the most rudimentary of cooking tools, THEN SO CAN YOU! All you need is a pot and a dream. Don't believe me? Well, opposite, is a photograph of my actual kitchen, the one I used to cook every single recipe in this book; the one I used to develop every recipe I've cooked on television. That is my oven. That is my tiny prep area (read: cutting board). And that is my sink. The one thing that you cannot see in this photo is my dishwasher, because that would be me.

You don't need a fancy kitchen to cook amazing meals. If I can do it in my humble galley kitchen, then so can you!

So, grab your sauté pan, and a handful of fresh seasonal ingredients, because together, we're going to be cooking some amazing food.

One season, one meal, one recipe at a time.

Great food starts now!

THANKS FOR THE GRILL, MOM!

# REFERENCE RECIPES

My recipes are based on a set of basic, primary ingredients such as homemade stock. These recipes are called for so often that, rather than repeat the steps to prepare these items in each recipe, I have consolidated them here.

## HOMEMADE STOCK

Stock is the lifeblood of most restaurants. It's the foundation for soups, sauces, and anything braised. Stock basically involves vegetables, water, a pot, and maybe some bones. If you can simmer water, then you can make delicious stock. My buddy Scott put it best when he said, "Why would you ever use water instead of stock? Why would you ever miss the opportunity to add flavor to a meal?" If you have a boxed stock from the store that you enjoy, stick with that as a quick turn-to when you're in a pinch for time. Keep in mind, though, that stock from the store potentially could contain sweeteners, a fair amount of sodium, and sometimes even artificial coloring. In fact, I have ruined meals using boxed stock from the store because unfortunately, the ones I used tasted terrible. That's why homemade stock is the way to go, not to mention that you can make homemade stock for close to nothing. Don't believe me? Go to your refrigerator and take a look in your crisper drawers. Seriously, I'll wait. (Cue sound of me whistling.) Let me guess what you have in there: wilted celery, flaccid carrots, perhaps some aging herbs? What about on your counter? Any vegetables? Some old onions and maybe a few cloves of garlic?

That is such great news! Don't toss those old vegetables in the trash; instead, let's use them for homemade stock. True, they may not look that great, but those limp vegetables still have plenty of flavor in them. After all, you've already paid money for those vegetables, right? So, don't throw them away; instead, save your money and gain flavor!

# VEGETABLE STOCK

5 large yellow onions, peeled and chopped roughly (2 pounds)

5 stalks celery, chopped roughly

5 large carrots, peeled and chopped roughly

1 cup roughly chopped mushrooms (preferably button, cremini, or shiitake)

5 sprigs fresh thyme

7 sprigs fresh flat-leaf Italian parsley

5 medium garlic cloves, peeled and crushed

1 teaspoon whole black peppercorns

1 teaspoon kosher salt

2 dried bay leaves

Since I have some very dear vegetarian friends, vegetable stock is the basis for many of my stews and risottos. Two things to keep in mind: the smaller you cut the vegetables, the faster you can extract the flavor from them, and the longer you simmer the stock, the more flavor your stock will ultimately have. I've found that 3 hours is perfect for a full flavored vegetable stock.

1. Combine the ingredients in a large pot.

2. Cover with 1 gallon (4 quarts, or 16 cups) of cold water. Place over high heat until just boiling. Once boiling, reduce the heat and simmer for 3 hours.

3. Strain the vegetable stock into another pot and enjoy right away, or let cool to room temperature. Once cooled, store any remaining stock in the refrigerator for up to 4 days or freeze for up to 6 months.

Notes: Mushrooms add a wonderful savory, meaty flavor to the vegetable stock, but be aware of any potential allergies to mushrooms your guests may have. This recipe is delicious without the mushrooms, too. Either way, you're good to go. Also, other vegetables that you can add to give flavor to your stock are fennel, shallots, and turnips.

1 (6- to 7-pound) chicken, giblets removed, rinsed, plus any necks or backs

5 large yellow onions, peeled and chopped roughly (2 pounds)

5 stalks celery, chopped roughly

5 large carrots, peeled and chopped roughly

5 sprigs fresh thyme

7 sprigs fresh flat-leaf Italian parsley

5 medium garlic cloves, peeled and crushed

1 teaspoon whole black peppercorns

1 teaspoon kosher salt

2 dried bay leaves

Note: After the stock has chilled completely, the fat will have risen to the top, solidified, and formed a cap which can be easily removed with a spoon. Discard this fat, or better yet, save it, covered, in the refrigerator for up to a few months. Chicken fat can be substituted for other types of fat, like butter, when a chicken flavor is preferred. We Southerners dig the stuff, for real. Some New York delis offer containers of it on their tables to spread on bread: they call it schmaltz, and it's gooood. Not good for you, of course, but darn tasty.

# CHICKEN STOCK

Chicken stock is as easy to make as vegetable stock—you just need a chicken plus some additional time. Both vegetable and chicken stock have plenty of flavor, true, but chicken stock has something that vegetable stock doesn't—a certain texture and fullness that comes in the form of gelatin which is extracted as collagen from the chicken bones. For a little extra punch of flavor, contact your local store to see if they also sell chicken necks and backs. If so, grab some of those too, because it's time to make some chicken stock!

1. Combine the ingredients in a large pot.

2. Cover with 28 cups (7 quarts) of cold water. Place over high heat until just boiling. Once boiling, reduce the heat and simmer gently for a minimum of 8 hours, or as many as 14 hours (the longer the better!). If you're planning on going for the longer times of, say, 10 to 14 hours, add 4 cups additional water at the 8-hour mark to keep the bones and vegetables covered by approximately 2 inches.

3. Strain the stock carefully into another pot, discarding any solids (vegetables, chicken, and bones). Enjoy your stock right away, or cool according to the instructions opposite. Homemade chicken stock will last in the refrigerator for up to 4 days or in the freezer for up to 6 months.

## COOLING INSTRUCTIONS

After the chicken stock has been strained carefully into a second metal pot, fill your kitchen sink about halfway with cold water and add plenty of ice to chill it down. If you have a small wire cookie rack (even a brick will do the trick), place it in the bottom of the sink. Carefully place the pot of strained chicken stock into the ice water. (The rack or brick keeps the cool water circulating freely under the pot.) Keep in mind that the ice water in the sink will rise significantly when you add the pot, so be careful that water doesn't overflow into your beautiful stock. Once the pot is safely in the sink, stir the ice water surrounding the pot occasionally to cool the stock faster.

## PROPER STORAGE

I keep a few large, thoroughly cleaned plastic yogurt containers handy for storing chilled stock. Once the stock is cool, I fill the containers four-fifths full to allow for expansion, close the lids tightly, and then transfer the containers into the freezer. Another option is to freeze some of your cooled stock in ice cube trays. Then, when completely frozen, simply remove the cubes of stock from the trays, transfer them into freezer bags and store them in the freezer. When you only need a small amount of stock, just add a few frozen cubes of stock. Bingo: instant flavor on the fly.

Note: Other vegetables that you can add to give flavor to your stock are fennel, shallots, and turnips.

1 loaf fresh bread, such as French baguette, sourdough, or ciabatta

Extra-virgin olive oil, for drizzling

Kosher salt, to taste

Freshly ground black pepper, to taste

# HOMEMADE CROSTINI: THREE WAYS

The thing I love about homemade crostini, besides, of course, how amazing they taste, is that they are easy to make. That said, you must promise me one thing: that you will not roam too far away from your oven or grill while making them. Promise? Good. You see, all three methods of making seasoned crostini include a good amount of heat. That is to say, I have seen some burned crostini in my day—tragic, I know. Still, although there is a little risk involved, I have a feeling that once you've tasted seasoned crostini, regular bread will just seem so, well, regular (sorry, bread). There's no question in my mind that it's well worth the risk for amazing flavor and texture.

### LOW RISK. SLOW AND STEADY. BAKED.

1. Adjust an oven rack to the middle position, then preheat the oven to 400°F.

2. Line a baking sheet with aluminum foil.

3. Using a bread knife, slice the loaf on a 25- to 45-degree angle (the greater the angle, the higher the surface area) half an inch thick.

4. Lay each piece, side by side, on the sheet pan in one layer, drizzle olive oil over each piece, then season them evenly with salt, and a few grinds of pepper.

5. Transfer the sheet pan to the oven and bake, uncovered, until the bread is lightly toasted, approximately 8 to 10 minutes.

6. Remove the pan, and carefully flip each piece over. Return the sheet pan to the oven and continue to bake, uncovered, until lightly toasted, approximately 2 minutes.

7. Remove from the oven and transfer the crostini to a plate until needed.

## MEDIUM RISK. FAST. BROILED.

1. Set your oven to broil.

2. Line a baking sheet with aluminum foil.

3. Using a bread knife, slice the loaf on a 25- to 45-degree angle (the greater the angle, the higher the surface area) half an inch thick.

4. Lay each piece, side by side, on the sheet pan in one layer, drizzle olive oil over each piece, then season them evenly with salt, and a few grinds of pepper.

5. Place the sheet pan under the broiler, and broil, uncovered, until the bread is lightly toasted. Keep a close eye on them—this could happen as quickly as 2 minutes.

6. Remove the pan and carefully flip each piece over. Return the sheet pan to the broiler until lightly toasted.

7. Remove from the oven and transfer the crostini to a plate until needed.

## HIGH RISK. VERY FAST WITH CHANCE OF COMBUSTION. GRILLED.

1. Set your grill to high. Once hot, clean the grill, then, using tongs, lightly dip a cloth in olive oil and wipe to coat the grill rack.

2. Line a baking sheet with aluminum foil.

3. Using a bread knife, slice the loaf on a 25- to 45-degree angle (the greater the angle, the higher the surface area) half an inch thick.

4. Lay each piece, side by side, on the sheet pan in one layer, drizzle olive oil over each piece, then season them evenly with salt and a few grinds of pepper. Arrange the slices on the grill and grill until lightly toasted with grill marks.

5. Flip the pieces and repeat.

6. Remove from the grill and transfer the crostini to a plate until needed.

Note: If using a round loaf of bread, be sure to cut the loaf in half first. Then, with the flat (cut) side facing down, starting from one side, cut straight down, making even slices. This method of slicing bread will prevent your slices from being smushed as you slice them.

For bonus material relating to this recipe, visit chefnathanlyon.com

# ROASTING, TOASTING, AND SPICING NUTS

## ALMONDS, WALNUTS, OR PECANS

1. Adjust an oven rack to the middle position, then preheat the oven to 350°F.

2. Spread out the nuts on a sheet pan in a single layer.

3. Bake, uncovered, for 15 to 17 minutes (almonds) or 13 to 14 minutes (walnuts or pecans), stirring occasionally for even cooking, until lightly colored. Be sure to set your timer. To test for doneness, break one nut in half and check for color. It should be a light golden brown color on the inside.

4. Remove from the oven and transfer the roasted nuts to a plate to cool, or toss in a bowl with a very light drizzle of extra-virgin olive oil and a good sized pinch (or two) of kosher salt.

## PINE NUTS

1. Adjust an oven rack to the middle position, then preheat the oven to 350°F.

2. Spread out the pine nuts on a sheet pan in a single layer.

3. Bake, uncovered, for 6 to 7 minutes, stirring occasionally for even cooking, until light golden in color. Be sure to set your timer.

4. Remove from the oven and transfer the roasted nuts to a plate to cool.

## CANDIED SPICED NUTS

1. Mix together the cinnamon, cumin, cayenne, salt, and a few good grinds of pepper in a small bowl.

2. Heat a medium sauté pan over medium heat for 1 minute or until hot.

3. Add 1 tablespoon oil and the nuts, and cook for approximately 2 minutes, stirring every 20 seconds to cook evenly.

4. Working quickly, add the spice mix to the sauté pan and stir to coat. Cook for 30 seconds, stirring once every five seconds.

5. Add the maple syrup very carefully, as it will bubble up, stirring to coat. Allow to cook 2 minutes more, stirring occasionally. Keep an eye on the nuts, and if they begin to smoke, turn down the heat a little and stir more often.

6. Remove from the heat and transfer the nuts to a sheet pan lined with parchment paper.

7. Working quickly, using two forks, separate the individual nuts, then allow to cool completely. Seriously. They're going to be hot.

## TOASTING SPICES

1. Add your chosen whole spices to a small sauté pan over medium-low heat.

2. Toast the spices by stirring frequently until they are just fragrant.

3. At the first sign of white wispy smoke, remove the spices from the hot pan to cool. Once cooled, you can either use them whole or grind them up.

**CANDIED SPICED NUTS**

½ teaspoon ground cinnamon

¼ teaspoon ground cumin

⅛ teaspoon ground cayenne pepper

¼ teaspoon kosher salt

Freshly ground black pepper, to taste

1 tablespoon grapeseed oil or extra-virgin olive oil

1¼ cups walnut halves, pecan halves, or whole raw almonds

3 tablespoons pure maple syrup, preferably Grade B

4 slices of bread

**HOMEMADE PUMPKIN PIE SPICE**

2 tablespoons ground cinnamon

1 teaspoon ground ginger

¼ teaspoon ground cloves

⅛ teaspoon ground cardamom

⅛ teaspoon ground nutmeg

**VANILLA SUGAR**

1 vanilla bean

3 cups granulated sugar

# HOMEMADE BREAD CRUMBS

1. Adjust an oven rack to the middle position, then preheat the oven to 300°F.

2. Lay each slice of bread side by side on a sheet pan in one layer. Bake, uncovered, for 30 minutes, until dry and light golden brown in color, flipping after 15 minutes. Remove the sheet pan from the oven and let the bread cool completely.

3. Place the bread in a 1-gallon zip-top bag, seal, and, using a rolling pin, pound the bread until desired texture is achieved.

# HOMEMADE PUMPKIN PIE SPICE

Mix together and there you go. Almost the perfect amount to refill an empty spice container.

# VANILLA SUGAR

In an airtight container, combine a scraped vanilla bean (also chop the entire pod into ½-inch pieces) with the sugar. After one week, the sugar will take on the heavenly flavor of vanilla. You like vanilla-flavored coffee? Me too. Use some vanilla sugar in place of your regular sugar, and you're all set.

# CRÈME FRAÎCHE

**YIELD: APPROXIMATELY 2½ CUPS**

2 cups heavy whipping cream

3 tablespoons buttermilk

1. Combine the heavy whipping cream with the buttermilk in a lidded container large enough to hold approximately 3 cups of liquid.

2. Rest the lid loosely on top, allowing the mixture to breathe.

3. Place the container on the counter, for 24 hours, undisturbed. The cream will thicken with time, and the flavor will become nutty and tangy. Voilà! Store crème fraîche in the refrigerator with the lid on tightly for up to 3 weeks.

# SEASONAL PRODUCE: HOW TO CHOOSE AND STORE

I have included this section on how to pick and store fresh, seasonal produce, drawing upon many years of working closely with Los Angeles-area farmers. Note that while I suggest using plastic bags as a method of storing certain produce, these bags can be washed, rinsed, dried, and re-used. An alternative to plastic bags is biodegradable food storage bags, which also get the job done.

## APPLES

Choose apples that have smooth skins, are firm, and are without any bruising, cracks, or soft spots.

Store unwashed apples in a perforated plastic bag in the crisper drawer of the refrigerator for up to 3 weeks. Rinse just before use.

## APRICOTS

Choose apricots that are uniform in color, forgiving (but not squishy) when gently squeezed, with unblemished skin, a sweet fragrance, and without cracks or bruising.

Soften unwashed apricots at room temperature. Once apricots give to gentle pressure, store in the crisper drawer of the refrigerator for up to 3 days. Rinse just before use. Apricots are most flavorful at room temperature.

## ARTICHOKES

Choose artichokes that are heavy for their size, with bright green leaves that are closed tightly and make a squeaking sound when you squeeze or rub them together.

Store unwashed artichokes in a sealed plastic bag in the refrigerator for up to 5 days. Rinse just before use.

## ARUGULA

Choose arugula with crisp, green leaves with no signs of wilting or decay.

Rinse and dry arugula and store wrapped in a dry paper towel inside a sealed plastic bag in the refrigerator for up to 5 days.

## ASPARAGUS

Choose crisp asparagus with tight, firm tips that have no signs of browning or decay.

Store unwashed asparagus wrapped in a damp paper towel inside a perforated plastic bag in the refrigerator for up to 5 days. Rinse just before use.

## AVOCADOS

Choose avocados that are either firm (under ripe) or slightly soft to the touch (ripe). Avoid avocados that are overly soft or bruised.

Store firm avocados at room temperature until just beginning to give to gentle pressure. Once they give to gentle pressure, store in the refrigerator for 3 to 4 days before use.

## BASIL

Choose basil with bright green leaves and no signs of decay, wilting, or browning.

Cut the bottom inch from the stems and store, unwashed, in a glass of water at room temperature, as you would fresh flowers. Rinse just before use.

## BEETS

Choose small- to medium-sized beets that are smooth in texture and have their bright greens still attached if possible.

Remove the greens from the beets. Tear the beet greens from the stems, discard the stems, rinse, dry, and then store the greens wrapped in a dry paper towel inside a sealed plastic bag for up to 5 days. Store the unwashed beets in a sealed plastic bag in the refrigerator for up to 2 weeks.

## BLACKBERRIES

Choose blackberries that are plump and dark in color without signs of mold, decay, or leaking.

Store unwashed blackberries in one layer, sandwiched between dry paper towels, in an airtight container in the refrigerator for up to 3 days. Rinse just before use.

## BLUEBERRIES

Choose blueberries that are firm and plump without any signs of decay or bruising.

Store unwashed blueberries in a brown paper bag in the refrigerator for up to 1 week. Rinse just before use.

## BROCCOLI

Choose broccoli that has tight, compact florets with no signs of bruising, wilting, or yellowing and very little cracking at the base where it was cut.

Store unwashed broccoli in a perforated plastic bag in the refrigerator for up to 5 days. Rinse just before use.

## BRUSSELS SPROUTS

Choose Brussels sprouts that are firm, heavy for their size, and without any signs of yellowing in the leaves.

Store unwashed Brussels sprouts in a paper bag in the refrigerator for up to 1 week. Rinse just before use.

## CABBAGE

Choose cabbage that is firm, heavy for its size, and without any signs of yellowing in the leaves.

Store unwashed cabbage in a perforated plastic bag in the crisper drawer of the refrigerator for up to 2 weeks. As the cabbage ages, peel away any yellowing leaves before use.

## CARROTS

Choose small to medium carrots that are firm, vibrant in color, with no cracking, soft spots, or signs of decay.

Remove and discard greens if attached, then store carrots, unwashed, in a sealed plastic bag in the refrigerator for up to 2 weeks. Rinse or peel just before use. Save older carrots for making homemade stock.

## CAULIFLOWER

Pick cauliflower with firm, white compact florets, bright green outer leaves, no black spots on the surface, and very little cracking at the base where it was cut.

Store unwashed cauliflower in a perforated plastic bag in the refrigerator for up to 1 week. Rinse just before use.

## CELERY

Choose celery that has crisp, firm stalks with the leaves still attached. The leaves are the best indicator of the celery's age; they should be bright green in color without any yellowing.

Store unwashed celery in a sealed plastic bag in the crisper drawer of the refrigerator for up to 1 week. Rinse just before use. Save older celery for making homemade stock.

## CHERRIES

Choose cherries that are large, firm, shiny, heavy for their size, and with stems still attached. Avoid cherries with soft spots, wrinkling, or splits.

Store unwashed cherries in a perforated plastic bag in the refrigerator for up to 5 days. Rinse just before use.

## CHIVES

Choose chives that are crisp and vibrant in color, with no signs of yellowing or wilting.

Store unwashed chives wrapped in a damp paper towel inside a perforated plastic bag in the crisper drawer of the refrigerator for up to 1 week. Rinse just before use.

## CILANTRO

Choose cilantro that is vibrant in color, with no signs of yellowing or decay.

Store unwashed cilantro wrapped in a damp paper towel inside a perforated plastic bag in the crisper drawer of the refrigerator for up to 1 week. Rinse just before use.

## CORN

Choose corn still in the husks, with plump, firm kernels that squirt juice when pressed with your thumbnail. The silk—the stringy filament at the top—gets darker and drier as it ages. Look for moist, lighter-colored silk.

Store corn in its husk in either a brown paper bag or perforated plastic bag in the refrigerator for up to 5 days. Corn can lose up to 50% of its sugar if left out on a warm day, so refrigerate as soon as possible.

## CUCUMBERS

Choose small- to medium-sized cucumbers that are slender in shape and firm to the touch with no soft spots, wrinkling, or yellowing.

Store unwashed cucumbers in a sealed plastic bag in the refrigerator for up to 1 week. Rinse just before use.

## DATES

Choose dates that are plump and slightly wrinkled. Avoid dates with powdery surface sugars or mold.

Store dates in a sealed, airtight container in the refrigerator for up to 6 months, or in the freezer for up to 1 year.

## EGGPLANT

Choose eggplants that are firm, smooth, shiny, evenly colored, and heavy for their size with a fresh looking cap and stem.

Larger ripe eggplants will leave a temporary imprint when pressed with your thumb.

Store unwashed eggplants in a paper bag in the crisper drawer of the refrigerator for up to 1 week. Rinse just before use.

## FENNEL

Choose fennel bulbs that are white in color, unblemished, firm when squeezed, and without any wrinkling or browning. The leaves, or fronds, should be bright green in color without any browning.
Store unwashed fennel in a sealed plastic bag in the refrigerator for up to 5 days. Rinse just before use. Save older fennel for making homemade stock.

## FIGS

Choose figs with firm stems that are just beginning to give to gentle pressure without any mold, decay, leaking, or wrinkling.

Ripen figs on a paper towel-lined plate at room temperature. Store unwashed figs in one layer, sandwiched between dry paper towels, in an airtight container in the refrigerator for up to 5 days. Rinse just before use.

## FRISÉE

Choose frisée with shiny, healthy green leaves without any signs of browning or decay.

Store rinsed and dried frisée leaves in a perforated plastic bag in the refrigerator for up to 1 week.

## GARLIC

Choose dry, papery, firm heads of garlic without any signs of decay or soft spots.

Store garlic in a cool, dark, well-ventilated place for up to 1 month. Remove any green sprouts that may appear over time prior to using.

## GINGER

Choose ginger that is very firm when squeezed, smooth, and heavy for its size without any signs of decay or softening.

Store unwashed ginger in the crisper drawer of the refrigerator for up to 3 weeks.

## GRAPEFRUIT

Choose grapefruit that is firm, heavy for its size with shiny skin, and is without soft spots, signs of decay, or wrinkling.

Store grapefruit in the crisper drawer of the refrigerator for up to 3 weeks. Grapefruits are most flavorful at room temperature.

## GRAPES

Choose grapes that are plump and firm to the touch without signs of decay or wrinkling. Avoid older grapes which will fall off their stems when shaken.

Store unwashed grapes in an airtight container in the refrigerator for up to 1 week. Rinse just before use.

## GREEN BEANS

Choose green beans that are firm, smooth, and snap cleanly when broken. There should not be any pronounced bulging of the seeds, and the tail end should be firm and without damage.

Store unwashed green beans in a brown paper bag in the crisper drawer of the refrigerator for up to 10 days. Rinse just before use.

## KALE

Choose kale with firm leaves that shows no signs of decay, yellowing, or drying.

Tear the greens from the stems (discarding the stems), rinse and dry, then store wrapped in a dry paper towel inside a sealed plastic bag for up to 1 week.

## KUMQUATS

Choose kumquats that are firm, heavy for their size with shiny skin, without any soft spots, signs of decay, or wrinkling.

Store unwashed kumquats in the crisper drawer of the refrigerator for up to 2 weeks. Rinse before use.

## LEEKS

Choose small to medium leeks that are firm, straight, and heavy for their size, without yellowing or other signs of decay, with as much white and light green as possible.

Store unwashed leeks in a perforated plastic bag in the crisper drawer of the refrigerator for up to 10 days. Rinse thoroughly just before use.

## LEMONS

Choose lemons that are firm, heavy for their size with shiny skin, and are without any soft spots, signs of decay or wrinkling.

Store lemons in the crisper drawer of the refrigerator for up to 2 weeks.

## LETTUCE

Choose lettuce with brightly colored, crisp leaves without any signs of decay, browning, or wilting.

Store unwashed lettuce in a sealed plastic bag in the refrigerator for up to 1 week. Rinse just before use.

## LIMES

Choose limes that are firm, heavy for their size with shiny skin, and are without any soft spots, signs of decay, or wrinkling.

Store limes in the crisper drawer of the refrigerator for up to 2 weeks.

## MELONS

Choose melons without soft spots and with a forgiving stem end when pushed gently. For cantaloupes, look for a thick lacing or netting on the skin. Melons will have a very sweet fragrance at the stem end when ripe.

Ripen melons at room temperature. Store ripe melons in the refrigerator for up to 3 days. Melons are most flavorful at room temperature.

## MINT
Choose mint that has bright green leaves with no signs of browning, withering, drying, or decay.

Store mint, unwashed, wrapped in a damp paper towel inside a sealed plastic bag in the refrigerator for up to 1 week. Rinse just before use.

## MUSHROOMS
Choose mushrooms that are firm, without signs of wetness, shriveling, or mold.

Store mushrooms in a brown paper bag in the refrigerator for up to 5 days. When ready to use, wipe clean with a damp cloth.

## NECTARINES
Choose nectarines that have matte (not shiny) skin, with tiny freckles (if possible), and little to no green color at the stem end.

Soften unwashed nectarines at room temperature, upside down, on their "shoulders." Once they give to gentle pressure, store ripe nectarines in the crisper drawer of the refrigerator for up to 3 days. Rinse just before use. Nectarines are most flavorful at room temperature.

## NEW POTATOES
Choose firm, smooth new potatoes without any soft spots, green patches, or sprouting.

Store unwashed new potatoes in a cool, dark, well-ventilated place for up to 1 week. Scrub or peel before use.

## ONIONS (WHITE, YELLOW, RED)
Choose onions that are firm, heavy for their size, and free from signs of decay, dampness, or sprouting.

Store onions in a cool, dark, well-ventilated place, away from potatoes, for up to 3 weeks. Save older onions for making homemade stock.

## ORANGES

Choose oranges that are firm, heavy for their size with shiny skin, and are without any soft spots, signs of decay, or wrinkling.

Store oranges in the crisper drawer of the refrigerator for up to 2 weeks.

## OREGANO

Choose oregano that has rich green leaves, a fresh herbaceous smell, with no signs of browning, withering, drying, or decay.

Store unwashed oregano, wrapped in a damp paper towel inside a perforated plastic bag in the crisper drawer of the refrigerator for up to 1 week. Rinse just before use.

## PARSLEY (FLAT-LEAF ITALIAN)

Choose parsley that has bright green leaves with no signs of browning, withering, drying, or decay.

Store unwashed parsley wrapped in a damp paper towel inside a sealed plastic bag in the refrigerator for up to 1 week. Rinse just before use.

## PARSNIPS

Choose parsnips that are firm, do not bend easily, and show no signs of cracking or decay.

Store unwashed parsnips in a sealed plastic bag in the crisper drawer of the refrigerator for up to 10 days. Rinse or peel just before use.

## PEACHES

Choose peaches with little to no green color at the stem end and with a sweet fragrance. Ripe peaches should show no signs of bruising, or cracking, and should give to a gentle pressure when squeezed.

Soften unwashed peaches at room temperature, upside down, on their "shoulders." Once they give to gentle pressure, store ripe peaches in the crisper drawer of the refrigerator for up to 3 days. Rinse just before use. Peaches are most flavorful at room temperature.

## PEARS

Choose pears that are smooth, without bruising, mold, or soft spots and barely give to a gentle pressure.

Ripen unwashed pears in a brown paper bag at room temperature. Once pears give to gentle pressure, store in a brown paper bag in the refrigerator for up to 3 days. Rinse just before use. Pears are most flavorful at room temperature.

## PEPPERS

Choose peppers that have a firm, smooth skin without any signs of decay, soft spots, or wrinkling.

Store unwashed peppers in a brown paper bag in the refrigerator for up to 1 week. Rinse just before use.

## PLUMS

Choose plums that are evenly colored, shiny, and firm (but not hard) to the touch, and show no signs of cracking, bruising, wrinkling, or decay.

Store unwashed plums in a brown paper bag in the crisper drawer of the refrigerator for up to 5 days. Rinse just before use. Plums are most flavorful at room temperature.

## POMEGRANATES

Choose brightly colored, firm pomegranates that are heavy for their size, slightly angular in shape, and without wrinkled skin.

Store whole pomegranates in the refrigerator for up to 1 month.

## POTATOES

Choose firm, smooth potatoes without any soft spots, green patches, or sprouting.

Store unwashed potatoes in a cool, dark, well-ventilated place, away from onions, for up to 1 month. Scrub or peel just before use.

## RADICCHIO

Choose brightly colored, crisp radicchio without any signs of decay or wilting.

Store unwashed radicchio in a perforated plastic bag in the refrigerator for up to 5 days. Rinse just before use.

## RASPBERRIES

Choose raspberries that are firm, plump, and dark red in color, without any signs of mold, decay, or leaking.

Store unwashed raspberries in one layer, sandwiched between dry, paper towels, in an airtight container in the refrigerator for up to 3 days. Rinse just before use.

## ROSEMARY

Choose rosemary that has fresh green leaves and feels sticky when rubbed between your fingers, with no signs of browning, withering, drying, or decay.

Store unwashed rosemary wrapped in a damp paper towel inside a perforated plastic bag in the crisper drawer of the refrigerator for up to 1 week. Rinse just before use.

## SAGE

Choose sage that has fresh silver-green leaves with no signs of browning, withering, drying, or decay.

Store unwashed sage wrapped in a damp paper towel inside a perforated plastic bag in the crisper drawer of the refrigerator for up to 1 week. Rinse just before use.

## SHALLOTS

Choose shallots that are firm when squeezed, not soft or sprouting, and with dry papery skin.

Store shallots in a cool, dark, well-ventilated place, for up to 3 weeks. Save older shallots for making homemade stock.

## SPINACH

Choose spinach that has bright firm leaves, with no signs of yellowing, wilting, or decay.

Store spinach, unwashed, in a perforated plastic bag in the refrigerator for up to 5 days. Rinse thoroughly just before use.

## SUGAR SNAP PEAS

Choose small- to medium-sized pea pods that are firm, shiny, and snap when broken. Avoid any with signs of softening.

Store unwashed sugar snap peas in a perforated plastic bag in the crisper drawer of the refrigerator for up to 5 days. Rinse just before use.

## SUMMER SQUASH / ZUCCHINI

Choose small to medium summer squash that is firm and without any soft spots or signs of wrinkling.

Store unwashed summer squash in a brown paper bag in the refrigerator for up to 1 week. Rinse just before use.

## STRAWBERRIES

Choose strawberries that are firm and shiny, with as much color as possible, and without any signs of mold, decay, or leaking.

Store unwashed strawberries in one layer, sandwiched between dry paper towels, in an airtight container in the refrigerator for up to 2 weeks. Rinse just before use.

## SWEET POTATOES

Choose sweet potatoes that are firm and smooth, with no soft spots or signs of decay.

Store unwashed sweet potatoes a cool, dark, well-ventilated place for up to 4 weeks. Scrub or peel just before use.

## THYME

Choose thyme that has numerous fresh green leaves per stem with no signs of browning, withering, drying, or decay.

Store unwashed thyme wrapped in a damp paper towel inside a perforated plastic bag in the crisper drawer of the refrigerator for up to 1 week. Rinse just before use.

## TOMATOES

Choose tomatoes that are heavy for their size, shiny, vibrant in color, and with no signs of bruising or decay.

Store ripe, unwashed tomatoes out of the sun, at room temperature, upside down on their "shoulders" for up to 5 days. Rinse just before use. Tomatoes should not be refrigerated as their flavor and texture will be compromised.

## TURNIPS

Choose turnips with firm, smooth skin, and with bright, crisp leaves still attached if possible.

Separate the leaves from the turnip. Tear the greens from their stems, discard the stems, rinse, dry, and then store the greens in a perforated plastic bag in the refrigerator for up to 5 days. Store unwashed turnips in a sealed plastic bag in the refrigerator for up to 1 week. Save older turnips for making homemade vegetable stock. Rinse or peel just before use.

## WATERCRESS

Choose watercress leaves that are crisp, with no signs of wilting or decay.

Rinse, dry, and store watercress wrapped in a dry paper towel inside a sealed plastic bag in the refrigerator for up to 3 days.

## WATERMELON

Choose a firm watermelon, heavy for its size, without any soft spots or cracks. When held in one hand and thumped with the other, watermelon should have a deep, clear, resonant sound.

Store watermelon in the refrigerator for up to 3 days.

## WINTER SQUASH

Choose hard winter squash that is firm, heavy for its size, with a matte skin (not shiny). The skin should be free from any soft spots or cracking.

Store winter squash in a cool, dark, well-ventilated place. Wrap any cut squash in plastic wrap and store in the refrigerator for up to 5 days.

# SPRING

ARTICHOKES
ASPARAGUS
AVOCADOS
BEETS
CARROTS
CAULIFLOWER
CELERY
CHERRIES
CHIVES
CILANTRO
FENNEL
FRISÉE
GARLIC
GINGER
GRAPEFRUIT
LEEKS
LETTUCE
MINT

NEW POTATOES
ONIONS
OREGANO
PARSLEY
PARSNIPS
ROSEMARY
SAGE
SHALLOTS
SUGAR SNAP PEAS
SPINACH
STRAWBERRIES
THYME
WATERCRESS

**YIELD: 3 SERVINGS**

1½ tablespoons unsalted butter, divided

¾ pound large asparagus, white fibrous bottoms discarded and bottom inch peeled

1 medium garlic clove, peeled and minced (½ teaspoon)

1½ tablespoons freshly squeezed lemon juice (juice of half a lemon)

Kosher salt, to taste

Freshly ground black pepper, to taste

3 large eggs

Parmigiano-Reggiano, not pre-grated, for serving

Extra-virgin olive oil, for drizzling

1 tablespoon finely chopped fresh flat-leaf Italian parsley

# PAN-ROASTED ASPARAGUS
## WITH SOFT-FRIED EGGS AND SHAVED PARMIGIANO

When the first asparagus of the season debuts at the farmers market, it's like a free-for-all. People arrive early, coffee in hand, for the very best selection. I mean, sure, I guess you could wait until lunch or dinner to enjoy them, but when served just barely charred and topped with a fried egg and some freshly shaved Parmigiano-Reggiano... for breakfast? If that isn't worth getting up early for, I don't know what is.

1. Add 1 tablespoon of butter to a large sauté pan, and heat over medium-high heat. The butter will foam up, and then subside.

2. After approximately 30 to 40 seconds, the butter will begin to turn golden brown. Immediately add the asparagus and shake the sauté pan gently to coat the asparagus in the butter.

3. Season with a good pinch of salt plus a few grinds of pepper and cook undisturbed for 1 minute.

4. Shake the sauté pan to rotate the asparagus, then add the garlic and shake the sauté pan again to distribute. Cook for 1 minute more.

5. Sprinkle the lemon juice over the asparagus and shake the pan to coat the asparagus evenly.

6. Turn off the heat and season to taste with salt and pepper. Cover the pan to keep the asparagus warm while you cook the eggs.

7. Heat the remaining butter in a medium nonstick sauté pan over medium-low heat until the butter is melted, swirling the pan to distribute the butter evenly.

8. Add the eggs one at a time until all the eggs are in the sauté pan.

9. Season lightly with salt and pepper, then cover with a lid. (Use a glass lid, if possible, so that you can see the egg's progress). Do not be tempted to increase the heat. I'm watching you.

10. Cook undisturbed for 3 to 4 minutes, or until the white is set and the yolk is still runny.

11. Remove the eggs from the heat when finished cooking and serve immediately.

12. To serve, distribute the asparagus evenly among 3 plates and top each plate with an egg.

13. Using a vegetable peeler, top each serving with some shavings of Parmigiano-Reggiano, then top with a drizzle of extra-virgin olive oil and a sprinkling of parsley. Serve immediately. Scootch over and hand me a fork.

*"Probably one of the most private things in the world is an egg before it is broken."* — M.F.K. FISHER

## ASPARAGUS SOUP

**YIELD: 6 TO 8 SERVINGS**

2 tablespoons unsalted butter, divided

2 tablespoons extra-virgin olive oil, divided

1 medium shallot, peeled and chopped roughly (3 tablespoons)

5 large garlic cloves, peeled and chopped roughly (1 tablespoon plus 2 teaspoons)

½ pound Yukon Gold potatoes, peeled and diced medium (2 medium potatoes)

4 cups vegetable or chicken stock (recipes on page 37 & 38)

5 sprigs fresh thyme

1 dried bay leaf

2 pounds asparagus, white fibrous bottoms discarded, bottom inch peeled, and cut into 1-inch pieces

2 tablespoons fresh goat cheese (chèvre)

2 teaspoons freshly squeezed lemon juice

Kosher salt, to taste

Freshly ground black pepper, to taste

Pecorino Romano or Parmigiano-Reggiano cheese, not pre-grated, for serving

Breadcrumbs (recipe on page 44), preferably homemade, optional, for garnish

2 tablespoons finely chopped fresh chives or fresh flat-leaf Italian parsley

# THREE SOUPS
## SAME METHOD

   Picture this: you're in a restaurant. You order a side of vegetables with your main course. When they arrive, what do you see? A bowl of bland, mushy, steamed cauliflower and broccoli. Wow. Again? It's just like the stereotypical bowl of underripe melon with half a grape passed off as a "side of fruit." How about we change things up a bit and turn those vegetables into a creamy soup? What do you say? Vegetables deserve better, and so do you. Go ahead. Pick a vegetable. Any vegetable.

# ASPARAGUS SOUP

1.  Combine 1 tablespoon butter and 1 tablespoon olive oil in a large saucepan and heat over medium-low heat until the butter is melted.

2.  Stir in the shallot and cook for 1 minute until it is soft and translucent.

3.  Add the garlic, and cook for 1 minute until fragrant.

4.  Stir in the potatoes, stock, thyme sprigs, and bay leaf.

5.  Cover and increase the heat to high until boiling, then reduce the heat to low and simmer over low heat for 10 minutes.

6.  Add the asparagus, re-cover, and continue simmering for 15 minutes, until the potatoes are cooked through and the asparagus is tender.

7.  Remove from the heat, then remove the thyme sprigs and bay leaf.

8.  Add the goat cheese, remaining butter, olive oil, and the lemon juice to the asparagus mixture.

9.  Using an immersion blender, regular blender, or food processor, blend or process the soup until smooth.

**CAULIFLOWER SOUP**

**YIELD: 6 TO 8 SERVINGS**

2 tablespoons unsalted butter, divided

2 tablespoons extra-virgin olive oil, divided

1 medium shallot, peeled and chopped roughly (3 tablespoons)

5 large garlic cloves, peeled and chopped roughly (1 tablespoon plus 2 teaspoons)

1 large head cauliflower (1½ pounds), leaves discarded, cored, and chopped into small pieces

¾ pound Yukon Gold potatoes, peeled and diced medium (3 medium potatoes)

2 cups vegetable or chicken stock (recipes on page 37 & 38)

2 cups whole milk

5 sprigs fresh thyme

1 dried bay leaf

2 ounces fresh goat cheese (chèvre) (¼ cup)

1 tablespoon freshly squeezed lemon juice

Kosher salt, to taste

Freshly ground black pepper, to taste

Pecorino Romano or Parmigiano-Reggiano cheese, not pre-grated, for serving

Breadcrumbs (recipe on page 44), preferably homemade, optional, for garnish

2 tablespoons finely chopped fresh chives or fresh flat-leaf Italian parsley

10. Season to taste with salt and pepper.

11. Serve in soup bowls, topped with freshly grated Pecorino Romano or Parmigiano-Reggiano, bread crumbs, chopped chives or parsley, and a grind of pepper.

## CAULIFLOWER SOUP

1. Combine 1 tablespoon butter and 1 tablespoon olive oil in a large saucepan and heat over medium-low heat until the butter is melted.

2. Stir in the shallot, and cook for 1 minute, until the shallot is soft and translucent.

3. Add the garlic and cook for 1 minute more, until fragrant.

4. Stir in the cauliflower, diced potatoes, stock, milk, thyme, and bay leaf.

5. Cover, increase the heat to high until simmering, then reduce the heat to low and continue to simmer for 25 minutes, until the potatoes are falling apart and the cauliflower is tender.

6. Remove from the heat, then remove the thyme sprigs and bay leaf.

7. Add the goat cheese, remaining butter, olive oil, and lemon juice to the cauliflower mixture.

8. Using an immersion blender, regular blender, or food processor, blend or process the soup until smooth.

9. Season to taste with salt and pepper.

10. Serve in soup bowls, topped with freshly grated Pecorino Romano or Parmigiano-Reggiano, bread crumbs, chopped chives or parsley, and a grind of pepper.

# BROCCOLI SOUP

1. Combine 1 tablespoon butter and 1 tablespoon olive oil in a large saucepan and heat over medium-low heat until the butter melts.

2. Stir in the shallot and cook for 1 minute, until the shallot is soft and translucent.

3. Add the garlic, and cook for 1 minute more, until fragrant.

4. Stir in the potatoes, stock, thyme, and bay leaf.

5. Cover, increase the heat to high until boiling, then reduce the heat to low and simmer for 10 minutes.

6. Add the broccoli florets, re-cover, and continue simmering for 15 minutes, until the potatoes are cooked through and the broccoli is tender.

7. Remove from the heat, then remove the thyme sprigs and bay leaf.

8. Add the goat cheese, remaining butter, olive oil, and lemon juice to the broccoli mixture.

9. Using an immersion blender, regular blender, or food processor, blend or process the soup until smooth.

10. Season to taste with salt and pepper.

11. Serve in soup bowls, topped with freshly grated Pecorino Romano, Parmigiano-Reggiano or aged Cheddar cheese, bread crumbs, chopped chives or parsley, and a grind of pepper.

**BROCCOLI SOUP**

**YIELD: 6 TO 8 SERVINGS**

2 tablespoons unsalted butter, divided

2 tablespoons extra-virgin olive oil, divided

1 medium shallot, peeled and chopped roughly (3 tablespoons)

5 large garlic cloves, peeled and chopped roughly (1 tablespoon plus 2 teaspoons)

½ pound Yukon Gold potatoes, peeled and diced medium (2 medium potatoes)

1 large head broccoli (1 pound), broken into bite-size florets

4 cups vegetable or chicken stock (recipes on page 37 & 38)

5 sprigs fresh thyme

1 dried bay leaf

2 tablespoons fresh goat cheese (chèvre)

2 teaspoons freshly squeezed lemon juice

Kosher salt, to taste

Freshly ground black pepper, to taste

Pecorino Romano, Parmigiano-Reggiano, or aged Cheddar cheese, not pre-grated, for serving

Breadcrumbs (recipe on page 44), preferably homemade, optional, for garnish

2 tablespoons finely chopped fresh chives or fresh flat-leaf Italian parsley

YIELD: 2 SERVINGS

1 large avocado, cut in half, lengthwise, pit removed

1 tablespoon extra-virgin olive oil, plus more for drizzling

1 tablespoon fresh lemon juice

¼ teaspoon ground cumin

Kosher salt, to taste

Freshly ground black pepper, to taste

Homemade Crostini (recipe on page 40)

Note: Try topping the crostini with fried eggs, sliced tomato and crème fraîche. Whoa. Yes, please.

## CUMIN AVOCADO ON CROSTINI

1. Scoop the flesh of an avocado out of its skin with a spoon and put it into a small bowl.

2. Add 1 tablespoon olive oil, the fresh lemon juice, and the cumin, and season to taste with salt and pepper.

3. Using the back of a fork, smash that avocado against the side of the bowl. Smash it like you mean it.

4. Adjust the seasoning with salt and pepper to taste once more, then slather 1 tablespoon of the avocado on each of the warm, crunchy crostini and drizzle a wee bit of olive oil over each one.

# GRILLED ARTICHOKES
## WITH LEMON-SHALLOT VINAIGRETTE

Did you know that the artichoke is actually a flower? Yup, it's true. Don't let this spiky blossom intimidate you though. He may seem all tough on the outside, but, truth be known, he's got a very sweet heart... a heart that pairs perfectly with a lemon-shallot vinaigrette.

1. In a small pot, add the chopped onion, garlic cloves, fresh thyme, lemon juice, bay leaf, white wine, peppercorns, salt, and enough water to fill the pot at least half way.

2. Turn the heat to high and bring this mixture to a boil, then reduce the heat to low to simmer.

3. Grab those three large artichokes and a serrated (bread) knife. Cut the stems off at the base of the artichokes. Again, using a serrated knife, cut the top third of each artichoke off and discard it. You can't eat that part anyway. Now cut each artichoke in half lengthwise.

4. Add the artichoke halves to the pot of simmering water. Top with an inverted plate, inverted old-school vegetable steamer, or a saucepan lid that is slightly smaller than the pot so that the artichokes stay submerged. Simmer until the bottoms of the artichokes can be pierced easily with a sharp knife and an outer leaf can be pulled out with little effort, about 25 minutes.

5. Drain the artichokes in a colander, cut side down, until they are cool enough to handle.

6. Meanwhile, preheat a grill to medium-high. Once hot, clean the grill, then, using tongs, lightly dip a cloth in a dish of olive oil and wipe to coat the grill rack.

**YIELD: 3 SERVINGS**

**GRILLED ARTICHOKES:**

3 large artichokes

1 large yellow onion, peeled and chopped into 8 pieces

3 large garlic cloves, peeled and crushed

7 sprigs fresh thyme

6 tablespoons freshly squeezed lemon juice (juice of 2 lemons)

1 dried bay leaf

1 cup dry white wine (preferably Sauvignon Blanc or Chardonnay)

1 tablespoon black peppercorns

2 tablespoons kosher salt

Extra-virgin olive oil, for preparing the artichokes

7. Using a spoon, gently remove the chokes (the sharp, feather-like leaves that sit in the middle of the artichoke, on top of the heart.)

8. Brush the cut sides of the artichoke halves with olive oil and grill them, face down, until slightly charred around the edges.

9. Remove from the grill and drizzle the lemon vinaigrette over the artichokes.

## VINAIGRETTE

In a medium container with a tight fitting lid, combine the vinaigrette ingredients, close the lid tightly, and shake well to combine. Or, whisk to combine the ingredients in a medium-sized bowl.

**VINAIGRETTE:**

1 large shallot, peeled and finely diced
(3 tablespoons)

6 tablespoons freshly squeezed lemon juice
(juice of 2 lemons)

¼ cup extra-virgin olive oil

Note: If you're not quite ready to crank up the grill for the season, no sweat. After simmering, draining, and brushing the artichoke halves with oil, simply place them under your broiler and cook until slightly charred.

# NOT YOUR MOM'S CHICKEN LIVER PÂTÉ

**YIELD: 4 SERVINGS**

2 tablespoons extra-virgin olive oil, divided

½ pound organic chicken livers

1 medium yellow onion, peeled and diced small (1 cup)

½ teaspoon roughly chopped fresh thyme

2 large garlic cloves, peeled and chopped roughly (2 teaspoons)

1 teaspoon sherry vinegar

4 teaspoons balsamic vinegar, divided

1½ tablespoons cold unsalted butter, cut into 3 pieces

Kosher salt, to taste

Freshly ground black pepper, to taste

Homemade Crostini (recipe on page 40)

My childhood nemesis: sautéed chicken livers with onions. You know what I'm talking about, right? Have you ever met a kid who came running when they heard that liver and onions were on the menu for dinner? However, over time (albeit a lifetime), I've grown quite fond of chicken livers, and I hope you've given them a chance, too. It turns out they're not gross at all. In fact, like most foods, they can be downright delicious when prepared correctly. Now, I still don't think most kids are going to rejoice when you tell them that they're having chicken livers for dinner, but perhaps, with this recipe, they might not go running for the hills.

1. Rinse the chicken livers, then remove and discard any connective tissue, veins, fat, or green spots. Pat the chicken livers dry.

2. Add 1 tablespoon extra-virgin olive oil to a medium sauté pan set over high heat and heat until shimmering; even a few wisps of smoke is okay.

3. Add the chicken livers and allow them to cook undisturbed for 2 minutes.

4. Using tongs, flip the livers, then continue cooking until nicely caramelized on all sides, approximately 2 additional minutes. Remove the tiny pieces slightly earlier and leave the very large pieces a few moments longer. A medium-sized liver should be light pink in color, but not raw, when cut into. Be careful not to overcook the livers, or else the flavor becomes too livery. Transfer the livers to a small plate.

5. Reduce the heat to medium-low. Using the same sauté pan, add the second tablespoon of oil, diced onion, and thyme. Cook for 6 to 8 minutes, stirring occasionally, until the onions are soft, translucent, and lightly caramelized.

6. Add the garlic and cook until fragrant, 1 minute.

7. Add the sherry vinegar, 3 teaspoons of the balsamic vinegar, and stir with a wooden spoon to loosen up the brown bits stuck to the bottom of the pan, then immediately remove from the heat.

8. Place the cooked livers, the caramelized onion plus any liquid from the pan, and the pieces of butter in a food processor fitted with the metal blade attachment, then blend until smooth.

9. Season to taste with salt and pepper and add the remaining balsamic vinegar.

10. Serve warm as an appetizer, or spoon the pâté into ramekins, cover with plastic wrap and refrigerate until chilled. Serve with crostini.

Note: Going for the chilled pâté option? Try this: serve with the crostini, capers, diced red onion, whole-grain Dijon mustard, a few lemon wedges, and cornichons, those tasty little pickles.

# BRAISED LENTIL FRISÉE SALAD

## LENTILS

1. Mix the lentils with the stock, bay leaf, and thyme in a medium saucepan over high heat.

2. Bring the saucepan to a boil, then reduce the heat to low and simmer for approximately 25 to 30 minutes, stirring occasionally, until the lentils are cooked through but not mushy. Drain. Discard the thyme sprigs and bay leaf.

## VINAIGRETTE

In a small container with a tight fitting lid, combine the vinaigrette ingredients, close the lid tightly, and shake well to combine. Or, whisk to combine the ingredients in a small bowl.

## SALAD

1. Add the bacon and 1 teaspoon of olive oil to a medium sauté pan over medium-low heat. Cook for approximately 5 to 6 minutes, stirring occasionally, until much of the fat has rendered off, and the bacon is just beginning to get nice and crispy.

2. Transfer the bacon to a side plate. Pour off and reserve half of the bacon fat and leave the other half in the pan.

**LENTILS:**

1 cup beluga lentils, rinsed well and drained

3 cups vegetable stock (recipe on page 37)

1 dried bay leaf

5 sprigs fresh thyme

**VINAIGRETTE:**

¼ cup plus 2 tablespoons extra-virgin olive oil

1 tablespoon red wine vinegar

⅛ teaspoon kosher salt

Freshly ground black pepper, to taste

½ teaspoon whole-grain Dijon mustard

**SALAD:**

1 teaspoon extra-virgin olive oil

2 strips bacon, halved lengthwise and then cut crosswise into ¼-inch slices (½ cup)

2 medium carrots, peeled and grated (1 cup)

1 small yellow onion, peeled and diced small (⅔ cup)

4 large garlic cloves, peeled and minced (1 tablespoon plus 1 teaspoon)

¼ teaspoon ground cumin

¼ cup roughly chopped fresh flat-leaf Italian parsley

2 tablespoons roughly chopped fresh mint

1 small head frisée, rinsed and dried, chopped or torn into bite-size pieces (2 cups)

Kosher salt, to taste

Freshly ground black pepper, to taste

3. Return the pan to medium-low heat and add the diced onions and grated carrots. Cook for 5 minutes, stirring occasionally.

4. Add the garlic and cumin and cook until fragrant, 1 minute. If it looks a little dry (or if you just happen to just really love bacon fat), add some of the reserved bacon fat back in.

5. In a large bowl, combine the contents of the sauté pan along with the lentils.

6. Grab the vinaigrette and give one more good shake, then pour half of it over the warm salad and gently mix with a large spoon.

7. Fold in the parsley, mint, frisée, and bacon. Season to taste with salt, pepper, and additional vinaigrette.

8. Serve on 4 plates.

Note: Leftover lentils are great for breakfast. Re-warm the lentils with a little water or vegetable stock, then fold in some feta cheese and top with a warm fried egg and grated Parmigiano-Reggiano.

# SPRING PEA AND SPINACH SOUP
## WITH CRÈME FRAÎCHE

When it comes to pea soup, where the integrity of the peas doesn't matter, use frozen peas instead of fresh. Most chefs do. Frozen peas are flash-frozen, so all that sweet flavor is locked into the peas. That, and freshly shucked peas are too delicate, too wonderful, and simply too expensive to blend into a soup. Salads? Sure. Risotto? Absolutely. But soup? Nah.

What about the color of pea soup? Normally, pea soup is an unpleasant muddy green. What's the secret of keeping my pea soup green, you ask? Add spinach. That's right—spinach. Again, use frozen spinach—flash-frozen means no loss of flavor. So grab a pot and open up that freezer, because soup's on!

1. Bring a large saucepan of water to boil.

2. Add the spinach and cook until it can be separated easily with a fork. Drain into a strainer over the sink, and cool quickly with cold running water. Continue to drain in the strainer and squeeze out as much of the water from the spinach as possible.

3. Add the bacon and 1 tablespoon of olive oil to a large saucepan over medium-low heat. Cook for approximately 5 to 6 minutes, stirring occasionally, until much of the fat has rendered off, and the bacon is just beginning to get nice and crispy.

4. Using a slotted spoon, remove the bacon, leaving the bacon fat in the saucepan, placing the cooked bacon on a paper towel to drain.

5. Add the onions to the saucepan and continue to cook over medium-low heat for 6 to 7 minutes, stirring occasionally, until the onions are soft and beginning to color.

**YIELDS: 4 TO 6 SERVINGS**

1 (10-ounce) block frozen spinach

1 tablespoon extra-virgin olive oil, plus more for drizzling

3 slices of bacon, halved lengthwise and then cut crosswise into ¼-inch slices (¾ cup)

1 medium yellow onion, peeled and diced small (1 cup)

3 large garlic cloves, peeled and chopped roughly (1 tablespoon)

1 (16-ounce) bag frozen peas

4 cups chicken stock (recipe on page 38)

1¼ teaspoon kosher salt, plus more to taste

¼ teaspoon freshly ground black pepper, plus more to taste

1½ tablespoons freshly squeezed lemon juice (juice of half a lemon)

8 medium fresh mint leaves, chopped roughly

2 tablespoons cold unsalted butter

Crème fraîche, for serving (recipe on page 45)

Fresh flat-leaf Italian parsley, for garnish

Note: You can make this dish vegetarian simply by replacing the bacon with 3 tablespoons extra-virgin olive oil. Swap out the chicken stock for vegetable stock.  Then, of course, you can always add some bacon.

6. Add the garlic, and cook until fragrant, 1 minute.

7. Add the peas and the chicken stock to the saucepan, raise the heat to high, bring to a boil, then reduce the heat to low and simmer for 5 minutes until the peas are cooked through.

8. Add the spinach and, using an immersion blender, purée until smooth.

9. Add the salt, pepper, lemon juice, mint leaves, and butter; continue to purée until fully incorporated.

10. Season to taste with salt and pepper.

11. Serve in individual bowls with a dollop of crème fraîche, a drizzle of olive oil, and a leaf of parsley. Then add a few crispy pieces of bacon if desired. Yum.

# MARINATED BABY ARTICHOKES

It was mid-April in 2009. One day before flying to New York City, I purchased three dozen baby artichokes from my friend Daisy, a farmer who sold her produce at the Santa Monica farmers market. Those artichokes were so beautiful, so fresh, that I just couldn't leave them behind in L.A. Two days after arriving in Manhattan, I prepared them for someone very special, in the best way I knew how.

Baby artichokes have no choke, so once they're cooked, you can dive right in with wild abandon, and eat the entire thing. You don't even need a fork. In fact, we ate ours, using our fingers, on a plane bound for the New Orleans Jazz Fest. Needless to say, we were the envy of those passengers around us.

Thank you, Daisy.

1. Fill a small bowl halfway with ice water, and add 2 lemon halves, squeezing each half as you add them. This is called acidulated water, and it will keep the artichokes from turning brown. When you are ready to cook the artichokes, drain them in a colander over the sink.

2. Remove and discard the outer leaves of each artichoke until you get to the more tender, yellow- or very light green-colored inner leaves. The darker green leaves are chewy when cooked and therefore must be removed.

3. Using a vegetable peeler, peel down the rough, outer portion of the stem and any tough fibrous area around the bottom of each artichoke.

4. Cut off and discard the top third of each artichoke, then cut each artichoke in half. Now you're all ready to cook.

**YIELD: 2 TO 4 SERVINGS**

12 baby artichokes

2 lemons cut in half, divided

¼ cup extra-virgin olive oil, divided

2 medium shallots, peeled and diced finely (6 tablespoons)

2 large garlic cloves, peeled and minced

3 sprigs fresh thyme

¼ cup dry white wine (Sauvignon Blanc)

1½ cups vegetable stock (recipe on page 37)

Kosher salt, to taste

Freshly ground black pepper, to taste

1 tablespoon balsamic vinegar

Parmigiano-Reggiano cheese, not pre-grated, for serving

2 tablespoons fresh flat-leaf Italian parsley, chopped roughly

5. As the artichokes are draining, add 2 tablespoons olive oil to a medium sauté pan, set it over medium-high heat, and heat until shimmering.

6. Add the drained artichokes and cook until lightly colored, 3 minutes, stirring every minute for even cooking.

7. Stir in the shallots, garlic, and thyme, and continue to cook for 1 minute.

8. Add the wine and cook until almost no liquid remains, about 1 minute.

9. Add the stock, a pinch of salt, and a few generous grinds of pepper.

10. Cover, increase the heat to high, bring to a boil, then reduce the heat to low, and simmer for approximately 15 minutes.

11. Remove the lid and continue to cook until the artichokes are easily pierced with the tip of a knife and very little liquid remains, approximately 10 to 15 minutes more, then remove from the heat, uncover, and discard the thyme sprigs.

12. To make the vinaigrette, whisk together 2 tablespoons olive oil, 1 tablespoon lemon juice, and the balsamic vinegar in a large bowl.

13. Stir the braised artichokes into the vinaigrette and, using a vegetable peeler, top with some shavings of Parmigiano-Reggiano. Sprinkle the Italian parsley over the still-warm artichokes and serve.

# Cauliflower Three Ways

I never knew that cauliflower could be so delicious. One of the first cauliflower recipes I really enjoyed was created by Chef Gloria Felix, owner and chef of Reservoir in Los Angeles. It was amazing: sliced thin and roasted at high heat with spices and butter. This got me thinking… if cauliflower can be this good roasted, how else can it be prepared? From that moment, my cauliflower quest had begun, creating recipes to satisfy everyone's taste, and I think I've done it! For example, my Dad is a huge fan of my roasted cauliflower with bread crumbs. He can empty half a bowl before I even get around to serving it. My friend Sarah in Richmond, Virginia loves my cauliflower purée with white truffle oil. In fact, she claims to dream about it. Strange, but true. My college roommate, Ewam, digs his cauliflower spicy—so spicy it is!

Three different people+three different tastes=cauliflower three ways. Everybody wins.

## White Truffle Cauliflower Purée

1. Bring the stock to a boil in a medium saucepan.

2. Add the cauliflower and garlic; reduce the heat to low and simmer for 25 to 30 minutes until the cauliflower is soft and can be very easily pierced with a fork. (Don't be surprised if there is very little stock remaining at this point.) Drain well in a colander.

3. Using an immersion blender or a food processor, purée the contents of the saucepan until smooth.

**WHITE TRUFFLE CAULIFLOWER PURÉE**

**YIELD: 2 TO 3 SERVINGS**

2 cups chicken or vegetable stock (recipes on page 37 & 38)

1 medium head cauliflower, leaves discarded, cored, and chopped into bite-size pieces

1 large garlic clove, peeled and chopped roughly (1 teaspoon)

3 tablespoons unsalted butter

Kosher salt, to taste

Freshly ground black pepper, to taste

Parmigiano-Reggiano, not pre-grated, for serving

White truffle oil, for drizzling

1 tablespoon finely chopped fresh flat-leaf Italian parsley

## SPICED ROASTED CAULIFLOWER

**YIELD: 4 SERVINGS**

1 medium head cauliflower, leaves discarded, cored, and chopped into bite-size florets

2 tablespoons extra-virgin olive oil

1 tablespoon unsalted butter, cut into small pieces

2 teaspoons yellow curry powder

1 teaspoon ground cumin

$\frac{1}{16}$ teaspoon ground nutmeg

$\frac{1}{8}$ teaspoon ground cayenne pepper

Kosher salt, to taste

Freshly ground black pepper, to taste

1 tablespoon red wine vinegar

$\frac{1}{4}$ cup roughly chopped fresh flat-leaf Italian parsley

$\frac{1}{4}$ cup grated Parmigiano-Reggiano cheese, not pre-grated

## ROASTED CAULIFLOWER WITH BREAD CRUMBS

**YIELD: 4 SERVINGS**

1 tablespoon kosher salt, plus more to taste

1 large head cauliflower, leaves discarded, cored, and chopped into bite-size florets

2 tablespoons extra-virgin olive oil

1 teaspoon ground cumin

Ingredients continued on next page »

4. Add the butter and process again, adding salt and pepper to taste.

5. Spoon into bowls and, using a vegetable peeler, add some shavings of Parmigiano-Reggiano. Drizzle truffle oil and sprinkle parsley over the top.

# SPICED ROASTED CAULIFLOWER

1. Adjust an oven rack to the middle position, then preheat the oven to 400°F.

2. Lay the slices of cauliflower evenly on a parchment paper- or aluminum foil-lined sheet pan.

3. Drizzle with 2 tablespoons of olive oil and dot with the pieces of butter.

4. Mix together the cumin, yellow curry powder, nutmeg, and cayenne and sprinkle evenly over the cauliflower; season to taste with salt and pepper.

5. Roast the cauliflower, uncovered, for approximately 25 minutes until it's lightly caramelized and can be easily pierced with a fork.

6. Remove the cauliflower from the oven, drizzle with the vinegar, sprinkle with the parsley, and top with the grated Parmigiano-Reggiano.

# ROASTED CAULIFLOWER
## WITH BREAD CRUMBS

1. In a medium saucepan set over high heat, bring to a boil enough water to submerge the cauliflower florets, then add 1 tablespoon salt.

2. Stir in the cauliflower florets, return the water to a boil, then reduce the heat to medium-low. Simmer for approximately 15 to 20 minutes until the cauliflower can be easily pierced with a fork, and drain well in a colander.

3. Transfer the cauliflower to a medium bowl and toss with the olive oil, cumin, a good pinch of salt and pepper, and the bread crumbs.

4. Meanwhile, adjust an oven rack to the middle position, then preheat the oven to 425°F.

5. Line a sheet pan with parchment paper, spread the cauliflower on it in a single layer and roast, uncovered, for 8 to 10 minutes, until the cauliflower is lightly toasted.

6. Sprinkle the cheese over the cauliflower and continue to roast for approximately 2 minutes more, until the cheese melts.

7. Remove the pan from the oven, return the cauliflower to the bowl, and toss it with the lemon juice and parsley.

8. Season to taste with salt and pepper and serve.

½ cup breadcrumbs (recipe on page 44), or panko (Japanese breadcrumbs)

¼ cup grated Parmigiano-Reggiano or Gruyère cheese, not pre-grated

2 tablespoons roughly chopped fresh flat-leaf Italian parsley

1½ tablespoons freshly squeezed lemon juice (juice of half a lemon)

Freshly ground black pepper, to taste

1 pound sugar snap peas, strings removed

1 tablespoon unsalted butter

15 medium-sized fresh mint leaves, chopped roughly

1 tablespoon freshly squeezed lemon juice

Kosher salt, to taste

Freshly ground black pepper, to taste

# BROWN BUTTER SUGAR SNAP PEAS
## WITH FRESH MINT

When I visit my brother in Colorado, I can always count on my niece, Mason, to be my sous-chef. We shop at the farmers market together, so why not cook together? Need pizza rolled out? No sweat. She's got it covered. Vegetables chopped? Please. Challenge her. How about sugar snap peas de-stringed? She can do it with one hand behind her back. Best of all, by the time Mason's finished prepping the sugar snap peas, I have the butter browned and ready to roll. Working together, Mason and I can have an amazing snack on the table for everyone to enjoy in seven minutes flat. Which just goes to show that two Lyons in the kitchen is always better than one.

1. In a large sauté pan over high heat, add the butter. The butter will foam up, subside, and after approximately 30 to 40 seconds, begin to turn golden brown. Brown butter has a slight nutty favor that works well with this dish.

2. Once the butter has turned golden brown, mix in the sugar snap peas. Cook, stirring occasionally, for 3 minutes.

3. Remove from the heat and add the mint and the lemon juice.

4. Season to taste with salt and pepper, mix together, then serve immediately.

# SLOW-ROASTED LEG OF LAMB
## WITH MINT AND CILANTRO PESTO

Roast leg of lamb is one of those wonderful spring dishes that exemplifies a certain elegance and sophistication, but sophisticated doesn't have to mean difficult—far from it.

Purchasing a leg of lamb for this recipe is easy. As a rule of thumb, go for a smaller leg. Larger legs can sometimes taste a bit on the gamey side. Shop around for the 3½- to 4-pound mark. A little lamb, as it were, like the one that Mary had. Also, when shopping, remember the acronym BRT, which stands for boned, rolled, and tied. The bone will be removed from the leg, the meat will be rolled up into a package, and it will all be held together with a stretchy mesh fabric.

Spring is in the air. Mary's no place to be seen. And sophistication? It never tasted so good.

1. Remove the leg of lamb from the mesh, unroll it, and cut it at the thinnest part so that the leg lays flat.

2. Pat the leg of lamb dry. Place it into a large bowl and season evenly on all sides with the salt and pepper.

3. Using a food processor, combine the remaining ingredients, and pulse until well blended, 15 seconds.

4. Pour the contents over the lamb and rub to coat the lamb all over. Cover with plastic wrap and allow to sit for 1 hour at room temperature.

5. Place the leg of lamb, fat side down, on an aluminum foil-lined sheet pan.

6. Turn the oven to broil. Once on, place the sheet pan with the leg of lamb under the broiler. Broil until nicely colored, 7 to 10 minutes, depending on how far the meat is from your oven's heat source.

**YIELD: 8 TO 10 SERVINGS**

**LAMB:**

1 boneless leg of lamb, 3½ to 4¼ pounds

2 teaspoons kosher salt

¾ teaspoon freshly ground black pepper

½ small yellow onion or 2 medium shallots, peeled and quartered

5 large garlic cloves, peeled

2 tablespoons roughly chopped fresh rosemary

1 tablespoon plus 1 teaspoon fennel seed

1 tablespoon finely chopped fresh thyme

1 teaspoon lemon zest (zest of 1 lemon), grated on a Microplane

1½ tablespoons freshly squeezed lemon juice (juice of half a lemon)

3 tablespoons extra-virgin olive oil

**MINT AND CILANTRO PESTO**

**YIELD: APPROXIMATELY 2 CUPS**

1 cup fresh mint leaves

½ cup fresh cilantro

3 tablespoons seasoned rice wine vinegar

1 tablespoon fresh ginger, peeled and grated on a Microplane

1 small garlic clove, peeled and grated into paste on a Microplane, ¼ to ½ teaspoon

2 tablespoons freshly squeezed lime juice (juice of 1 lime)

⅓ cup grapeseed oil

¼ teaspoon kosher salt

⅛ teaspoon freshly ground black pepper

7.  Check on the progress of the lamb every couple of minutes. A char is fine; burning, not so much.

8.  When the lamb is nicely colored, flip the leg with tongs and continue to broil until nicely colored on the fat side, 5 to 7 minutes. Your kitchen should smell a little bit like garlic-rosemary heaven. Remove the leg from the broiler.

9.  Adjust an oven rack to the middle position and set the oven to 300°F.

10. Insert an oven-safe digital thermometer probe horizontally into the middle of the leg (still fat side up), and set the alarm to sound at 127°F.

11. Once the oven is preheated, transfer the leg to the oven and cook, uncovered, until the thermometer alarm goes off. For medium-rare, that's approximately 35 to 40 minutes.

12. Remove the leg from the oven and transfer to a cutting board. Tent loosely with foil and allow to rest at least 20 minutes prior to slicing.

13. Slice thinly against the grain of the meat and serve with the mint-cilantro pesto on the side.

Note: If you prefer your lamb cooked to medium or even barely a medium-well, not to worry. The smaller end pieces will be cooked more than the thicker center parts. There's something for everyone.

## MINT AND CILANTRO PESTO

Mint jelly is so 1970s. Here, try this instead.

1.  Place all of the ingredients in a food processor and blend for 20 seconds.

2.  Using a rubber spatula, scrape down the sides, then blend for 20 seconds more.

**VINAIGRETTE:**

1 large garlic clove, peeled and minced (1 teaspoon)

1 medium shallot, peeled and diced finely (3 tablespoons)

¼ teaspoon finely chopped fresh oregano

1½ tablespoons freshly squeezed lemon juice (juice of half a lemon)

2 tablespoons red wine vinegar

¼ cup extra-virgin olive oil

Kosher salt, to taste

Freshly ground black pepper, to taste

**SALAD:**

2 (5-ounce) cans of premium yellowfin tuna in extra-virgin olive oil, undrained

1 (15-ounce) can of white beans (Great Northern beans), rinsed and drained

2 tablespoons capers, rinsed and drained

1 (12-ounce) jar artichoke hearts, drained

¼ cup roughly chopped fresh flat-leaf Italian parsley, plus some whole leaves for garnish

Kosher salt, to taste

Freshly ground black pepper, to taste

4 cups arugula, rinsed and dried

Parmigiano-Reggiano cheese, not pre-grated, for serving

# Tuna and White Bean Salad

No offense to my oven, but there are days when I just don't feel like turning on the heat. Maybe you feel the same way. Not to say my relationship with my oven isn't amazing, but sometimes you just need some space, you know? Of course, we still have to eat. How about this? Grab a few cans of olive oil-packed tuna and a can of white beans from your pantry, and combine them with a few other ingredients—and bingo! You're good to go. Seriously. It's that fast. It's darn tasty, and substantial, too, not foofy—all without turning on the oven. Nothing like a good pantry raid to get the flame back into your relationship. With your oven, I mean.

1. In a medium container with a tight fitting lid, combine the garlic, shallot, oregano, lemon juice, vinegar, and olive oil, close the lid tightly, and shake well to combine. Or, whisk to combine the ingredients in a medium bowl. Season to taste with salt and pepper.

2. Open the cans of tuna and put them into a small bowl. Use a fork to break up the tuna, then season to taste with salt and pepper. It will need some seasoning—trust me.

3. Mix the white beans, capers, artichoke hearts, and chopped parsley with half the vinaigrette; season to taste with salt and pepper.

4. Serve one cup of arugula on a plate with a scoop of the bean salad and one quarter of the tuna. Use a vegetable peeler to top with some shavings of Parmigiano-Reggiano, then sprinkle with the whole parsley leaves. Drizzle any remaining vinaigrette over the salad, if desired.

**GREMOLATA:**

1 teaspoon lemon zest (zest of 1 lemon), grated on a Microplane and chopped finely

1 medium garlic clove, peeled and minced (½ teaspoon)

3 tablespoons finely chopped fresh flat-leaf Italian parsley

Kosher salt, to taste

Freshly ground black pepper, to taste

**LEEKS:**

½ pound leeks

1 small bulb fennel, sliced into 8 equal wedges

Kosher salt, to taste

Freshly ground black pepper, to taste

1 tablespoon extra-virgin olive oil

1 tablespoon unsalted butter

5 sprigs fresh thyme

1 large garlic clove, peeled and minced

1 cup dry white wine (preferably Sauvignon Blanc)

1 cup vegetable stock (recipe on page 37)

1½ tablespoons of fresh lemon juice (juice of half a lemon)

2 tablespoons roughly chopped fresh flat-leaf Italian parsley

# PAN-FRIED TILAPIA
## WITH BRAISED LEEKS AND GREMOLATA

## GREMOLATA

1. In a small bowl, combine the lemon zest, garlic, and parsley and mix well.

2. Season to taste with salt and pepper, stir, and cover with plastic wrap.

## LEEKS

1. Cut off the root ends and dark green parts of the leeks, halve them, and clean them carefully in a sink or large bowl full of water; drain the leeks.

2. Season the cut side of the leeks lightly with salt and pepper.

3. In a sauté pan large enough to accommodate the leeks, combine 1 tablespoon olive oil and 1 tablespoon butter and heat over medium-high heat until the butter just begins to brown.

4. Add the leeks, cut side down, and the fennel and cook undisturbed for 3 minutes, or until nicely caramelized.

5. Using tongs, flip the leeks and fennel; continue to cook until caramelized, 1 minute.

6. Stir in the white wine, stock, thyme, and garlic and bring to a simmer. Reduce the heat to low and cook until the leeks are beginning to soften and give when pressed, approximately 15 minutes.

7. Squeeze in the lemon juice, and reduce the liquid until ¼ cup remains, approximately 15 additional minutes.

8. Season to taste with salt and pepper, discard the thyme sprigs, stir in the parsley, and cover and keep warm.

## TILAPIA FILLETS

1. While the vegetables are braising, pat the fillets dry and season them lightly, on both sides, with salt and pepper.

2. Sprinkle the flour onto a plate, then dredge the fillets in the flour, shaking them lightly to remove any excess.

3. When the vegetable braising liquid is reduced to approximately 1 cup, combine the olive oil and butter over medium-high heat in a large sauté pan until the butter begins to brown.

4. Carefully add the fillets, and let cook until nicely browned, approximately 3 minutes. Using a wide spatula, flip the fillets, and continue to cook for 2 to 3 minutes more. The fish should look opaque, and just begin to flake, but still be moist.

5. Squeeze the lemon juice over the fillets, then serve immediately on a bed of the braised vegetables (with the tasty braising liquid) and a generous sprinkling of gremolata over the top of the entire dish.

**TILAPIA FILLETS:**

2 tilapia fillets, 1 inch thick at the thickest point (about ¾ pound)

Kosher salt, to taste

Freshly ground black pepper, to taste

½ cup unbleached all-purpose flour

1 tablespoon unsalted butter

1 tablespoon extra-virgin olive oil

1½ tablespoons fresh lemon juice (juice of half a lemon)

YIELD: 4 SERVINGS

**DIJON CRÈME FRAÎCHE:**

1 tablespoon whole-grain Dijon mustard

¼ cup crème fraîche (recipe on page 45)

Place the mustard and crème fraîche in a small bowl and stir until combined.

**SALMON:**

1 pound salmon fillet, 1½ inches thick, skin on, cut into 4 equal pieces

1 tablespoon lemon zest (zest of 3 lemons), grated on a Microplane

2 teaspoons roughly chopped fresh thyme

1 tablespoon extra-virgin olive oil

1 teaspoon unsalted butter

Kosher salt, to taste

Freshly ground black pepper, to taste

# PAN-SEARED SALMON
## WITH DIJON CRÈME FRAÎCHE

When I was in culinary school, my fellow students and I were each presented with a magnificent salmon, approximately twelve pounds in weight, with the assignment to prepare it in a number of ways using a variety of different cooking methods. Yet, before our teacher, Chef Coker, allowed us to make the first cut, he reminded us that this beautiful salmon, only days prior, was swimming along its merry way, perhaps humming a little salmon tune, and was, indeed, very much alive. Looking down at our salmon on the cutting board before us, we all agreed that they were now, in fact, quite dead. Chef Coker slowly (and dramatically, I might add) gazed at us all, leaned forward and very deliberately said, "Do not kill them twice." From that point forward I vowed to never overcook, waste, or disrespect my food, be it fish, chicken, lamb, beef, or vegetable.

I'm happy to say that for this recipe, I have developed a surefire cooking method that'll have your salmon cooked to perfection. In fact, I think even Chef Coker would be impressed.

1. Pat the salmon dry, then pat the non-skin side with the lemon zest and chopped thyme, season lightly with salt and pepper, and allow the salmon to sit for 30 minutes at room temperature.

2. Heat a large sauté pan over high heat until hot; add 1 tablespoon of olive oil and the butter to the sauté pan. The butter will bubble up, turn brown and perhaps even smoke. Swirl the sauté pan to distribute, then add the salmon, skin side up.

3. Cook undisturbed for 1 minute, flip to skin side down and continue cooking for 30 seconds.

4. Cover the sauté pan and immediately push the sauté pan off the heat. Turn off the heat and allow the salmon to rest undisturbed for 15 minutes.

5. Serve with a dollop of Dijon crème fraîche and revel in the glow of your happy guests' contentment.

Note: I love lentils with salmon. Try pairing this dish with my braised lentil-frisée salad (recipe on page 73). Delicious!

**SALSA VERDE:**

1 cup packed roughly chopped fresh cilantro

1 cup packed roughly chopped fresh flat-leaf Italian parsley

1½ tablespoons capers, rinsed and drained

2 small anchovy fillets (packed in olive oil), rinsed and chopped

1 medium garlic clove, peeled and minced (½ teaspoon)

1½ tablespoons fresh lemon juice (juice of half a lemon)

½ teaspoon red wine vinegar

Kosher salt, to taste

Freshly ground black pepper, to taste

½ cup extra-virgin olive oil

1 medium shallot, peeled and diced finely (3 tablespoons)

**HALIBUT:**

1 pound California or Alaskan halibut fillet (1- to 1 ½ -inch thick), patted dry and halved

Kosher salt, to taste

Freshly ground black pepper, to taste

Extra-virgin olive oil, for rubbing the halibut

1 tablespoon unsalted butter

# PAN-ROASTED HALIBUT
## WITH SALSA VERDE AND ASPARAGUS

### SALSA VERDE

1. Combine the cilantro, parsley, capers, anchovy, garlic, lemon juice, red wine vinegar, salt, and pepper in a food processor. Process for a few seconds then scrape down the sides.

2. Add the olive oil, and process for a few more seconds.

3. Spoon into a small bowl and stir in the shallots.

4. Season to taste with salt and pepper.

### HALIBUT

1. Adjust an oven rack to the middle position, then preheat the oven to 375°F.

2. Pat the halibut dry, then season both sides lightly with salt and pepper and allow to sit for 20 minutes at room temperature. While the halibut is resting prepare the ingredients for the pan-roasted asparagus.

3. After 20 minutes, rub each halibut fillet with olive oil, just enough to coat.

4. Over medium-high heat, add the butter to a large, ovenproof sauté pan. The butter will foam up, subside, then begin to turn golden brown in color.

5. Immediately add the halibut and allow to cook, undisturbed, for 2 minutes.

6. Flip the halibut over and immediately transfer the sauté pan to the oven.

**ASPARAGUS:**

1 tablespoon unsalted butter

¾ pound large asparagus, white fibrous bottoms discarded, and bottom inch peeled

1½ tablespoons freshly squeezed lemon juice (juice of half a lemon)

1 medium garlic clove, peeled and minced (½ teaspoon)

Kosher salt, to taste

Freshly ground black pepper, to taste

7. Roast, uncovered, for 3 minutes. After 3 minutes, remove the sauté pan and transfer the fish to a side plate so it won't overcook, or serve immediately.

## ASPARAGUS

1. Add the butter to a large sauté pan and heat over medium-high heat. The butter will foam up, subside, then begin to turn golden brown in color.

2. Add the asparagus and gently shake the sauté pan to coat the asparagus in the butter.

3. Season evenly with a good pinch of salt, some pepper, and cook undisturbed for 1 minute.

4. Shake the sauté pan, then sprinkle in the minced garlic.

5. Using tongs, rotate the asparagus and cook for 2 additional minutes, giving the sauté pan a little shake after the first minute.

6. Squeeze the lemon juice over top of the asparagus and (you guessed it) give the pan a little shake. Remove from the heat and season to taste with salt and pepper.

7. To plate, spoon the salsa verde on the plate first, followed by 3 to 5 spears of asparagus, and finally, top with the halibut.

Note: For a quick appetizer, serve the asparagus and salsa verde with some Parmigiano-Reggiano cheese.

# Red Beans and Rice... A Classic

A timeless classic—beans and rice. An unassuming dish. Almost humble, if you will. Well, this recipe may be modest, but it's flavored boldly and it will satisfy a hungry crowd while providing plenty of nutrition. What's more? You can have this meal on the table within half an hour. It's no wonder that this simple and inexpensive combination is a popular favorite around the world. I guess there's a reason why the classics stand the test of time.

1. In a medium saucepan or rice cooker, prepare the rice according to the package directions.

2. In a medium saucepan, add the bacon and one teaspoon of olive oil and place over medium-low heat. Cook, stirring occasionally for approximately 5 to 6 minutes until much of the fat has rendered off, and the bacon is just beginning to get nice and crispy.

3. Add the onions, bell pepper, and celery. Cook, stirring occasionally, for 5 minutes until soft.

4. Add the sausage and cook for 3 minutes, breaking up the sausage into small pieces with the back of a wooden spoon as it cooks.

5. Stir in the garlic, cumin, coriander, bay leaves, thyme, oregano, and chile flakes and cook until fragrant, 1 minute.

6. Add the red beans, tomatoes, and stock and stir well.

7. Increase the heat to high until simmering, then reduce the heat to low and continue to simmer for 25 minutes to allow the flavors to blend.

**YIELD: 6 SERVINGS**

2 cups brown rice

2 slices of hickory smoked bacon, halved lengthwise and then cut crosswise into ¼-inch slices (½ cup)

1 teaspoon extra-virgin olive oil

2 medium yellow onions, peeled and diced small (2 cups)

1 large red bell pepper, cored and diced small (1¼ cups)

2 celery stalks, diced small (1 cup)

¾ pound fresh sweet sausage (pork or turkey), removed from casing, approximately 2 to 3 links

9 large garlic cloves, peeled and minced (3 tablespoons)

1 teaspoon ground cumin

¼ teaspoon ground coriander, optional

2 dried bay leaves

1 teaspoon finely chopped fresh thyme

⅛ teaspoon finely chopped fresh oregano

⅛ teaspoon crushed red chile pepper (chile flakes), or to taste

2 (15-ounce) cans red kidney beans, rinsed and drained

1 (15-ounce) can diced tomatoes, undrained, preferably fire-roasted, or 2 medium tomatoes, cored and chopped roughly

Ingredients continued on next page »

2 cups chicken stock (recipe on page 38)

Kosher salt, to taste

Freshly ground black pepper, to taste

Crème fraîche (recipe on page 45), for serving

Green onions, thinly sliced, for serving

1 lime, quartered, for serving

Fresh cilantro, for serving

A bottle of your favorite hot sauce on the side, optional

8. Remove the bay leaves and season to taste with salt and pepper.

9. Serve in soup bowls, adding the cooked rice in first. Then pile on the beans. To garnish, add a dollop of crème fraîche, a sprinkling of green onions, a squeeze of lime juice, and some cilantro. Don't forget your favorite hot sauce. Oh, yeah. Now that's good stuff.

# CINCINNATI CHILI

You never saw a man so insulted in your life. My buddy Scott, a native of Tennessee, pulled his car over to the side of the road, shut the engine off, turned in his seat to face me, and scoffed, "Chili... with beans and pasta? Nathan, what did chili ever do to YOU?"

I first learned of Cincinnati chili while eating lunch with my dad in my hometown of Arlington, Virginia. Now, Virginia isn't known for its chili like Texas or Tennessee, but in that chili restaurant, my dad and I discovered something amazing when we began to eat. There was no five-alarm heat, no burning mouth, no tears like other chili experiences I've had in the past. Far from it. This chili had depth, texture, and a wonderful sweet fragrance. Now for all you die-hard chili fans out there, like my buddy Scott from Tennessee, you may not consider this to be a true chili because it has "fillers" such as beans and tomatoes. Nevertheless, this dish can be enjoyed by adults and kids alike without the requisite milk chaser. For what it's worth, when Scott finally tasted my Cincinnati chili, he sat up, put down his fork, crossed his arms, nodded and said, "Pretty good." Assuming he'd had enough, I went to remove his plate. Before I could take it away, however, he stopped me. "That's okay, I'll finish it." Translation? Love at first bite.

1. Add 3 tablespoons oil and the onions to a small pot set over medium heat. Cook, stirring occasionally, for 8 to 10 minutes, until the onions are soft and translucent.

2. Stir in the garlic and cook until fragrant, 1 minute.

**YIELD: 4 TO 6 SERVINGS**

3 tablespoons extra-virgin olive oil, plus more for drizzling

1¼ pounds ground beef (85% lean)

2 large yellow onions, peeled and diced small (3 cups)

5 large garlic cloves, peeled and chopped roughly (1 tablespoon plus 2 teaspoons)

2 tablespoons tomato paste

1¼ teaspoons chili powder

1 teaspoon ground allspice

1 teaspoon ground cinnamon

1 teaspoon ground cumin

⅛ teaspoon ground cayenne pepper, or to taste

2 tablespoons plus 1 teaspoon kosher salt, divided, plus more to taste

1½ tablespoons natural unsweetened cocoa powder

1 (14-ounce) can diced tomatoes, undrained, preferably fire-roasted

1 tablespoon Worcestershire sauce

1½ tablespoons apple cider vinegar

2 cups chicken or vegetable stock (recipes on page 37 & 38)

1 (15-ounce) can red kidney beans, rinsed and drained

Freshly ground black pepper, to taste

1 (16-ounce) package spaghetti

Chili two ways: add grated Cheddar cheese

Chili three ways: chili two ways plus chopped raw white onions or shallots

3. Add the beef and cook, breaking up the beef with a wooden spoon into small pieces until beginning to brown, for 3 minutes.

4. Add the tomato paste and continue to cook, stirring occasionally, for 3 minutes.

5. Stir in the chili powder, allspice, cinnamon, cumin, cayenne, 1 teaspoon salt, unsweetened cocoa, tomatoes, Worcestershire sauce, vinegar, stock, and beans.

6. Reduce the heat to medium-low and continue cooking for 30 minutes, stirring occasionally, while the chili simmers slowly. Taste the chili; the flavors should be well-balanced and the chili still somewhat watery. Season to taste with salt and pepper.

7. Bring a small pot of water to a rolling boil, then add 2 tablespoons of salt.

8. Add the spaghetti to the boiling water and cook, stirring occasionally, until *al dente* (almost done, or "to the tooth").

9. Drain well, drizzle some extra-virgin olive oil on the pasta, stir to coat, and serve in pasta bowls, topped with a healthy scoop of Cincinnati Chili. Add additional toppings of your choice (see sidebar).

# Roasted Rosemary-Lemon Chicken

**YIELD: 4 SERVINGS**

1 whole chicken, 3 to 3½ pounds

Kosher salt, for seasoning

Freshly ground black pepper, for seasoning

2 tablespoons unsalted butter

1 teaspoon finely chopped fresh rosemary

2 (5-inch) sprigs fresh rosemary

1 teaspoon finely chopped fresh thyme

5 sprigs fresh thyme

2 small lemons, halved

1 teaspoon extra-virgin olive oil

When I was a child, a few times every year, my family and I would drive out to the Shenandoah Valley to visit the family farm where my great-grand-mother, Mema Hattie, lived. With its red barn, grazing cows, and huge chicken coop, it was an endless source of enjoyment for my brothers and me.

In their well-groomed side yard, which sloped gently towards the two-lane country road, sat a brick, two-level grill. The wood was piled into the pit, lit aflame, and burned until deep red in color. Then, when the temperature was just right, the chickens went on the grill. They were the best-tasting chickens I ever had—juicy and succulent, with a salty, crispy skin. Now, I may not have a double-decker grill, but this is one recipe that I think my great-grandmother would have enjoyed just the same.

1. Adjust an oven rack to the middle position, then preheat the oven to 400°F.

2. Remove any giblets from inside the chicken. Pat the chicken dry, inside and out.

3. Season the inside cavity of the chicken liberally with 1 teaspoon salt and a few really good grinds of pepper. Let sit at room temperature for 30 minutes.

4. Mix together the butter, 1 teaspoon chopped rosemary, 1 teaspoon chopped thyme, ¾ teaspoon salt, and a few generous grinds of pepper in a small bowl.

5. Gently pull the skin away from the breast, being careful not to tear the skin, and push the butter mixture between the skin and the breast. Repeat for the thighs.

> *"Cooking is not about being the best or most perfect cook, but rather it is about sharing the table with family and friends."*
> — SKYE GYNGELL

6.  Stuff the cavity of the chicken with the lemons, squeezing the juice in the cavity first, seeds and all, then following with the rosemary and thyme sprigs. It's going to get juicy, folks.

7.  Season the outside of the chicken with salt and pepper, then truss per instructions on the next page.

8.  Heat a large oven-safe sauté pan over medium-high heat until hot. When hot, add the olive oil, swirl to distribute evenly, and immediately put the chicken, breast side up, into the sauté pan and transfer to the oven.

9. Roast the chicken, uncovered, for approximately 17 minutes per pound, or until a digital thermometer inserted into the thigh and not touching the bone reads 160°F. Do not open the oven or baste the chicken during roasting. When the chicken is cooked properly, the juices will run clear when the thigh is pierced with a knife. For a 3-pound chicken, exactly 50 minutes is perfect. For a 3½-pound chicken, 1 hour on the dot.

10. Remove the pan from the oven and lift the chicken onto a cutting board. Allow the chicken to rest for 15 minutes prior to carving.

## TRUSSING THE CHICKEN

Trussing a chicken is super easy. All you need is the chicken and a knife.

1. Position the chicken breast side up, with the tail of the chicken facing you and the wings facing away from you.

2. Take your knife and cut a small slit in the left middle portion/flap of skin, just above the tail and to the left of it.

3. Imagine that you want the chicken to sit cross-legged. Take the left leg if you're right-handed (the right leg if you're left-handed), and cross it to the right side. Now, take the right leg, and fold it over the left, tucking the leg into and through the small slit that you've cut.

4. Fold the tips of the wings back behind the chicken and you're good to go.

For bonus material relating to this recipe,
visit chefnathanlyon.com

# TAPENADE-ENCRUSTED RACK OF LAMB

**YIELD: 4 SERVINGS**

1 rack of lamb, just over 1 pound, silver skin removed (see note)

Kosher salt, for seasoning

Freshly ground black pepper, for seasoning

1 tablespoon extra-virgin olive oil

2 tablespoons black olive tapenade (recipe on page 265)

For parties, I often serve my tapenade-encrusted rack of lamb as a simple, yet impressive appetizer. Seared on the stove top, slathered with tapenade (a southern French spread made of black olives and capers), and finally, slow-roasted just to medium rare in the oven, this recipe has "delicious" written all over it. Once cooked, you can slice each rack into 8 individual servings and place them on a platter for an elegant appetizer. Give it a try; I guarantee it'll be the talk of the party!

1. Pat the lamb dry, then season the lamb rack on all sides, using ¼ teaspoon salt total and a few generous grinds of pepper. Allow to sit at room temperature for 30 minutes.

2. After 15 minutes, adjust an oven rack to the middle position, then preheat the oven to 400°F.

3. Heat a large sauté pan over medium-high heat until hot. Add one tablespoon extra-virgin olive oil (the oil will likely smoke), swirl the pan to distribute the oil evenly.

4. Immediately add the lamb, fat side down, to the pan and sear on each side until nicely colored, approximately 2 minutes per side.

5. Place the rack of lamb on a parchment lined sheet pan, fat side facing up (bones will be arching down). Smear the lamb meat with two tablespoons of tapenade.

6. Transfer the sheet pan to the oven and roast, uncovered, for approximately 13 minutes.

7. Remove the sheet pan from the oven and transfer the lamb rack to a cutting board. Cover the lamb loosely with aluminum foil and allow to rest 15 minutes prior to slicing between the bones.

8. Grab a bone, and enjoy.

Note: Similar to the iridescent color of a pearl, silver skin is the inedible connective tissue that covers a portion of the meat. Unlike the thin layer of fat on the rack, silver skin is too tough to pull off with your bare hands. The silver skin can be removed using your knife of choice, by simply filleting it off. Do this by cutting just under the silver skin with the tip of your knife, angling your knife slightly upwards, then cutting the silver skin off in strips. Alternatively, you can ask your butcher to remove the silver skin.

For bonus material relating to this recipe, visit chefnathanlyon.com

---

*"My doctor told me I had to stop throwing intimate dinners for four unless there are three other people."* — ORSON WELLS

# SWEET CRÊPES
## WITH CHOCOLATE GANACHE

It was a crisp, late fall afternoon in Paris, 1995. I was in the middle of a backpacking trip across Europe—a college graduation present to myself. Eating chocolate in Bruges, drinking Guinness in Dublin, sipping espressos in Florence… all memorable experiences.

However, it was the Musée Rodin in Paris that I will never forget. Armed with a warm Latte in one hand and a freshly wrapped banana-Nutella crêpe in the other, I entered the courtyard of the Musée Rodin. Under a thick blanket of gray clouds, I took a seat on a cold wrought iron bench in front of Rodin's ornate doorway called the Gates of Hell. What a moment it was: the taste of the creamy hazelnut chocolate and warm bananas in the crêpe, the soft milk foam on my lips, the cool wind on my face, the late colorless autumn afternoon, the scent of decaying leaves in the air… so still, and so perfect.

I do hope to go back someday. Not to relive that moment, which I know is impossible, but because, well… because that crêpe was just so darn good.

1. Place the eggs in a large bowl and whisk until the eggs are mixed.

2. Add the milk, flour, butter, granulated sugar, and salt and whisk gently until well combined.

3. Allow the batter to sit, covered, for 30 minutes. During this time, the flour will absorb the liquid, swell, and result in a better textured crêpe. The crêpe batter texture will be that of heavy whipping cream.

4. While the crêpe mixture is resting, prepare the ganache (see recipe on the next page).

5. Strain the batter through a fine mesh strainer into a medium-sized bowl.

**YIELD: 4 TO 6 SERVINGS**

**CRÊPES:**

3 large eggs

1¼ cup whole milk

1 cup unbleached all-purpose flour

2 tablespoons unsalted butter, melted

1 teaspoon granulated sugar

1/16 teaspoon kosher salt

Bananas, peeled and sliced

Strawberries, hulled and sliced

Confectioners' sugar, for garnish

**CHOCOLATE GANACHE:**

9 ounces chocolate (containing between 60% to 72% cocoa solids), chopped finely

1 cup heavy whipping cream

6. Place a crêpe pan or small nonstick sauté pan over medium-low heat.

7. Once hot, measure approximately ¼ cup batter (you can use a 2-ounce ladle for this), and pour into the center of the pan.

8. Quickly rotate and tilt the pan to spread the batter evenly, just enough to cover the bottom of the pan.

9. Cook for 30 to 45 seconds, then flip the crêpe over. (You may have to use your fingers to do this.) The crêpe should be cooked, maybe even very lightly golden brown in color, but not dry or crispy. One telltale sign of when to flip the crêpe is when the edges of the crêpe start to turn upwards in the pan, a great place to grab hold with your fingers and flip.

10. Cook the second side for approximately 15 to 30 seconds, then transfer to a plate.

11. Serve with a slathering of chocolate ganache and some sliced strawberries and bananas.

12. Fold the edges inward, then dust with confectioners' sugar, if desired.

## CHOCOLATE GANACHE

1. Place the chopped chocolate into a medium bowl.

2. Pour the cream into a small saucepan over medium heat, stirring until it just starts to slowly simmer.

3. Pour the warmed cream over the chopped chocolate.

4. Cover with plastic wrap or aluminum foil and allow the chocolate to sit undisturbed for 2 minutes. Be patient

5. Uncover and stir slowly. Like magic, the chocolate will melt and the ganache will become dark and smooth.

6. Look around the kitchen to make sure no one is watching, and if you are alone, go ahead and lick the spoon clean. No one will be the wiser. Say you washed it. Trust me.

Note: Layer any remaining cooked crêpes between parchment paper, place into a plastic 1 gallon bag, and store in the refrigerator for up to 3 days. Prefer a savory crêpe? No problem: simply omit the sugar and proceed as normal. Fill with a variety of vegetables, such as sautéed mushrooms, spinach, or different cheeses, like ricotta or Brie.

# Vanilla Cherry Clafoutis

Clafoutis is the love child of a steamy relationship between a crêpe and a custard, two delicious desserts beloved by all. Yet, unlike a crêpe, one clafoutis will serve eight people, and unlike a custard, a clafoutis doesn't need a waterbath. Simplicity, great taste, and a sexy texture, all in one dessert? Clafoutis, je t'aime.

1. Adjust an oven rack to the middle position, then preheat the oven to 425°F.

2. Combine the eggs with 3 tablespoons of granulated sugar on low speed in a blender for 10 seconds.

3. Gradually add the flour, lemon zest, salt, vanilla, and milk until well blended, 30 seconds.

4. Let rest undisturbed for at least 5 minutes. This time allows the flour to absorb the liquid resulting in a better finished texture.

5. Combine the butter, cherries, and the remaining granulated sugar in a medium, oven-safe, non-stick sauté pan, over medium heat. Cook, stirring occasionally, for approximately 5 minutes until the cherries are soft and a syrup has formed.

4. Pour the egg mixture evenly over the sweet, hot cherries (sounds sexy, right?). Transfer the sauté pan into the oven and bake, uncovered, for approximately 15 minutes, or until the crispy brown edges have puffed up and the middle of the clafoutis is golden brown.

5. Remove from the oven and, using a spatula, slide the clafoutis out onto a cutting board.

6. Slice and serve on dessert plates dusted with confectioners' sugar.

**YIELD: 8 SERVINGS**

4 large eggs

4 tablespoons granulated sugar, divided

¾ cup unbleached all-purpose flour

1 teaspoon grated lemon zest (zest of 1 lemon), grated on a Microplane

⅛ teaspoon kosher salt

1 teaspoon pure vanilla extract

1 cup whole milk

2 tablespoons unsalted butter

1 pint fresh sweet cherries, halved and pits removed (2 cups)

Confectioners' sugar, for serving

Note: If you happen to be a bigger fan of orange than lemon, feel free to substitute the zest of 1 large orange (1 tablespoon) for the lemon zest, and substitute 1 teaspoon Grand Marnier for the vanilla extract.

**FRUIT:**

2 cups fresh sweet cherries, halved and pits removed

2 pints strawberries, hulled and quartered

1 pint blueberries, raspberries, blackberries, or a combination

5 large fresh mint leaves, chopped finely (2 tablespoons) plus 4 large whole mint leaves for garnish

1 teaspoon granulated sugar

**VANILLA WHIPPED RICOTTA:**

1 (16-ounce) container whole-milk ricotta cheese, drained

1 teaspoon pure vanilla extract

⅓ cup confectioners' sugar

2 tablespoons honey, preferably orange blossom

# FRESH FRUIT
## WITH HONEY VANILLA WHIPPED RICOTTA

1. In a medium bowl, toss to combine the fruit salad ingredients.

2. Put the ricotta, vanilla extract, confectioners' sugar, and honey in the bowl of a food processor or mixer. Process or whip until smooth. Refrigerate until it's time for dessert.

3. To serve, divide the fruit into bowls, top with a generous spoonful of the Honey Whipped Vanilla Ricotta and garnish with a mint leaf.

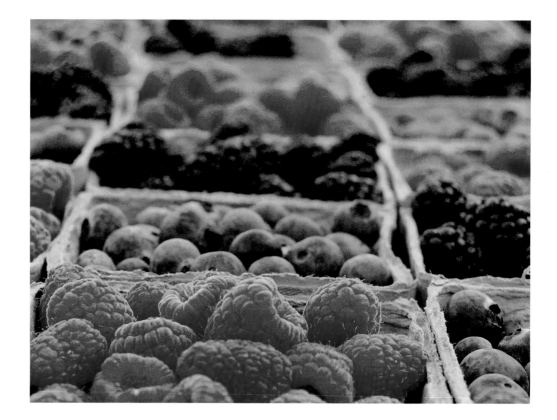

# LEMON-VANILLA RICOTTA CHEESECAKE
## WITH GINGERSNAP CRUST

YIELD: 12 SERVINGS

CRUST:

10 ounces gingersnaps (such as Mi-Del brand), ground very finely (2 cups)

5 tablespoons unsalted butter, melted

Nonstick spray

MERINGUE:

3 egg whites

1 cup granulated sugar, divided

Take my hand; we'll get through this together. Don't be intimidated by the number of steps. Read through it once and you'll quickly realize that it's not a difficult process. In fact, it's simple and well worth the effort.

This is the best cheesecake I have ever made. It took me nine times to perfect it. That's a lot of cheesecake, right? Don't get me wrong; the first eight were good, so say my friends down the block who enjoyed every step of this cheesecake evolution. Each cheesecake got progressively better, progressively easier, yet it was the ninth attempt, this very recipe, that took the cake.

Now, it's your turn. Take this recipe and go. Make this cheesecake and enjoy every last bite. But, first? You gotta let go of my hand. Wow. That's quite a grip you got there.

1. Adjust an oven rack to the middle position, then preheat the oven to 300°F.

2. Prepare a 9-inch springform pan with 3-inch sides by wrapping the outside with enough plastic wrap to ensure that water added to the roasting pan prior to cooking doesn't accidentally leak into the cheesecake. (Now is not the time to skimp on plastic wrap.)

3. Cover the plastic wrap with two layers of aluminum foil. Spray the insides and bottom of the pan with nonstick spray.

4. Combine the gingersnap crumbs in a small bowl with the melted butter and mix thoroughly.

5. Turn the crumb mixture into the middle of the prepared springform pan and give it a little shake to distribute the crumbs evenly.

**FILLING:**

2 (8-ounce) packages regular cream cheese

1 (16-ounce) container whole milk ricotta cheese, drained

3 large eggs

1 tablespoon cornstarch

¼ teaspoon kosher salt

1 teaspoon lemon zest (zest of 1 lemon), grated on a Microplane

2 tablespoons freshly squeezed lemon juice

2 teaspoons pure vanilla extract

6. Using the (washed) inverted plastic cap of the nonstick spray can, press the crust evenly only into the bottom of the pan—not up the sides.

7. Transfer to the freezer to chill.

8. Whisk the egg whites in a clean and dry mixing bowl on high until frothy.

9. Stop the mixer and add 1 tablespoon of sugar, then continue to whisk until medium peaks are formed. This is your meringue.

10. Transfer the meringue into a bowl and cover with plastic wrap.

11. Swap out the whisk attachment for the paddle attachment. Add the cream cheese, ricotta cheese, and remaining sugar to the original bowl used for whisking the egg whites.

12. Mix on medium-high until smooth in texture.

13. Slowing the mixer to medium-low, add 1 egg. Do not add the next egg until the first egg is incorporated.

14. Repeat, one egg at a time, until all 3 eggs are incorporated, then stop the mixer and scrape down the sides and bottom of the bowl with a spatula.

15. Turn the mixer to medium-low and add the corn starch by sifting it through a small sieve to evenly distribute into the fluffy mixture. Mix.

16. Add the salt, lemon zest, lemon juice, and vanilla extract and mix until just combined.

17. Remove the mixing bowl from the electric mixer, and with a spatula, gently fold the meringue into the cheese mixture until fully incorporated. If you see some liquid egg white at the bottom of the bowl, simply grab your whisk and whisk by hand until incorporated.

Note: To achieve those perfect slices of cheese-cake like you see in the stores and restaurants, remove the springform pan sides and place the chilled cheesecake in the freezer for a few hours. Once frozen, transfer to a cutting board. Use a knife to separate the cheesecake from the pan bottom. Heat the blade of a large knife in a large container filled with very hot water. Wipe the knife blade dry, then immediately slice the cheesecake into wedges. Heat the knife again as needed, then dry prior to each slice. Transfer the slices into the refrigerator, until thawed, then serve.

18. Pour the airy lemon-vanilla cheesy mixture into the prepared springform pan that's been in the freezer. Spread the mixture evenly and level the top.

19. Place the springform pan, uncovered, into a roasting pan.

20. Carefully pour very hot water into one corner of the roasting pan (without spilling any water into the cheesecake) to a depth of 1 inch, then transfer the roasting pan into the pre-heated oven.

21. Set your digital timer for 1 hour and 25 minutes. After the alarm sounds, the center of the cheesecake should have just a little wobble to it.

22. Turn off the oven, and allow the cheesecake to relax in its warm water bath in the oven, undisturbed, for 1 hour.

23. Remove the roasting pan from the oven, transfer the springform pan onto a cooling rack, and allow to rest at room temperature for an additional 1 hour.

24. Cover with plastic wrap and refrigerate for 8 hours before serving (see note in the sidebar).

25. Slice and serve topped with the cherry and vanilla bean compote, or enjoy as is.

# HOMEMADE CHERRY AND VANILLA BEAN COMPOTE

1. Combine the sugar, vanilla bean (if using) and the water (which will look like wet sand) in a heavy saucepan and cover with a glass lid.

2. Place over medium-low heat. After approximately 8 to 10 minutes, you will see the color of the sugar darken slightly to a light golden tan. Give the pan a small swirl to ensure that one part of the caramel doesn't cook faster than another part.

3. Reduce the heat to low, and continue to cook until a light brown caramel color is achieved, swirling the pan as necessary.

4. With the heat still on low, carefully add the cherries. Stir continuously with a wooden spoon and cook until the cherries begin to give off their liquid, 1 minute.

5. Remove from the heat and stir in the vanilla extract, if using.

6. Serve or cool to room temperature.

7. Any leftover compote can be stored in the refrigerator for up to 1 week.

**YIELD: 4 SERVINGS**

1 cup granulated sugar

3 tablespoons water

1 pound fresh sweet cherries, halved and pits removed

1 teaspoon pure vanilla extract, or ½ vanilla bean, halved and scraped

# SUMMER

| | |
|---|---|
| APRICOTS | NECTARINES |
| ARUGULA | NEW POTATOES |
| AVOCADOS | ONIONS |
| BASIL | OREGANO |
| BLACKBERRIES | PARSLEY |
| BLUEBERRIES | PEACHES |
| CELERY | PEPPERS |
| CHERRIES | PLUMS |
| CHIVES | RASPBERRIES |
| CILANTRO | ROSEMARY |
| CORN | SAGE |
| CUCUMBERS | SHALLOTS |
| EGGPLANT | SPINACH |
| FENNEL | SUMMER |
| FIGS | SQUASH/ZUCCHINI |
| GARLIC | THYME |
| GINGER | TOMATOES |
| GRAPES | WATERMELON |
| GREEN BEANS | |
| MELONS | |

1¼ cup unbleached all-purpose flour

3 tablespoons granulated sugar, divided

2 tablespoons dark brown sugar

1¼ teaspoons baking powder

½ teaspoon baking soda

¼ teaspoon kosher salt

2 large eggs, separated

1¼ cups buttermilk

3 tablespoons unsalted butter, melted

1 tablespoon pure vanilla extract

½ cup whole-milk ricotta cheese, drained

1 teaspoon lemon zest (zest of 1 lemon), grated on a Microplane

1 pint blueberries (2 cups)

Confectioners' sugar, for serving

Pure maple syrup, Grade B if possible, for serving

# BLUEBERRY-RICOTTA PANCAKES
## WITH PURE MAPLE SYRUP

Fresh blueberries always remind me of time spent with my grandfather, Papa, at his cottage near the Outer Banks of North Carolina. My trusty dog, Heineken, and I would scan the grounds to see if the carrots were ready to be pulled, the figs ripe enough to be picked, or the blueberries gathered. Most years, we arrived too late for the blueberries; the blue jays had already stripped the bushes clean. Sometimes, however, they would leave us with a few meager cups—just enough to make fresh blueberry pancakes the following morning. Over the years, my love for blueberries hasn't faltered, nor has my desire for blueberry pancakes. Let me tell you, if I had this recipe of blueberry pancakes back then, there's no question that Heiny and I would have given those blue jays a run for their money. They're that good.

1. Whisk together the flour, 2 tablespoons granulated sugar, brown sugar, baking powder, baking soda, and salt in a medium bowl.

2. In a large bowl, whisk together the egg yolks, buttermilk, melted butter, vanilla extract, ricotta, and lemon zest.

3. Using an electric mixer or the whisk attachment of your immersion blender, whisk the egg whites until just barely foamy, in a third (clean and dry) bowl.

4. Add the remaining 1 tablespoon granulated sugar and continue whisking to medium-firm peaks.

5. Whisk the flour mixture by hand into the egg yolk mixture.

6. Fold in the egg whites gently just until incorporated.

7.  Add 1 teaspoon butter to a nonstick griddle or a large nonstick sauté pan and place over medium-low heat until the butter foams up, subsides, and begins to brown.

8.  Make 3 pancakes using a ¼-cup measuring cup or 2-ounce ladle of pancake batter for each pancake.

9.  Dot the pancakes with a few blueberries, pressing them into the batter if necessary; don't go crazy with the berries.

10. Cover with a glass lid to monitor the progress. Cook for exactly 3 minutes on the first side, remove the lid and gently flip the pancake. Cook, uncovered, for an additional 2 minutes on the second side. The edges will be dry, and when lifted the bottom should be a light golden brown.

11. Serve on warm plates with a pat of butter, some confectioners' sugar, and a drizzle of warm maple syrup.

Note: To keep the pancakes warm, place them in a single layer on parchment paper-lined baking sheets and put them into a 180°F oven. Either that, or cook with two sauté pans at a time.

# Eggs Four Ways

My two older brothers, Eric and Craig, used to let me tag along when they went out to parties, long before I even had a driver's license. I always loved the parties, sure, but it was the after-party that I looked forward to most: the old-school 24-hour breakfast joints—late night meals, their treat. The concept of breakfast at any time is something I've never outgrown. Scrambled eggs with sautéed vegetables for breakfast, a Southwestern omelet for lunch, and a cheeseburger with sliced avocado, tomatoes and lettuce topped with a fried egg for dinner—yum! Maybe not all in the same day, mind you. Nowadays, when my brothers and I get together, we'll still make time to swing by those same 24-hour breakfast joints for a late night meal just like old times, and if I'm lucky, they'll even let me drive.

## Soft-Fried Egg

1. Melt the butter in a nonstick sauté pan over low heat. The butter will foam a little.

2. Once the foam subsides, crack in the eggs and sprinkle the thyme and oregano over the top of the egg; season lightly with salt and pepper, then add the grated cheese.

2. Cover with a lid and cook undisturbed for 3 to 4 minutes, or until the white is set and the yolk is still runny.

3. Uncover, transfer to a plate, then top with the basil and parsley. Serve immediately.

Note: Using a lid while cooking the eggs will cook the top side of the eggs gently. Use a glass lid, if possible, to check on the egg's progress as it cooks.

**YIELD: 1 SERVING**

**SOFT-FRIED EGG**

1 teaspoon unsalted butter

2 large eggs

⅛ teaspoon finely chopped fresh thyme

⅛ teaspoon finely chopped fresh oregano

½ tablespoon grated Parmigiano-Reggiano, Asiago, or Gruyère cheese, not pre-grated

Kosher salt, to taste

Freshly ground black pepper, to taste

¼ teaspoon finely chopped fresh basil

¼ teaspoon of finely chopped fresh flat-leaf Italian parsley

**SCRAMBLED EGGS**

1 teaspoon unsalted butter

3 large eggs, whisked with a fork

¼ teaspoon finely chopped fresh thyme

¼ teaspoon finely chopped fresh oregano

Kosher salt, to taste

Freshly ground black pepper, to taste

1 tablespoon grated Parmigiano-Reggiano, Asiago, or Gruyère cheese, not pre-grated

¼ teaspoon finely chopped fresh basil

¼ teaspoon finely chopped fresh flat-leaf Italian parsley

# SCRAMBLED EGGS

When scrambling eggs, use low heat and chopsticks, to keep them moving in the pan, then remove the eggs while they still look a bit wet. Believe me, it works. For a small curd of egg, stir continuously. For a larger curd, stir occasionally.

1. Melt the butter in a nonstick sauté pan over medium heat. The butter will foam a little.

2. Once the foam subsides, add the whisked eggs and sprinkle the thyme and oregano over the top of the egg; season lightly with salt and pepper.

3. Using the chopsticks or a heat-proof spatula, immediately begin to stir the eggs; continue stirring until the eggs are mostly cooked and still a touch moist.

4. Add the cheese, stir, and immediately transfer to a plate.

5. Top with the basil and parsley and serve.

# Perfectly Cooked "Hard-Boiled" Eggs

Hard-boiled eggs aren't really supposed to be boiled because boiling eggs increases the chance of rubbery, over-cooked eggs. We don't want to do that to our eggs. Eggs are our friends. Instead, you want the water to come just to a gentle bubbling, then turn off the heat—like a hot tub for eggs. Better than boiling, for sure.

1. Place the eggs into a 3½ quart saucepan, then fill with cold tap water just to half an inch over the tops of the eggs.

2. Cook on high heat until you first hear the sound of an egg just barely clunking on the bottom of the saucepan or when you see the first really BIG bubbles appear magically from under the eggs, approximately 13 minutes.

3. Turn off the heat, and allow to sit undisturbed for 14 minutes.

4. Immediately remove the eggs from the hot water and transfer them into the bowl of cold water. Let sit for 5 minutes to stop the eggs from cooking any further.

5. That's it. Perfect every time. Crack one open under cold running water, grab some kosher salt and pepper, and have at it.

Note: Older eggs work better for "hard-boiled" eggs; as the pH of eggs changes with age, the eggs become easier to peel. Fresher eggs are harder to peel, so take a quick look at which eggs are older and use those.

YIELD: 6 EGGS

**PERFECTLY COOKED "HARD-BOILED" EGGS**

6 large eggs

1 medium bowl of ice water

Kosher salt, to taste

Freshly ground black pepper, to taste

3 large eggs

½ teaspoon kosher salt

# POACHED EGGS

1. Crack each egg into separate ramekins or small bowls.

2. Fill a large nonstick sauté pan with approximately 1½ inches of water, and bring it just barely to a simmer.

3. Sprinkle in the salt.

4. Working one at a time, slowly lower each ramekin gently into the hot water by lowering the lip just under the surface of the hot water. The hot water will slowly fill the ramekin so that the egg can float freely into the sauté pan. Repeat with the remaining 2 eggs.

5. If the water is simmering too much, the eggs will break apart, so adjust the temperature accordingly. Cook for approximately 4 to 5 minutes, or just until the whites are set but the yolks are not. Lift the eggs from the water with a slotted spoon, allow to drain for a few seconds and serve immediately.

Note: Just as older eggs work best for hard (not quite) boiled eggs, fresher eggs work best for poaching as the eggs will stay more compact as they cook.

# SPRING VEGETABLE FRITTATA
## WITH FRESH BASIL

YIELD: 4 TO 6 SERVINGS

3 tablespoons extra-virgin olive oil, plus more for drizzling

1 medium yellow onion, peeled and diced small (1 cup)

2 small zucchini, diced small (2 cups)

1 cup thinly sliced mushrooms

½ teaspoon finely chopped fresh thyme

¼ teaspoon kosher salt

Freshly ground black pepper, to taste

7 large eggs, whisked with a fork

¾ cup crumbled feta cheese

7 medium fresh basil leaves, stacked, rolled, and sliced very thinly

1. Adjust an oven rack to the middle position, then preheat the oven to 325°F.

2. Set a large, oven-safe, nonstick sauté pan over medium heat and add 3 tablespoons olive oil; heat until shimmering.

3. Add the onions, zucchini, mushrooms, and thyme, and season with ¼ teaspoon salt and a few really good grinds of pepper.

4. Cook, stirring occasionally, until the onions are transparent and the veggies are looking ready for that eggy bath, 10 minutes.

5. Add the eggs, half the basil, and the feta. Shake the pan to distribute the ingredients, cook for 30 seconds, then transfer the sauté pan into the oven.

6. Bake, uncovered, for 12 to 14 minutes or until the eggs are just set.

7. Remove the frittata from the oven, slide out onto a cutting board, slice into 6 pieces, and serve topped with the remaining sliced basil and a drizzle of olive oil.

Note: Other types of cheese that would work wonders include Gruyère and Parmigiano-Reggiano. Also, a wonderful topping for this dish is a mixture of diced, seeded tomatoes, plus a splash of olive oil and a drizzle of balsamic vinegar. It's a goodie.

2 cups chopped watermelon, seeds removed, rind discarded

3 small cucumbers (Persian or Japanese) peeled, seeded, chopped roughly (1½ cups)

1 small yellow or red bell pepper, seeded and chopped roughly (1 cup)

1 medium tomato, seeded and quartered

½ small jalapeno, seeded, deveined, and chopped roughly (1 tablespoon, or more to taste)

15 medium-sized fresh mint leaves, chopped roughly

¼ cup roughly chopped fresh cilantro, plus whole leaves for garnish

½ small red onion, peeled and chopped roughly (⅓ cup)

1 tablespoon plus 1 teaspoon red wine vinegar

1½ tablespoons freshly squeezed lemon juice (juice of half a lemon)

¼ cup extra-virgin olive oil

1½ teaspoons kosher salt, plus more to taste

⅛ teaspoon freshly ground black pepper, plus more to taste

# SPICY WATERMELON GAZPACHO

In my high school years, my best friend Jason and I would spend countless hours searching for the perfect watermelon. We considered it a kind of sport. Holding the watermelons in one hand, we would thump them with the knuckles of the other hand, listening for that tell-tale tone: a slightly deep, yet hollow, resonant sound. Jason and I would happily thump our way through 20 to 30 watermelons before agreeing on the perfect one. We would later split the watermelon in half. Then, sitting on my parent's front porch, spoons in hand, we would proceed to devour the entire watermelon. It took some effort on our part, but over the course of an afternoon, we finished the whole thing. What then? Well, our idea of reckless teenage fun was to drive, watermelon rinds in tow, under the cover of night, to the home of one of our teachers, Steve, and jam the rinds of the watermelon under his van's back tires, rendering his ride temporarily immobile. All the while, we were busting our guts laughing, as silently as we could possibly manage, so as not to get caught. No, we weren't the wildest teenagers the world has ever seen, but man, did we laugh… and it all began with the exciting sport of watermelon thumping.

1. Add all the above ingredients to a blender or food processor (It's gonna be full—work in two batches if necessary).

2. Beginning with the slowest speed, blend or pulse until the desired consistency is achieved. I find that it's perfect after blending for approximately 30 seconds. Enjoy your gazpacho with more texture? Blend less.

3. Adjust the seasoning with salt and pepper and refrigerate until chilled. Serve topped with a cilantro leaf.

¼ cup extra-virgin olive oil

2 medium yellow onions, peeled and diced small (2 cups)

3 large garlic cloves, peeled and minced (1 tablespoon)

1 (28-ounce) can diced tomatoes, undrained, preferably fire-roasted

½ teaspoon finely chopped fresh oregano

1 cup black olives, pitted and chopped roughly

2 tablespoons capers, rinsed, drained, and chopped roughly

⅛ teaspoon crushed red chile pepper (chile flakes), or to taste

½ teaspoon ground fennel seed

1 dried bay leaf

2 small anchovy fillets (packed in olive oil) rinsed and mashed into a paste

2 teaspoons balsamic vinegar

Toasted pine nuts, for garnish (recipe on page 42)

3 tablespoons roughly chopped fresh flat-leaf Italian parsley

5 medium-sized fresh basil leaves, stacked, rolled and sliced very thinly

Parmigiano-Reggiano cheese, not pre-grated, for serving

Kosher salt, to taste

Freshly ground black pepper, to taste

Homemade Crostini (recipe on page 40)

# CROSTINI ALLA PUTTANESCA

This past March, one of my friends, Emilia, a successful writer in Los Angeles working on developing a character for a television show, asked me a cooking question. "What would a bachelor, with almost nothing in his kitchen, cook at the last minute? Something gourmet, but out of relatively thin air?"

Immediately I responded, "Puttanesca. A gourmet dish that can be made in a flash, using items a bachelor may have in his pantry." In fact, items that all of us might have in our pantry, bachelor or not. Turns out, Emilia loved the idea, the bachelor made Puttanesca for his date, and nobody went to bed hungry. Sigh... I love a happy ending.

1. Add ¼ cup of olive oil, the onions, and a pinch of salt in a medium saucepan over medium-low heat, and cook, stirring occasionally, for 6 to 8 minutes, until the onions are soft and translucent.

2. Add the garlic, chile flakes, and ground fennel, stir and cook until fragrant, 1 minute. Add the tomatoes, stir and bring to a simmer.

3. Stir in the black olives, capers, bay leaf, and anchovy. Simmer on low heat for 15 minutes.

4. Stir in the fresh oregano and vinegar and continue to cook, stirring occasionally, for 15 minutes more.

5. Remove the bay leaf and season to taste with salt and pepper.

6. Serve the puttanesca in a bowl with the crostini on the side. Top the puttanesca with the pine nuts, parsley, basil and then use a vegetable peeler to top with some shavings of Parmigiano-Reggiano.

Note: Leftovers? Serve puttanesca tossed with pasta for one heck of a tasty dinner.

**VINAIGRETTE:**

1 small shallot, peeled and diced finely (1½ tablespoons)

Kosher salt, to taste

Freshly ground black pepper, to taste

2 tablespoons balsamic vinegar

3 tablespoons extra-virgin olive oil

**ZUCCHINI:**

2 tablespoons extra-virgin olive oil

4 medium-sized zucchini, sliced lengthwise in ¼-inch slices using a mandoline or vegetable peeler

Kosher salt, to taste

Freshly ground black pepper, to taste

8 ounces fresh mozzarella cheese (or burrata if available), drained and sliced thinly

6 medium-sized fresh basil leaves, stacked, rolled, and sliced very thinly

Homemade Crostini (recipe on page 40)

# GRILLED ZUCCHINI AND MOZZARELLA CROSTINI

1. Preheat a grill to medium-high. Once hot, clean the grill, then, using tongs, lightly dip a cloth in olive oil and wipe to coat the grill rack.

2. In a small bowl combine the shallot, a pinch of salt and pepper, and the balsamic vinegar. Whisk in 3 tablespoons of olive oil.

3. Drizzle 2 tablespoons olive oil over the sliced zucchini. Using your hands, coat each piece evenly with the oil; season with salt and pepper. Taste a piece to see if it needs more seasoning, adding more to taste.

4. Grill the zucchini with the cover closed until nicely colored, 5 minutes per side. Do not move the zucchini slices for the first few minutes.

5. Once nicely caramelized, flip each piece and continue cooking until equally caramelized on the second side.

6. Transfer the cooked zucchini into a large bowl and drizzle over the vinaigrette, carefully and gently tossing to coat. Season to taste with salt and pepper.

7. To serve, top the crostini with thin slices of mozzarella. Season the mozzarella lightly with salt and pepper. Place a few slices of the grilled zucchini on top of the mozzarella and finish with the basil.

Note: If using a firm mozzarella, give this a try: about a minute before your bread is toasted on the second side, place a thin slice of the cheese on the crostini and allow it to get all melty.

# Heirloom Tomato and Mozzarella Salad

1. In a medium container with a tight fitting lid, combine the vinaigrette ingredients, close the lid tightly, and shake well to combine. Or, whisk to combine the ingredients in a medium-sized bowl.

2. Place the cherry tomatoes, half the basil, and half the parsley in a medium bowl. Combine gently with half the vinaigrette. Season to taste with salt and pepper.

3. To serve, put some of the mozzarella on each plate and top with sliced heirloom tomatoes; season with salt and pepper. Top the heirloom tomatoes with more mozzarella, then some of the cherry tomato mixture. Sprinkle the remaining basil and parsley over each plate, and drizzle over additional vinaigrette to taste.

**YIELD: 4 TO 6 SERVINGS**

**VINAIGRETTE:**

1 medium shallot, peeled and diced finely (3 tablespoons)

2 tablespoons balsamic vinegar

1 tablespoon red wine vinegar

5 tablespoons extra-virgin olive oil

**SALAD:**

1 pint cherry tomatoes, halved

10 medium-sized fresh basil leaves, stacked, rolled, and sliced very thinly, divided

½ cup fresh flat-leaf Italian parsley, picked and chopped roughly, divided

Kosher salt, to taste

Freshly ground black pepper, to taste

1 (8-ounce) container fresh mozzarella cheese, drained and sliced thinly

3 large heirloom tomatoes, cored and sliced into medium-sized wedges

YIELD: 2 TO 4 SERVINGS

½ cantaloupe, seeded, rind removed, and sliced into 1-inch sections

2 pints strawberries, hulled and quartered

2 tablespoons of balsamic OR white wine vinegar

15 medium-sized fresh mint leaves, chopped finely

Freshly ground black pepper, to taste

1 cup crumbled feta cheese

2 tablespoons extra-virgin olive oil

# STRAWBERRY CANTALOUPE SALAD
## WITH FRESH MINT — TWO WAYS

Gather 'round, friends. Let's name off some summertime culinary classics, shall we? Strawberries with aged balsamic? That's a goodie. Cantaloupe with fresh mint? Another winner. What about slices of cantaloupe sprinkled with a little salt? Uh-huh. So (pondering)... what about a salty cheese, like feta, paired with cantaloupe? Would that work? Or, how about adding strawberries to the cantaloupe and feta? Hey, come to think of it, what if everybody got together in the same bowl and had a little summertime party? What do you think? Would it work? Turns out... yes, yes, it does! Aren't friends just the greatest?

1. Gently toss the cantaloupe, strawberries, vinegar of choice, pepper, and olive oil in a large bowl.

2. Add the feta and chopped mint to the bowl just prior to serving and toss.

Note:  If you prefer the flavor of the strawberries to pop, go with a nice balsamic. If you're more of a cantaloupe person, go with the white wine vinegar. Both work great.

# SPICED ROASTED EGGPLANT TOMATO SOUP
## WITH FRESH GOAT CHEESE

One of the wonderful flavor combinations found worldwide is eggplant paired with tomato. Whether they're deep fried, grilled, baked, or sautéed, one thing's for sure: eggplant and tomato make quite a pair... and they're good for you. Add to this perfect nightshade duo some chile flakes for heat, garam masala spice blend for an earthy depth, and fresh goat cheese for a tangy, sweet finish, and you've got something really special. Don't just take my word for it, though. Grab a spoon and see for yourself! The world awaits.

1. Adjust an oven rack to the middle position, then preheat the oven to 450°F.

2. In a large bowl, toss the eggplant with 3 tablespoons olive oil, and season well with some salt and pepper.

3. Lay the eggplants in a single layer on two sheet pans lined with parchment paper. Place into the oven, and roast, uncovered, until lightly colored, approximately 30 minutes, stirring after 15 minutes.

4. Add 4 tablespoons olive oil and the onions to a small pot over medium heat, and cook, stirring occasionally, for 8 to 10 minutes, until the onions are soft and translucent.

5. Stir in the garlic, thyme, garam masala, chile flakes, bay leaf, and paprika, and cook until fragrant, 1 minute.

6. Pour in the tomatoes and stock and add the salt and pepper.

7. Turn the heat to high, bring to a boil, then reduce the heat to low and simmer for 20 minutes.

**YIELD: 8 SERVINGS**

1 large Italian eggplant, peeled and diced medium (approximately 7 to 8 cups)

7 tablespoons extra-virgin olive oil, divided, plus more for drizzling

½ teaspoon kosher salt, plus more to taste

¼ teaspoon freshly ground black pepper, plus more to taste

2 large yellow onions, peeled and diced small (3 cups)

6 large garlic cloves, peeled and chopped roughly (2 tablespoons)

1 tablespoon finely chopped fresh thyme

¾ teaspoon garam masala (see note)

⅛ teaspoon crushed red chile pepper (chile flakes), or to taste

1 dried bay leaf

1 teaspoon ground paprika

1 (28-ounce) can diced tomatoes, undrained, preferably fire-roasted

4 cups chicken or vegetable stock (recipes on page 37 & 38)

2 tablespoons freshly squeezed lemon juice, plus more to taste

Ingredients continued on next page »

2 tablespoons finely chopped fresh flat-leaf Italian parsley

2 tablespoons finely chopped fresh mint

Fresh goat cheese (chèvre), for serving

Homemade Crostini, optional (recipe on page 40)

8. Check the eggplants; if they are lightly colored, remove them from the oven.

9. Add the eggplants and the stock to the tomato mixture and stir. Increase the heat to high and bring to a simmer.

10. Remove from the heat and discard the bay leaf.

11. Using an immersion blender, blend until smooth.

12. Add lemon juice, a healthy pinch of salt, and a few really good grinds of pepper. Blend once more. Taste and adjust seasoning once more with additional lemon juice, salt, and pepper.

13. Serve in soup bowls with a drizzle of olive oil, a few pieces of goat cheese, a sprinkling of the chopped parsley and mint, and crostini on the side.

Note: Garam masala is an Indian spice blend that lends a wonderful warm sweetness to any dish. These spices may include, but are not limited to: cinnamon, cloves, cardamom, fennel, cumin, and black pepper.

*"Shipping is a terrible thing to do to vegetables. They probably get jet-lagged, just like people."* — ELIZABETH BARRY

**VINAIGRETTE:**

2 tablespoons white wine vinegar

2 tablespoons freshly squeezed lemon juice

1 medium shallot, peeled and diced finely
(3 tablespoons)

3 tablespoons extra-virgin olive oil

Freshly ground black pepper, to taste

**SALAD:**

3 small zucchini

Kosher salt, to taste

3 tablespoons extra-virgin olive oil

1 tablespoon capers, rinsed and drained

Pecorino Romano or Parmigiano-Reggiano
cheese, not pre-grated, for serving

¼ cup roughly chopped fresh flat-leaf
Italian parsley

# SUMMER SQUASH SALAD
## WITH LEMON, CAPERS, AND PECORINO ROMANO CHEESE

Wet, flaccid, and bland—yikes. Not good descriptors, regardless of the subject. Well, that is exactly what my inner childhood Nathan remembers about summer squash and zucchini, no matter the household, no matter the sleepover. I would always see the same baked dish: sliced spongy squashes baked with onions and lots of cheese. Ugh! Oh, geeze, why? The resulting taste and texture was, shall we say, less than desirable to my nine-year-old palate, so my aversion to baked squash—or any squash, really—runs deep—so deep it took me a long, long time to come around. Almost thirty years.

It turns out that squash, when prepared the right way, is delicate, light, and flavorful. "Impossible!" shouts my inner childhood Nathan. Don't get me wrong: summer squash that is grilled, sautéed, or broiled over high heat, then drizzled with a balsamic vinaigrette is great. Oh, yes. Even my nine-year-old self would enjoy that. This method, though, of very thinly sliced summer squash, served raw, with capers, shaved Pecorino Romano and extra-virgin olive oil? Wow!

Simple, fresh, and delicious: now those are descriptors that any summer squash or zucchini can stand up and be proud of.

1. In a small container with a tight fitting lid, combine the vinaigrette ingredients, close the lid tightly, and shake well to combine. Or, whisk to combine the ingredients in a small bowl.

2. Using a mandoline or your vegetable peeler, carefully slice the zucchini lengthwise into $\frac{1}{16}$-inch thick slices lengthwise. The slices will resemble wide pasta noodles. Season to taste with salt and pepper.

3. Place the zucchini in a medium bowl.

4.  Whisk the olive oil into the shallot mixture and add the capers. On a plate, loosely arrange some zucchini slices into a small pile, then spoon some of the caper vinaigrette over the top.

5.  Lastly, using a vegetable peeler, top with some shavings of cheese and some of the parsley.

# CREAMED SUMMER CORN SOUP
## WITH CHOPPED CILANTRO AND AGED CHEDDAR

Even though this recipe is called "creamed" summer corn soup, it doesn't actually contain any cream. The cream comes from the corn through a process called "creaming." Creaming is when you cut off the kernels, then, using the back of your knife, press against the cob while pushing the knife down the length of the cob, top to bottom. This extracts the sweet, creamy "milk" of the cob. The thickening comes from potatoes. The resulting flavor and texture will be the sweetest and creamiest corn soup you've ever had.

1. Heat 4 tablespoons of the olive oil in a small pot over medium heat.

2. Add the onion, a pinch of salt, and a few grinds of pepper and cook, stirring occasionally, for 8 to 10 minutes, until the onions are soft and translucent.

3. Stir in the garlic, thyme, and chile flakes and cook until fragrant, 1 minute.

4. Add the corn (and their cobs), the diced potato, and the stock, then cover. Turn the heat to high and bring to a boil.

5. Reduce the heat to low and simmer for approximately 25 to 30 minutes until the potatoes are cooked through.

6. Remove from the heat, then remove and discard the corn cobs.

7. Add the butter to the soup and, using an immersion blender, blend continuously until smooth. Add the lime juice and season to taste with salt and pepper.

8. Serve warm and garnish each bowl with grated cheese, a drizzle of olive oil, a good sprinkle of chopped cilantro, and a grind of pepper. Ouch, that's good.

**YIELD: 5 TO 6 SERVINGS**

¼ cup extra-virgin olive oil, plus more for drizzling

2 large yellow onions, peeled and diced small (3 cups)

Kosher salt, to taste

Freshly ground black pepper, to taste

3 large garlic cloves, peeled and minced (1 tablespoon)

2 teaspoons roughly chopped fresh thyme

⅛ teaspoon crushed red chile pepper (chile flakes), or to taste

4 ears corn, kernels sliced off the cob (2 cups), reserving cobs

1 medium yellow potato, peeled and diced medium (¾ to 1 cup)

4 cups chicken or vegetable stock (recipe on page 37 & 38)

2 tablespoons unsalted butter, cut into 4 pieces

2 tablespoons freshly squeezed lime juice (juice of 1 lime)

Aged cheddar cheese, not pre-grated, for serving

2 tablespoons finely chopped fresh cilantro

For bonus material relating to this recipe, visit chefnathanlyon.com

1 large Italian eggplant, peeled and diced medium (approximately 7 to 8 cups)

2 medium yellow onions, peeled and diced small (2 cups)

7 tablespoons of extra-virgin olive oil, divided

3 large garlic cloves, peeled and minced (1 tablespoon)

1 teaspoon ground cumin

1 teaspoon ground fennel seed

¼ teaspoon crushed red chile pepper (chile flakes), or to taste

1 fennel bulb, diced small (1 cup)

1 large red, yellow, or orange bell pepper, cored and diced small (1¼ cup)

2 medium tomatoes, cored and diced medium (2 cups), or 1 (14-ounce) can diced tomatoes, undrained, preferably fire-roasted

3 tablespoons capers, rinsed, drained, and chopped roughly

1 cup green olives, pits removed and chopped roughly

2 tablespoons balsamic vinegar

Kosher salt, to taste

Freshly ground black pepper, to taste

⅓ cup roughly chopped fresh flat-leaf Italian parsley

Ingredients continued on next page »

# ROASTED EGGPLANT CAPONATA

Caponata is one of those wonderful versatile Italian dishes that gets better over time, when the flavors are allowed to blend effortlessly. It's also one of those multi-talented dishes that can be served in a variety of mouth-watering ways. You see, although caponata is typically served as an appetizer, you can serve leftover caponata with pasta and shaved Parmigiano- Reggiano for an impromptu dinner party, the following morning, with eggs, for a delicious caponata omelette brunch gathering, or serve it warm over baby mixed greens. Breakfast, appetizer, salad, or dinner… there's nothing this dish can't do.

1. Adjust two oven racks to the middle position, then preheat the oven to 450°F.

2. In a large bowl, toss the eggplant with 3 tablespoons of olive oil, and season well with salt and pepper.

3. Spread out the eggplant in one layer onto two parchment paper-lined sheet pans. Roast, uncovered, in the oven for 15 minutes. Remove the sheet pans from the oven, stir the eggplant, then place the sheet pans back in the oven, this time on opposite racks. Bake 15 minutes more, until the eggplants are lightly colored and cooked through.

4. After the eggplant has been cooking for 15 minutes, stir the diced onion with ¼ cup of olive oil in a large saucepan over medium heat. Cook for approximately 8 to 10 minutes, stirring occasionally, until the onions are soft, translucent, and lightly caramelized.

5. Next, stir in the garlic, cumin, ground fennel, and chile flakes and cook until fragrant, 1 minute.

6. Add the diced fennel and the bell pepper and cook until they begin to soften, stirring occasionally, 5 minutes.

7. Stir in the tomatoes, capers, olives, vinegar, and baked eggplant. Cook until the caponata has thickened, approximately 15 minutes, then remove from the heat, season to taste with salt and pepper, and stir in the parsley and basil.

8. Serve with crostini for one heck of an appetizer.

7 medium-sized fresh basil leaves, stacked, rolled and sliced very thinly

Homemade Crostini (see page 40)

6 medium to large tomatoes

2 tablespoons extra-virgin olive oil, plus more for drizzling

½ pound fresh spicy Italian sausage (pork or turkey), removed from casing, approximately 2 to 3 links

1 medium yellow onion, peeled and diced small (1 cup)

3 medium garlic cloves, peeled and minced (1½ teaspoons)

1 tablespoon finely chopped fresh basil leaves

1¼ teaspoons finely chopped fresh oregano

2 tablespoons finely chopped fresh flat-leaf Italian parsley

½ teaspoon finely chopped fresh thyme

½ cup breadcrumbs (recipe on page 44), or panko (Japanese breadcrumbs)

1 cup grated Parmigiano-Reggiano cheese, not pre-grated

½ cup mozzarella cheese, grated from a whole piece

3 tablespoons toasted pine nuts (recipe on page 42)

Kosher salt, to taste

Freshly ground black pepper, to taste

# STUFFED TOMATOES
## WITH SPICY ITALIAN SAUSAGE AND PINE NUTS

1. Adjust an oven rack to the middle position, then preheat the oven to 375°F.

2. Remove the cores from the tomatoes and scoop out the insides with a teaspoon. Season the insides of the tomato shells with salt and pepper.

3. Add the olive oil, sausage, and onions to a medium saucepan and cook over medium-low heat for 10 minutes until the onions are soft and translucent, breaking up the sausage into small pieces with the back of a wooden spoon as it cooks.

4. Add the garlic, basil, oregano, parsley, and thyme. Stir to combine, and cook for 1 minute.

5. Remove from the heat and transfer to a medium bowl, and mix in the breadcrumbs, cheeses, and toasted pine nuts. Season to taste with salt and pepper.

6. Stuff the tomatoes evenly with the sausage stuffing, mounding any excess stuffing on each tomato. Arrange the stuffed tomatoes in a lightly oiled casserole dish, drizzle the tops lightly with olive oil, and bake, uncovered, until the tops are browned, approximately 20 minutes. Serve.

Note: Here's a tip: when coring the tomato, cut the top of the tomato large enough to easily accommodate the teaspoon.

1 medium peach, pit removed and diced
small

1 medium nectarine, pit removed and
diced small

1 pint strawberries, hulled and quartered

1 plum, pit removed and diced small

1 pint red raspberries

Large fresh mint leaves, to taste

½ vanilla bean, seeds and pod: slice down
the length of the pod, spread open,
and scrape out the flesh by pressing with
a butter knife

½ cup Grand Marnier

1 bottle Viognier white wine, chilled

1 bottle sparkling rosé wine, chilled

Notes: Sangría is derived from the Spanish word
for "blood" and is classically made with red wine
and fruit. That said, sometimes the mid-summer
heat demands that a crisp white wine be served.
Also keep in mind that people love the alcohol-
soaked pieces of fruit, so be sure to cut the fruit
into bite-size pieces. Substitute or add other ripe
seasonal fruits: apricots, blackberries, or cherries.

# SPARKLING ROSÉ-WHITE SANGRÍA
## WITH GRAND MARNIER AND FRESH MINT

1. Combine the peach, nectarine, strawberries, plum, raspberries, mint, vanilla seeds and pod, Grand Mariner, and Viognier in a large container.

2. If time permits, refrigerate for a few hours to allow the fruit to chill.

3. Pour into a pitcher or punch bowl, then just before serving, add the bottle of sparkling rosé.

4. Serve in rocks glasses, wine glasses, or in the bride's designer hand-crafted sequined bridal shoes.

# GRILLED SWEET CORN
## WITH BUTTER, SALT, AND CILANTRO

I know that people are used to soaking their corn before tossing them onto a hot grill to keep them from burning. To that, I say, "Let em' BURN!" Okay, maybe not burn-burn, but a nice char can be a wonderful thing. It imparts a wonderful smoky flavor to the corn. It's like tough love for produce. That said, you do have to protect the corn from cooking too much, or else those plump, juicy kernels will shrivel up, dry out, and get chewy. Nobody wants that, right? How about we split the difference and prepare the corn so that we can enjoy that smoky flavor while keeping all the juice? Forget the soak, and bring on the flame because sometimes a little tough love is just what's needed.

1. Preheat your grill to medium-high.

2. Shuck the corn, leaving 1 layer of husk covering the cob.

3. Place the corn on the grill, close the lid, and grill for a total of 15 minutes, rotating the corn one-third turn every 5 minutes, until the corn is cooked and the husks are slightly charred.

4. Remove the corn from the grill, carefully shuck the corn (hot!), and enjoy with butter, salt and cilantro.

5. Floss.

**YIELD: 6 SERVINGS**

6 ears of corn, whole and unshucked

2 tablespoons unsalted butter

Kosher salt, to taste

3 tablespoons roughly chopped fresh cilantro

For bonus material relating to this recipe, visit chefnathanlyon.com

**GRILLED VEGETABLES:**

3 small Japanese or Chinese eggplants, cut lengthwise into ¼-inch slices

2 zucchini or yellow squash, cut lengthwise into ¼-inch slices

3 red, yellow, or orange bell peppers, cored, seeded and cut lengthwise into ½-inch slices

½ pound asparagus, white fibrous bottoms discarded and bottom inch peeled

1 large portabella mushroom, cut into ½-inch slices

Extra-virgin olive oil, for drizzling

Kosher salt, to taste

Freshly ground black pepper, to taste


**VINAIGRETTE:**

3 tablespoons balsamic vinegar

¼ cup extra-virgin olive oil

1 medium shallot, peeled and diced finely (3 tablespoons)

½ teaspoon finely chopped fresh oregano

1 large garlic clove, peeled and minced finely (1 teaspoon)

Kosher salt, to taste

Freshly ground black pepper, to taste

# MARINATED GRILLED SUMMER VEGETABLES

It's summertime! The sun is out, you're whistling a catchy little tune, and you seem to have a surplus of fresh veggies (it's true). I, for one, say we toss those bad boys on the grill, drizzle over a fresh marinade while they're still hot and proceed to make an almost endless variety of foods! Don't believe me? How about marinated grilled vegetables tossed with pasta, shaved Parmesan and torn herbs? Or served on a sandwich with a slathering of fresh goat cheese? Piled on a vegetable plate with some fresh pesto and mozzarella? I mean, who wouldn't want that? I'll fire up the grill, you make the marinade, and together, we'll make those fresh vegetables sing!

1. Heat a grill to medium-high. Once hot, clean the grill, then, using tongs, lightly dip a cloth in olive oil and wipe to coat the grill rack.

2. Combine the eggplant, zucchini, bell pepper, asparagus and mushroom in a large bowl. Drizzle with just enough olive oil to coat (not too much) and season well with salt and pepper. Toss the vegetables to coat evenly.

3. Distribute the vegetables on the grill (or use a grill basket) and cook until they are just tender and well marked, 5 to 6 minutes per side. A light char is good, but if they begin to burn, turn down the heat a little.

4. In a medium container with a tight fitting lid, combine the vinaigrette ingredients, close the lid tightly, and shake well to combine. Or, whisk to combine the ingredients in a medium-sized bowl.

5. When the vegetables finish grilling, transfer them back into the original large bowl, drizzle over the vinaigrette and toss to coat. Serve.

2 avocados, cut in half, pit discarded

½ small red onion, peeled and diced small (⅓ cup)

2 tablespoons freshly squeezed lime juice (juice of 1 lime)

¼ cup finely chopped fresh cilantro

¼ cup finely chopped fresh flat-leaf Italian parsley

2 medium tomatoes, cored, seeded, and diced small (1 cup)

1 small jalapeño pepper, seeded, deveined, and diced finely (1 tablespoon)

3 tablespoons extra-virgin olive oil

Kosher salt, to taste

Freshly ground black pepper, to taste

Homemade Crostini (recipe on page 40)

# SPICY GUACAMOLE

1. Scoop the avocados out of their skin with a spoon onto a cutting board and cut into small cubes.

2. Mix the avocados with the onion and lime juice in a medium-sized bowl.

3. Fold in the cilantro, parsley, tomato, jalapeno, and olive oil, and season to taste with salt and pepper.

4. Serve in a bowl with crostini on the side.

# GERMAN-STYLE POTATO SALAD

**YIELD: 4 SERVINGS**

2 pounds small white or new red potatoes, scrubbed

6 tablespoons extra-virgin olive oil, divided

3 strips applewood-smoked bacon, halved lengthwise and then cut into ¼-inch slices, crosswise (¾ cup)

4 medium shallots, peeled and diced small (¾ cup)

3½ tablespoons white wine vinegar

2 tablespoons capers, rinsed, drained, and chopped roughly

3 tablespoons whole-grain Dijon mustard

¹⁄₁₆ teaspoon crushed red chile pepper (chile flakes), or to taste

4 celery stalks, diced small (2 cups)

6 tablespoons mayonnaise

4 hard boiled eggs, peeled and diced medium (recipe on page 125)

¾ cup roughly chopped fresh flat-leaf Italian parsley

Kosher salt, to taste

Freshly ground black pepper, to taste

It was the night before the BIG GAME: World Cup soccer 2010: Argentina versus Germany. The problem was, I wanted Argentina to win, while my friend Jen was cheering for Germany. Thinking Germany might lose, I thought to myself, "be nice, Nathan. Cook something tasty for your friend to help ease the pain when Argentina wins." So I did exactly that. I donned my Argentina soccer jersey and proceeded to cook a five course meal consisting of grilled olive bread with marinated olives and goat cheese, grilled vegetable ratatouille, marinated grilled artichokes, white bean tuna salad, and finally... my vinegar based German-style potato salad.

Unfortunately, Argentina did not win that day. All was not lost, though! Both Jen and I agreed that the feast was a complete success, and, if there had to be a star of the menu? A dish that scored the most points overall? Well, I must admit, the German-style potato salad won that day, too.

1. Put the potatoes in a medium saucepan and fill with cool water, enough to cover the potatoes.

2. Over high heat, bring the water to a boil. Reduce the heat to low and simmer for approximately 20 minutes, or until the potatoes can be easily pierced with the tip of a knife.

3. Drain the potatoes, then cut each potato into medium cubes.

4. Meanwhile, add the bacon and 1 tablespoon of olive oil, to a medium sauté pan. Place the sauté pan over medium-low heat. Cook for approximately 5 to 6 minutes, stirring occasionally, until much of the fat has rendered off, and the bacon is just beginning to get nice and crispy. Transfer the bacon to a side plate, and if you're from the South, like me, save the bacon fat for another use.

5. In a medium container with a tight fitting lid, make a vinaigrette by combining the shallots, vinegar, capers, mustard, chile flakes, and remaining olive oil, close the lid tightly, and shake well to combine. Or, whisk to combine the ingredients in a medium-sized bowl.

6. In a large bowl, gently fold to combine the warm cubed potatoes, vinaigrette, celery, mayonnaise, diced egg, parsley, and bacon. Season to taste with salt and pepper.

7. Cover with plastic wrap, then refrigerate until chilled. Once chilled, season to taste with salt and pepper before serving.

**YIELD: 2 CUPS**

2 pounds cherry or grape tomatoes, halved

1 head garlic, separated into cloves, unpeeled

1½ tablespoons roughly chopped fresh thyme

½ teaspoon kosher salt

Freshly ground black pepper, to taste

¼ cup extra-virgin olive oil

# SLOW-ROASTED TOMATOES
## WITH FRESH THYME AND GARLIC

Late summer, when tomatoes are plentiful and literally bursting from the fields—or your garden—is the best time to roast these little gems. Now, I know that three and a half hours seems like a long time, but it's well worth the time, because once roasted, there's so much you can make. Toss them with fresh pasta, add some to a vegetable frittata, or make a batch of slow-roasted tomato pesto for sandwiches. Sound good? Great! Now grab those tomatoes and let's get started… three and a half hours—I can hardly wait!

1. Adjust an oven rack to the middle position, then preheat the oven to 225°F.

2. Place the tomato halves, flesh-side up, and all of the garlic cloves on a parchment paper-lined sheet pan. Season the tomatoes evenly with the thyme, salt, and pepper and drizzle over the olive oil.

3. Roast in the oven, uncovered, until lightly colored, soft and slightly collapsed, around 3½ hours… or more. The total roasting time will depend upon the size of the tomato used.

4. Remove from the oven. Squeeze each garlic clove to remove the sweet, soft insides, and add to the tomatoes. Serve and enjoy.

Note: When roasting for long periods of time, keeping skins on the garlic allows them to steam in their skins and remain sweet, whereas peeled garlic can get bitter. Any leftover tomatoes, garlic, and oil can be transferred into a container, topped off with more olive oil, and stored in the refrigerator for up to a week.

**SUN-DRIED TOMATO PESTO**

YIELD: 1 CUP

1 (8.5-ounce) jar sun-dried tomatoes in olive oil, drained

1 large garlic clove, peeled and roughly chopped

¼ cup pine nuts, toasted (recipe on page 42)

½ cup extra-virgin olive oil, plus more to taste

¼ cup grated Parmigiano-Reggiano, not pre-grated

1 tablespoon water

Kosher salt, to taste

Freshly ground black pepper, to taste

**SLOW ROASTED TOMATO PESTO**

YIELD: 1 CUP

1 cup slow-roasted tomatoes (recipe on page 156)

2 tablespoons pine nuts, toasted (recipe on page 42)

¼ cup extra-virgin olive oil

¼ cup grated Parmigiano-Reggiano, not pre-grated

Kosher salt, to taste

Freshly ground black pepper, to taste

# PESTO – THREE WAYS

Of the many things I've cooked over the years for television, few things compare to the flavor and simplicity of a really good pesto. The day I made my three-minute recipe for a fresh basil pesto on set, the camera crew (brothers Carl and David Pennington) quickly leaned in to inspect the dish. They drawled in a thick Georgia accent, "Wait. That was it? That was so easy. Wow! That's good stuff! Can we get the recipe?"

Add a dollop of pesto to pasta, poached eggs, grilled chicken, roast turkey, or my favorite—a melted mozzarella, pesto and tomato sandwich—and you've got culinary greatness in just seconds! All of this can be yours with just the press of a button. Now that is easy.

## SUN-DRIED TOMATO PESTO

In a food processor, process together the tomatoes, garlic, pine nuts, olive oil, Parmigiano-Reggiano, and water until the desired texture is achieved. Season to taste with salt and pepper.

## SLOW ROASTED TOMATO PESTO

In a food processor, process the tomatoes, garlic, pine nuts, olive oil, and cheese. Process to the desired texture, and season to taste with salt and pepper.

CLASSIC BASIL PESTO

YIELD: 1 CUP

2 ¼ packed cups fresh basil leaves

½ cup extra-virgin olive oil

2 large garlic cloves, peeled and chopped
roughly (2 teaspoons)

½ cup pine nuts

½ cup grated Parmigiano-Reggiano,
not pre-grated

Kosher salt, to taste

Freshly ground black pepper, to taste

Note: Care for a nuttier flavor in your pesto?
Try using toasted pine nuts (recipe on page 42).

# CLASSIC BASIL PESTO

In a food processor, process to combine, the basil, ¼ cup oil, garlic, and pine nuts. Scrape down the sides, then add the remaining ¼ cup oil, and the cheese. Process until the desired texture is achieved, seasoning to taste with salt and pepper. For the record, I add about ½ teaspoon salt and a few good cranks of pepper. No need to rush; taste as you go. Take your time and enjoy.

# SALADE NIÇOISE

1. Pat the tuna dry with a paper towel, then lightly season each piece of tuna with salt and pepper. Let the tuna sit for 30 minutes at room temperature.

2. Bring a small pot of water to a rolling boil, then add the salt. Add the green beans and cook until still firm to the bite, or *al dente*, 5 to 7 minutes.

3. Without turning off the heat, remove them from the boiling water with a slotted spoon or tongs. Do not throw away the water. Transfer the beans to the bowl of ice water. Once the beans are cooled, drain well and transfer them to a large bowl.

4. Meanwhile, put the potatoes into the boiling water, and cook until they are easily pierced with a knife, 10 to 15 minutes, depending on their size.

5. Drain the potatoes, halve them lengthwise, and transfer them into the bowl with the beans. It's cool. They're friends.

6. Heat a medium sauté pan over medium-high heat until very hot. Once very hot, add the olive oil and swirl the pan to distribute. The oil should shimmer, perhaps even smoke.

7. Add the tuna to the pan and allow to sear for 30 seconds. Flip the tuna and continue to sear the tuna for another 30 seconds.

8. Transfer the tuna to a cutting board, let cool slightly, and slice across the grain into ¾-inch slices.

**YIELD: 4 TO 6 SERVINGS**

**SALAD:**

2 tablespoons kosher salt, plus more to taste

1 pound fresh ahi tuna, 1¼ inches thick

½ pound green beans, stem ends removed

1 pound mixed baby potatoes, scrubbed

1 teaspoon extra-virgin olive oil

1 pint cherry tomatoes, halved

1 (12-ounce) jar marinated artichoke hearts, drained

¼ cup fresh flat-leaf Italian parsley, whole leaves or chopped roughly

1 (15-ounce) can garbanzo beans (chickpeas), rinsed and drained

1 tablespoon capers, rinsed and drained

1 cup Niçoise or Kalamata olives, pitted and chopped roughly

3 hard-boiled eggs, peeled and halved (recipe on page 125)

Freshly ground black pepper, to taste

Bowl of ice water

9. In a medium container with a tight fitting lid, combine the vinaigrette ingredients, close the lid tightly, and shake well to combine. Or, whisk to combine the ingredients in a medium-sized bowl.

10. Add the tomatoes, artichoke hearts, parsley, garbanzo beans, capers, and olives to the bowl of beans and potatoes. Gently toss to combine with just enough dressing to coat, and season to taste with salt and pepper.

11. Serve family-style on a large platter with the hard-boiled eggs and tuna placed on top, or divide equally onto individual salad plates.

**VINAIGRETTE:**

1 small shallot, peeled and diced finely (1½ tablespoons)

1 large garlic clove, peeled and minced (1 teaspoon)

1 tablespoon balsamic vinegar

1 tablespoon red wine vinegar

1½ tablespoons freshly squeezed lemon juice (juice of half a lemon)

1 teaspoon whole-grain Dijon mustard

½ teaspoon finely chopped fresh oregano

¼ cup extra-virgin olive oil

Kosher salt, to taste

Freshly ground black pepper, to taste

*"The colors of a fresh garden salad are so extraordinary, no painter's palette can duplicate nature's artistry."* — DR. SUNWOLF

2 tablespoons kosher salt, plus more to taste

3 tablespoons extra-virgin olive oil

2 large yellow onions, peeled and diced small (3 cups)

1 pound linguini

5 large garlic cloves, peeled and minced (1 tablespoon plus 2 teaspoons)

1 cup dry white wine, such as Sauvignon Blanc

2 pounds mussels, scrubbed and de-bearded

2 pounds small hard shell clams, scrubbed

1½ tablespoons freshly squeezed lemon juice (juice of half a lemon)

3 tablespoons finely chopped fresh flat-leaf Italian parsley

Freshly ground black pepper, to taste

Note:  For a truly insane culinary experience, make yourself a fresh batch of my classic basil pesto (recipe on page 160) then stir the pesto into the still hot, drained pasta.  Serve the mussels and clams over top the pasta. One word: wow.

# LINGUINI AND SHELLFISH
## WITH GARLIC WHITE WINE SAUCE

1. For the pasta, bring a small pot of water to a rolling boil.

2. While waiting for the water to boil, in a second small pot, large enough to hold the mussels and clams, add the olive oil and heat over medium heat until shimmering. Add the onions and cook, stirring occasionally, for 8 to 10 minutes, until the onions are soft and translucent.

3. Now, back to the pasta. Once the water has come to a rolling boil, add the salt. Stir the linguini into the boiling salted water and cook, stirring occasionally, until *al dente* (almost done, or "to the tooth").

5. Add the garlic to the onions in the second small pot and cook until fragrant, 1 minute.

6. Add the wine to the second pot, increase the heat to high and bring to a boil.

7. Stir in the clams and mussels then cover with a lid. Reduce the heat to medium-high and cook for approximately 5 to 6 minutes, stirring after 3 minutes, until almost all of the shells have opened.

8. Remove from the heat and stir in the lemon juice and chopped parsley.

9. Drain the pasta, then add the drained pasta back into the same pot you cooked it in. Season to taste with salt and pepper. Pour the warm mussels and clams over the pasta and stir. If the pasta is finished cooking prior to the mussels being done, simply drizzle a little olive oil over the pasta and stir to prevent the pasta from sticking. Cover and wait for the mussels to jump in.

10. Serve in pasta bowls.

# SAUTÉED CUMIN SHRIMP
## WITH ORZO AND FETA SALAD

I just like the name: oorrrrrrrrrrrzo. Made of semollllliiiiiiiina. It sounds so romantic. See how it feels rolling off of the tongue just saying it? Now imagine eating it. Well, actually, you don't have to imagine it. Here's a refreshing orzo recipe that's sure to please. Who knows? After the first bite, you may just fall in love, too.

1. Bring a small pot of water to a rolling boil then add the salt. Add the orzo to the boiling water and cook, stirring occasionally, until *al dente* (almost done, or "to the tooth").

2. Once done, drain without rinsing, transfer to a large bowl, then stir with a good drizzle of extra-virgin olive oil to keep the orzo from sticking.

3. Heat the butter and 1 tablespoon of olive oil in a large sauté pan over medium heat until the butter foams up, subsides, and begins to turn a light golden brown.

4. Stir in the ground cumin and ground fennel and cook until fragrant, 1 minute. Add the shrimp and garlic, and stir to coat.

5. Continue to cook the shrimp for approximately 3 minutes until just pink, stirring often for even cooking.

6. Drizzle over 1½ tablespoons lemon juice and season lightly with salt and pepper. Continue to cook for 1 minute, stirring occasionally. Add the shrimp to the bowl of orzo.

7. To complete the salad, fold in the shallots, bell pepper, tomatoes, olives, garbanzo beans, and feta in with the shrimp and orzo.

**YIELD: 6 TO 8 SERVINGS**

2 tablespoons kosher salt, plus more to taste

1 cup orzo pasta

3 tablespoons extra-virgin olive oil, divided, plus more for drizzling

2 tablespoons unsalted butter

½ teaspoon ground cumin

½ teaspoon ground fennel seed

⅛ teaspoon crushed red chile pepper (chile flakes), or to taste

5 large garlic cloves, peeled and minced (1 tablespoon plus 2 teaspoons)

1 pound medium shrimp (16-to-20 count), shelled and deveined

2 medium shallots, peeled and diced small (6 tablespoons)

1 large yellow or orange bell pepper, cored, seeds discarded, and diced small (1¼ cups)

1 pint cherry tomatoes, three quarters halved, remaining kept whole

1 cup Kalamata olives, drained and pits removed, chopped roughly

1 (15-ounce) can garbanzo beans (chickpeas), rinsed and drained

1½ cups crumbled feta cheese

2½ tablespoons white wine vinegar

Ingredients continued on next page »

3 tablespoons freshly squeezed lemon juice (juice of 1 lemon), divided

½ cup fresh basil leaves, stacked, rolled and sliced very thinly

½ cup roughly chopped fresh flat-leaf Italian parsley

¼ cup roughly chopped fresh mint leaves

Freshly ground black pepper, to taste

8.  Whisk 2 tablespoons olive oil with the vinegar and the remaining 1½ table-spoons lemon juice in a small bowl and drizzle evenly over the salad.

9.  Fold in the herbs, season with salt and pepper to taste, gently toss to combine, and serve.

# Red Snapper En Papillote

YIELD: 2 SERVINGS

2 portioned fillets of red snapper
(¾ pound)

Kosher salt, to taste

Fresh ground black pepper, to taste

1 large lemon, zested on a Microplane and then sliced very thinly

1 lemon, halved

3 tablespoons unsalted butter, divided

1 tablespoon extra-virgin olive oil, plus more for drizzling

1 small fennel bulb, halved lengthwise and sliced thinly

3 large shallots, peeled and sliced thinly lengthwise

½ teaspoon ground fennel seed

2 large garlic cloves, peeled and minced (2 teaspoons)

1 cup cherry tomatoes, halved

2 teaspoons capers, rinsed and drained

6 sprigs fresh thyme

3 tablespoons dry white wine (such as Sauvignon Blanc) or Pernod, divided

1. Adjust an oven rack to the middle position, then preheat the oven to 425°F.

2. Pat the fish fillets dry, then season lightly on both sides with salt, pepper, and the zest. Let sit at room temperature for 20 minutes.

3. In a medium sauté pan set over medium-low heat, add 1 tablespoon butter and 1 tablespoon olive oil, then heat until the butter stops foaming.

4. Add the fennel, shallots, and ground fennel. Cook, stirring occasionally, until the shallots are just transparent, 4 to 5 minutes.

5. Stir in the garlic, and cook until fragrant, 1 minute. Remove from the heat.

6. Place an inverted sheet pan in the oven.

7. Cut pieces of parchment to 24 inches by 16 inches. Fold each in half, then cut each fold into half a heart as big as the paper allows. Unfold each piece; it will look like a heart.

8. Make a little bed for the fish using the cooked onion mixture, tomatoes and capers, near the seam of the fold. Top each bed with a piece of fish.

9. Cover each fish with 3 sprigs thyme, half of the lemon slices and the remaining 2 tablespoons butter (cut each tablespoon into very small pieces).

10. Close the heart over the fish with the bottom tip of the heart facing you. Starting at the lowest point of the heart, fold the bottom tip approximately an inch towards the center of the heart (away from the seam) as if marking the page in a book. Folding the paper in the same way towards

Note: This dish can be prepared through step 10 a few hours ahead of time and put in the refrigerator. Before cooking in the oven, let the papillote sit for 45 minutes at room temperature, then proceed according to the instructions.

For bonus material relating to this recipe, visit chefnathanlyon.com

the spine of the heart (starting at the bottom of the heart), make small, creased, overlapping folds around the filling, sealing the parchment tight. Follow the curve of the heart and stop a few inches from sealing the paper heart at the top.

11. Pour half of the wine into each paper heart, then finish each papillote by sealing the last paper fold (at the top of the heart) under the bag.

12. Carefully place the prepared envelopes on the hot sheet pan already in the oven. Cook for 10 to 12 minutes (depending on the thickness of the fish), or until the paper is brown and puffed up.

13. Remove the envelopes from the oven, transfer to a plate, tear open, and serve immediately with a drizzle of olive oil and a squeeze of lemon.

6 tablespoons extra-virgin olive oil, divided

2 tablespoons unsalted butter

2 medium yellow onions, peeled and diced small (2 cups)

⅛ teaspoon crushed red chile pepper (chile flakes), or to taste

¼ teaspoon ground cumin

¼ teaspoon ground coriander

2 large garlic cloves, peeled and minced (2 teaspoons)

Kernels cut from 4 ears of fresh corn (approximately 3 cups)

Kosher salt, to taste

Freshly ground black pepper, to taste

1 (15-ounce) can black beans, rinsed and drained

1 large red, yellow, or orange bell pepper, seeded and diced small (1¼ cup)

1 large tomato, seeded and diced small (1¼ cups), or ½ pint cherry tomatoes, halved

1 small jalapeño pepper, seeds and veins discarded, diced finely, or to taste

1 head romaine lettuce, rinsed, dried, and chopped finely

¼ cup roughly chopped fresh cilantro

Ingredients continued on next page »

# SPICY CORN AND BLACK BEAN SALAD
## WITH GRILLED LEMON GARLIC CHICKEN

To me, this recipe represents the quintessential summer corn salad. Fresh corn, sautéed with butter and salt, tossed with black beans, some crumbled feta cheese, chopped fresh herbs, and a pinch of chile flakes for a subtle touch of heat. Is that it? Could it get any better? Let's fire up the grill and top that salad with juicy slices of grilled marinated chicken. Whoa. If that's not a summer salad, I don't know what is.

1. In a large sauté pan set over medium heat, add 2 tablespoons olive oil and 2 tablespoons butter, and heat until the butter begins to turn brown. Add the onions, plus the chili flakes, cumin, and coriander and cook, stirring occasionally, for 8 to 10 minutes, until the onions are soft, translucent, and lightly caramelized.

2. Add the garlic, plus the corn and season lightly with salt and pepper. Stir, and cook for an additional 4 minutes, until the corn is heated through.

3. Meanwhile, combine the black beans, bell pepper, tomato, jalapeño, chopped romaine, cilantro, and parsley in a large bowl, and toss to mix.

4. In a small bowl, whisk the lime juice, vinegar, and the remaining 4 tablespoons of olive oil together. Add half of the dressing to the salad. Toss again, and season with salt and pepper to taste.

5. Fold in the warm corn mixture, feta and avocado. Adjust the seasoning with additional dressing, salt, and pepper.

6. Serve, topped with thin slices of the marinated grilled lemon garlic chicken.

½ cup roughly chopped fresh flat-leaf Italian parsley

2 tablespoons freshly squeezed lime juice (juice of 1 lime)

2 tablespoons white wine vinegar

1 cup crumbled feta cheese

2 avocados, halved, pit discarded, flesh scooped out with a spoon and diced

Marinated grilled lemon garlic chicken (recipe on page 172)

For bonus material relating to this recipe, visit chefnathanlyon.com

*"Food for thought is no substitute for the real thing."*
— WALT KELLY

¼ cup extra-virgin olive oil

1½ tablespoon finely chopped fresh rosemary

1 teaspoon finely chopped fresh oregano

1 teaspoon finely chopped fresh thyme

5 large garlic cloves, peeled and minced (1 tablespoon plus 2 teaspoons)

1 teaspoon kosher salt

¼ teaspoon freshly ground black pepper

1 teaspoon lemon zest (zest of 1 lemon), grated on a Microplane

3 tablespoons freshly squeezed lemon juice (1 lemon)

3 pounds boneless, skinless chicken thighs

# MARINATED GRILLED LEMON GARLIC CHICKEN

1. Combine the olive oil, rosemary, oregano, thyme, garlic, salt, pepper, lemon zest, and lemon juice in a quart size zip-top bag. Close the bag and shake well to mix the marinade.

2. Pat the chicken thighs dry, then add them to the bag. Re-close the bag, and massage the bag to distribute the marinade. Place the bag into a bowl (just in case the bag leaks), and allow to sit at room temperature for 45 minutes.

3. Meanwhile, heat the grill to a medium-high flame. Once hot, clean the grill, then, using tongs, lightly dip a cloth in olive oil and wipe to coat the grill rack.

4. Using tongs, add the chicken thighs to the grill. Do not reposition the chicken once on the grill. Cook the chicken for about 4 minutes, rotating 90 degrees after 2 minutes, to get those awesome crosshatch marks.

5. Flip the thighs, and continue cooking for another 4 minutes (again, rotating after 2 minutes), until well marked and cooked through. Discard the marinade. How do you know when they're properly cooked? Simple. Remove one and cut into it; the juices should run clear.

6. Remove the chicken and place them on a cutting board to rest for 5 minutes, loosely covered with aluminum foil.

Note: Don't have a grill? That's what your oven's broiler setting is for. Adjust the level of the oven rack approximately 5 inches from the heat source. Grab a sheet pan, line it with foil (for easy cleanup), and turn your oven to broil. Place the chicken thighs on the sheet pan, uncovered, and slide the sheet pan under the broiler. My chicken thighs took approximately 9 minutes per side, to cook to perfection. Again, the time will vary slightly from oven to oven.

# GRILLED LEMON ROSEMARY CHICKEN PAILLARD
## WITH PEACH CHUTNEY

1. Heat your grill to medium-high. Once hot, clean the grill, then, using tongs, lightly dip a cloth in olive oil and wipe to coat the grill rack.

2. Pat the chicken breasts dry. Using a mallet, rolling pin, or the back of a saucepan, pound each chicken breast between two sheets of plastic wrap until ⅓-inch thick.

3. Remove the chicken from the plastic wrap, then season equally with rosemary, lemon zest, garlic, salt, and pepper. Drizzle lightly with the olive oil, just enough to coat both sides, rubbing to coat evenly.

4. Grill the first side for 3 minutes. Flip the chicken and grill the other side 1-2 minutes, until juices run clear when poked with a fork.

**YIELD: 4 SERVINGS**

**GRILLED CHICKEN:**

4 large boneless, skinless chicken breasts (approximately 2 pounds)

1½ tablespoons finely chopped fresh rosemary

2 teaspoons lemon zest (zest of 2 lemons), grated on a Microplane

3 large garlic cloves, peeled and minced (1 tablespoon)

1 teaspoon kosher salt

¼ teaspoon freshly ground black pepper

Extra-virgin olive oil, for drizzling

**PEACH CHUTNEY:**

**YIELD: 2¼ CUPS**

2 tablespoons extra-virgin olive oil

1 medium yellow onion, peeled and diced small (1 cup)

1 small red bell pepper, seeded and diced small (1 cup)

¼ teaspoon kosher salt, plus more to taste

1/16 teaspoon freshly ground black pepper, plus more to taste

1 large garlic clove, peeled and minced (1 teaspoon)

3 medium peaches, pit removed and chopped roughly

1/16 teaspoon crushed red chile pepper (chile flakes), or to taste

1 teaspoon ground cinnamon

1 tablespoon dark brown sugar

2 tablespoons golden raisins

2 tablespoons white wine vinegar

⅛ teaspoon ground nutmeg

½ tablespoon fresh ginger, peeled and grated on a Microplane

## PEACH CHUTNEY

1. In a medium saucepan set over medium-low heat, add the oil, onions, red bell pepper, and the salt and pepper, stir to combine, and cook 6 to 8 minutes until transparent, stirring occasionally.

2. Add the garlic and cook until fragrant, 1 minute.

3. Add the remaining ingredients, reduce the heat to low, and cook, stirring occasionally, for 10 minutes. Season to taste with salt and pepper.

4. Remove from the heat and use immediately, or allow to cool, then transfer to a large container then store in the refrigerator for up to a week.

# SLOW-COOKED BABY BACK RIBS
## WITH HOMEMADE SPICE RUB

From Virginia to the Carolinas, from Tennessee to Texas, my friends and I have always been huge fans of slow-cooked pork ribs. Maybe it's a texture thing, or maybe it's the simple fact that, when prepared just right, they're juicy, fatty, sweet, and spicy in every lip-smackin', finger-lickin', bone-nibblin' bite. Of course, just the notion of taking a fairly inexpensive, tough piece of meat and transforming it into an ever-so-tender, fall-off-the-bone thing of beauty is exciting. Sure, my friends who live in the Southern states tease me for using my oven to prepare slow cooked pork ribs, and not an outdoor smoker for barbecue, but I don't own a smoker. My oven is the next best thing. After some spice rub, a few hours in the oven plus a slathering of homemade barbecue sauce, you can bet that your friends won't be teasing you any more—because they'll be too busy eating.

1. To make the spice rub, mix together the salt, pepper, cumin, paprika, brown sugar, oregano, garlic powder, and cayenne in a small mixing bowl.

2. Place the ribs on a cutting board and pat dry all over. Remove the membrane (see note in the sidebar on the next page) and rub the slabs evenly with the spice rub—all over, front and back. Let sit, meat side up, for 45 minutes at room temperature.

3. Adjust an oven rack to the middle position, then preheat the oven to 250°F.

4. Transfer the ribs to a roasting pan. Brush the meat side of each slab evenly with 2 tablespoons barbecue sauce.

**YIELD: 6 SERVINGS**

**RIBS:**

2 slabs of baby back ribs
(2½ pounds each)

1 cup freshly pressed apple cider

**SPICE RUB:**

1½ tablespoons kosher salt

½ teaspoon freshly ground black pepper

1¼ teaspoon ground cumin

1 teaspoon paprika

2 tablespoons brown sugar

2 teaspoons dried oregano

2 teaspoons garlic powder

½ teaspoon ground cayenne pepper

Note: You will first want to remove the thin membrane that is on the back, or rib side of the slab. I've found the best way to accomplish this is to begin with a clean dish towel, a sharp knife, and a butter knife. Starting at the center of the slab, using the sharp knife, score the membrane the width of the rack, along one of the bones. Then, work the flat tip of the butter knife just under the membrane, and tease up an edge. Hold the slab down, then, while grabbing the membrane with the towel, gently pull it up and back against itself and off. Repeat with the other side. Or, ask the person behind the meat counter to do it. They're there to help you.

For bonus material relating to this recipe, visit chefnathanlyon.com

**BARBECUE SAUCE:**

**YIELD: APPROXIMATELY 2 CUPS**

1 cup organic ketchup

1 tablespoon whole-grain Dijon mustard

1 teaspoon Worcestershire sauce

¼ cup apple cider vinegar

¼ teaspoon hot pepper sauce, or to taste (optional)

2 tablespoons unsulfured dark molasses

5. Pour the apple cider around the ribs, then cover completely with plastic wrap. It's okay; plastic wrap can safely go into the oven at 250°F. Now wrap completely in aluminum foil.

6. Place the roasting pan in the oven and set the timer for 3 hours.

7. Remove the sheet pan from the oven, carefully remove and discard the foil and the plastic wrap, so the ribs are totally exposed.

8. Using two spatulas, transfer the racks to a sheet pan, meat side up. Brush over a thin layer of barbecue sauce. Turn the oven to broil and place the baking sheet under the broiler.

9. Being careful not to burn the sauce, broil the ribs just enough to give them some color. Remove from the broiler. Strain the braising liquid from the roasting pan into a separate container; you may want to add a little to your barbecue sauce.

10. Transfer the ribs to a cutting board, slice between the bones, and dig in.

## BARBECUE SAUCE

Whisk or stir the ingredients together in a small container. Well, that was easy, right? Pour out 4 tablespoons sauce into a small bowl to use for brushing the ribs.

1½ pounds ground beef (chuck), 82% lean

1 medium shallot, peeled and minced
(3 tablespoons)

1 teaspoon kosher salt

¼ teaspoon freshly ground black pepper

4 ounces crumbled blue cheese, divided

2 ounces arugula, rinsed and dried

6 hamburger buns, lightly toasted on the grill

1 recipe homemade tomato mostarda (recipe
on this page)

Note: If you measure each burger using a ½ cup
measuring cup, each burger will be approximately ¼ pound. If you don't have blue cheese,
my second runner-up would be an aged cheddar.
Other possible topping suggestions: spicy gua-
camole (recipe on page 152) hickory smoked
bacon, grilled red onions, sautéed mushrooms,
and sliced tomato.

# GRILLED HAMBURGER
## WITH TOMATO MOSTARDA, ARUGULA, AND BLUE CHEESE

1. Heat your grill to medium-high. Once hot, clean the grill, then, using tongs, lightly dip a cloth in olive oil and wipe to coat the grill rack.

2. In a large bowl, gently mix to combine the meat with the shallot, salt, and pepper. Do not over mix. Form into patties, then using your thumb or the back of a tablespoon, gently press into the middle of each burger. This small indentation will ensure that the center of the burger doesn't puff up as it cooks.

3. If you enjoy your burgers medium-rare, grill the burgers for 3 minutes on one side, with the lid closed, until nicely colored, then flip the burgers, close the lid again, and cook 3 minutes more on the second side. Transfer to a sheet pan to rest.

4. While the burgers are resting, place the hamburger buns face down on the grill until lightly toasted. Once the buns are toasted, assemble the burgers, adding the mostarda, cheese, and arugula to your heart's desire. Now, that's a darn good burger!

## TOMATO MOSTARDA

After making my tomato mostarda, I swear, you'll never want ordinary ketchup again. I'm just sayin'—it's that good.

1. Put the tomatoes, vinegar, salt, pepper, sugar, tomato paste, and mustard in a food processor and process until the tomatoes are broken down.

2. Transfer the contents to a large saucepan, add the bay leaves, bring the liquid to a boil, reduce the heat to medium, and cook, stirring occasionally, for 30 minutes.

3. After 30 minutes, begin stirring more frequently until the mostarda thickens and very little liquid remains, approximately 15 minutes more.

4. Remove from heat and take out the bay leaves. Give it a taste. It should taste bright, sweet, and vibrant, like ketchup. If it's a little flat, add a touch more vinegar and re-taste.  A touch of salt or pepper, perhaps? Re-taste.

5. Allow to cool before serving. Store in the refrigerator for up to two weeks.

**TOMATO MOSTARDA:**

**YIELD: APPROXIMATELY 1½ CUPS**

2 pounds cherry or grape tomatoes, halved

⅓ cup red wine vinegar, plus more to taste

2 teaspoons kosher salt, plus more to taste

¼ teaspoon freshly ground black pepper, plus more to taste

⅓ cup granulated sugar

3 tablespoons tomato paste

2 tablespoon whole-grain Dijon mustard

3 dried bay leaves

**SKIRT STEAK:**

**YIELD: 4 TO 6 SERVINGS**

2 pounds skirt steak

Kosher salt, for seasoning

Freshly ground black pepper, for seasoning

2 tablespoons extra-virgin olive oil

# GRILLED SKIRT STEAK
## WITH CHIMICHURRI SAUCE

You have to love Argentina: wonderful people, amazing wine, and the best grass-fed beef. Now, what goes perfectly with beef? Well, in Argentina they would say chimichurri: an herbal condiment with garlic, a touch of heat, and a zingy finish from vinegar. It's perfect because flavorful meats like beef taste best when paired with a firm contrast in flavor. For this dish, chimichurri is just the thing, plus it's super simple to make using ingredients that you may already have in your kitchen right now. So, let's grill that steak, grab a glass of Malbec, and toast our friends to the south for whom we have to thank for this amazing sauce. *¡Besos, Argentina!*

1. Pat the steak dry, then season the steak lightly (both sides) with salt and pepper.

2. Rub with 2 tablespoons olive oil and allow to sit at room temperature for 30 minutes.

3. Prepare your grill by heating it to medium-high. Once hot, clean the grill, then, using tongs, lightly dip a cloth in olive oil and wipe to coat the grill rack.

4. Arrange the steaks on the grill; do not move them for at least 2 minutes; this will help them not stick to the grill.

5. After 4 to 6 minutes, depending upon the thickness of your steaks, flip the steaks with tongs and grill for 4 to 6 minutes more. The steaks should be well marked and still a touch soft to the touch when pressed with your finger.

4. Transfer the steaks from the grill to a cutting board, and allow them to rest (loosely covered with aluminum foil) for 10 minutes prior to slicing, thinly, against the grain (perpendicular to the fibers) of the meat. To do so, you may have to cut each skirt steak into smaller, more manageable lengths.

## CHIMICHURRI SAUCE

1. Combine all of the ingredients except the water and olive oil in a medium mixing bowl and mix together. Allow to sit for 5 minutes, during which time the wonderful flavors will marry.

2. After 5 minutes, whisk in the water, then the olive oil. There you go—fresh chimichurri sauce. Serve immediately or store in the refrigerator for up to 2 weeks.

Note: I think chimichurri is best when prepared by hand. That said, it can also be made on the quick in a food processor. Combine all of the ingredients except for the olive oil and water and process for a few seconds. Let sit for 5 minutes, then add the water and oil, and process for a few more seconds. Zip!

**CHIMICHURRI SAUCE:**

**YIELD: APPROXIMATELY 1½ CUPS**

6 large garlic cloves, peeled and minced (2 tablespoons)

½ small red onion, peeled and diced small (⅓ cup)

½ teaspoon crushed red chile pepper (chile flakes), or to taste

1 cup roughly chopped fresh flat-leaf Italian parsley

2 teaspoons finely chopped fresh oregano

4 tablespoons red wine vinegar

3 tablespoons freshly squeezed lemon juice (juice of 1 lemon)

1 teaspoon kosher salt

¼ teaspoon freshly ground black pepper

2 tablespoons water

1 cup extra-virgin olive oil

**TOMATO SAUCE:**

¼ cup extra-virgin olive oil

2 large yellow onions, peeled and diced small (3 cups)

12 large garlic cloves, peeled and chopped roughly (¼ cup)

3 tablespoons tomato paste

1 (28-ounce) can crushed tomatoes, undrained, preferably fire-roasted

1 teaspoon finely chopped fresh oregano

2 tablespoons fresh basil leaves, chopped finely

1 dried bay leaf

¾ teaspoon kosher salt, plus more to taste

⅛ teaspoon freshly ground black pepper, plus more to taste

⅛ teaspoon crushed red chile pepper (chile flakes), or to taste

¼ teaspoon ground fennel seed

# HOMEMADE ITALIAN PIZZA

For a wiener dog, Heiny sure did love pizza. Together, Heiny and I would put in some serious hours on campus in the basement of Duke Hall at James Madison University, during the days of when I was pursuing a degree in fine arts (stained glass, if you're curious). The automated canine clock that he was, Heiny would whimper around midnight, his cue for me to call out for a whole-wheat vegetable pizza—our favorite. When the pizza arrived, I would put down my glass project, wash up, and together we would enjoy a relaxing dinner. Nowadays, with the aid of my sixteen-year-old bread machine, pizza can be a reality anytime, not just after midnight. Had Heiny only known...

1. Heat the olive oil in a large saucepan over medium-low heat. Add the onions and cook, stirring occasionally, for 10 to 12 minutes, until the onions are soft and translucent.

2. Add the garlic, stir and cook until fragrant, 1 minute.

3. Stir in the tomato paste and cook for 3 minutes more.

4. Add the remaining ingredients and continue cooking, uncovered, for 25 to 30 minutes, stirring occasionally, reducing the heat to low and stirring more often as the sauce thickens.

5. Once thick, remove the bay leaf and, using a food processor or blender, carefully process until smooth. Season to taste with salt and pepper. Then, let cool completely before using.

## DOUGH

1. Place the ingredients in a bread maker in the order they are listed.

2. Close the lid, select the dough setting, and press start. After the allotted amount of time (mine takes an hour and thirty minutes), your pizza dough will be ready.

## PIZZAS

1. Adjust an oven rack to the middle position, place a pizza stone or two stacked, inverted sheet pans in the oven, then preheat the oven to 500°F. (If using a stone, preheat for 15 minutes longer than usual before you put the first pizza in the oven. This will ensure that the pizza stone has also reached a high enough temperature so that the bottom of the pizza will be crisp.)

2. Divide the dough into four equal portions, using a knife. Lightly flour both your work table and a rolling pin.

3. Working with one portion of dough at a time, while covering the other pieces with plastic wrap, roll out the dough to as thin as you can get it, around ⅛-inch thick, and rotating the dough in quarter turns as you roll to ensure evenness.

4. Place the rolled pizza dough on a lightly floured pizza peel, or on the back of a lightly floured sheet pan.

**DOUGH:**

¾ cup very warm water

3 tablespoons extra-virgin olive oil

1½ teaspoons kosher salt

1 teaspoon granulated sugar

2¼ cups unbleached all-purpose flour

1½ teaspoons active dry yeast

5.  Spread 2 tablespoons of tomato sauce evenly over the dough, keeping 1 inch of space from the edge of the pizza free of sauce. Top as desired, but not too much—when it comes to thin crust pizza, less is more.

6.  Carefully but quickly slide the dough onto the pizza stone or inverted sheet pan heating in the oven and bake until the edges of the dough are golden brown in color and the bottom is crisp and lightly toasted, approximately 8 minutes.

7.  Transfer to a cookie rack until ready to serve, to keep the pizza crust from getting soggy. Finish the pizza with a drizzle of extra-virgin olive oil.

8.  Transfer to a cutting board, cut, and serve.

## TOPPING SUGGESTIONS

Thinly sliced fresh tomatoes, mozzarella cheese, goat cheese, fresh oregano, fresh basil, fresh egg, ham, prosciutto, sausage (both fresh and dry), olives, fresh mushrooms, thinly sliced red onions, arugula, classic basil pesto (recipe on page 160).

*"First we eat, then we do everything else."* — M.F.K. FISHER

**PANNA COTTA:**

1 packet powdered unflavored gelatin
(2 teaspoons)

3 tablespoons cold water

1 cup heavy whipping cream

⅓ cup honey, preferably orange blossom

2½ cups buttermilk

1 teaspoon pure vanilla extract

Nonstick spray

# HONEY BUTTERMILK PANNA COTTA

I first fell for panna cotta back in the day while traveling solo through Europe (cue romantic music and soft lighting). It happened in Florence, Italy, in late November, 1995, and it was love at first spoonful. The luscious, creamy texture of panna cotta (Italian for "cooked cream") was reminiscent of a wild fling I had the year prior, back in the US with crème brûlée. Crème brûlée was too needy, though: "stove top" this, and "water bath" that, and eventually we went our separate ways. Panna cotta is different: elegant, simple to prepare, and it can even be made several days in advance of an intimate gathering. Also, because panna cotta sets in the refrigerator, there's no need to turn on the oven. What a dessert! At the end of the day, as much as I desired otherwise, I just couldn't keep panna cotta all to myself. One thing's for sure: no one ever forgets their first panna cotta.

1. Prepare eight 4-ounce ramekins by lightly spraying nonstick spray into each and wiping gently with a paper towel to distribute the spray evenly along the sides and bottom.

2. Add the gelatin to the cold water in a medium bowl, and allow to bloom (soften) for 5 minutes; do not stir.

3. Meanwhile, stir the heavy whipping cream and honey together in a small saucepan set over medium heat. Heat, stirring occasionally, until the honey is fully dissolved at just barely a simmer.

4. Slowly add the warm honey cream to the gelatin and stir until the gelatin is fully dissolved.

5. Pour the buttermilk into a large bowl (or a large pitcher for easier pouring) and, stirring continuously, slowly pour the warm cream mixture into the buttermilk.

6. Stir in the vanilla.

7. Fill the ramekins equally and refrigerate uncovered for approximately 5 hours until chilled and completely set.

8. To unmold the panna cotta, dip the bottom of each ramekin into very hot water for 45 seconds, or until you can see the panna cotta just beginning to melt around the sides. You may also take a knife and run it around the inner circumference of each ramekin. Place a dessert plate on top of the ramekin, then holding both the ramekin and plate, simply invert. Sometimes you may have to give it a little shake—not you, the ramekin. Remove the ramekin and serve each panna cotta with either fresh berries or preserves sauce (recipe below).

**PRESERVES SAUCE:**

½ cup 100%-fruit strawberry or raspberry preserves

2 tablespoons water

## PRESERVES SAUCE

Over low heat, in a small saucepan, mix together the preserves with the water until warm. Strain the warm preserves though a small strainer, pushing on the preserves with the back of a spoon to strain out the seeds.

# WARM NECTARINE BLACKBERRY COBBLER

**YIELD: 8 TO 10 SERVINGS**

**FRUIT COBBLER:**

10 large nectarines, cut into bite-size pieces, pits discarded (8 cups)

2 pints blackberries (4 cups)

1 teaspoon lemon zest (zest of 1 lemon), grated on a Microplane

3 tablespoons freshly squeezed lemon juice (juice of 1 lemon)

2 teaspoons pure vanilla extract

3 tablespoons dark brown sugar

1½ tablespoons cornstarch

When I was seven, my brothers, mom, and I all piled into the family van and drove up to Vermont to visit a family friend, Barbara, who lived in a super-cool geo-dome in the middle of a forest in who-knows-where Vermont. Think Hansel and Gretel. Down the sharply winding hill from Barbara's place was a wide, slow-moving river with pockets of still water, where my brothers and I would sit and watch the rainbow and brown-nosed trout swim effortlessly along the shallow bottom. The best part of our visit, though, was the endless supply of fresh, wild blackberries that seemed to grow in abundance everywhere we looked. By the end of the day, our fingertips, lips, and teeth were stained deep violet and our arms were adorned with small red welts and scrapes from picking through the berry bushes' sharp thorns—the price of admission to reach the juiciest of berries buried deep inside the twisted branches. I learned a great lesson during that trip: some things in life are worth the extra effort, mostly when they're this delicious.

1. Adjust an oven rack to the middle position, then preheat the oven to 375°F.

2. Combine the fruit, lemon zest, lemon juice, vanilla, and dark brown sugar in a large bowl and fold together to mix.

3. Using a little fine mesh sieve (such as for dusting confectioners' sugar), dust the cornstarch over the fruit evenly and fold together gently.

**COBBLER TOPPING:**

½ cup old-fashioned oats (not instant)

1 cup whole raw almonds

⅓ cup unbleached all-purpose flour

2 teaspoons ground cinnamon

⅓ cup dark brown sugar

¼ teaspoon kosher salt

5 tablespoons unsalted butter, melted

## COBBLER TOPPING

1.  Combine the oats, almonds, flour, cinnamon, brown sugar and salt, in the order they are listed, in a food processor and process for 5 seconds.

2.  Transfer into a medium bowl, then stir in the melted butter until well combined.

3.  Butter the sides and bottom of a 13 x 9 x 2-inch casserole dish.

4.  Pour the fruit into the prepared baking dish and top evenly with the crumb topping.

5.  Bake, uncovered, for 30 minutes until the cobbler looks nice and bubbly. The topping should be a light golden brown.

6.  Serve warm with ice cream or chilled with whipped cream. This cobbler also doubles as a great breakfast treat.

# AUTUMN

| | |
|---|---|
| APPLES | ONIONS |
| ARUGULA | OREGANO |
| BROCCOLI | PARSLEY |
| CAULIFLOWER | PEARS |
| CELERY | PLUMS |
| CHIVES | POMEGRANATES |
| CORN | ROSEMARY |
| CUCUMBERS | SAGE |
| DATES | SHALLOTS |
| EGGPLANT | SPINACH |
| FENNEL | SWEET POTATOES |
| FIGS | THYME |
| GARLIC | TOMATOES |
| GINGER | WINTER SQUASH |
| GRAPES | |
| KALE | |
| LEEKS | |
| MUSHROOMS | |
| NECTARINES | |

**WAFFLES:**

1 small sweet potato (about ¾ pound)

1½ cups unbleached all-purpose flour

1 tablespoon baking powder

1 teaspoon kosher salt

2 teaspoons pumpkin pie spice (see recipe on page 44)

1 tablespoon ground cinnamon

¹⁄₁₆ teaspoon ground nutmeg

2 large eggs

1¼ cups 2% or whole milk

2 teaspoons pure vanilla extract

5 tablespoons unsalted butter, melted

¼ cup pure maple syrup, preferably Grade B

1 tablespoon orange zest (zest of 1 large orange), grated on a Microplane

Extra-virgin olive oil, for preparing the sweet potato

Nonstick spray

# SWEET POTATO WAFFLES
## WITH HONEY BUTTER

Everyone has a few extra sweet potatoes loitering around the kitchen with nothing to do during the holidays, right? How about this for an idea of what to do with them: waffles—seriously. Go with me on this one. Waffles with real flavor. One little cooked sweet potato is all you'll need to cook up an entire batch. Once made, these waffles really shine with a slathering of honey butter and a drizzle of pure maple syrup. Got nothing to do, little sweet potato? Well, now you do. It's called breakfast, and you're it!

1. Adjust an oven rack to the middle position, then preheat the oven to 400°F. Rub a thin layer of olive oil on the sweet potato, set on a parchment paper-lined sheet pan, and bake for 45 to 60 minutes, or until a knife inserted through the skin doesn't stick.

2. Peel and mash the baked sweet potato. Measure 1 cup and place in a large bowl. Using a small spoon, eat any extra mashed sweet potato when no one is looking.

3. Whisk together the flour, baking powder, salt, pumpkin pie spice, cinnamon, and nutmeg in a medium bowl.

4. Whisk the eggs, milk, vanilla, butter, maple syrup, and orange zest into the bowl with the mashed sweet potato.

5. Slowly whisk the flour mixture into the sweet potato egg mixture until just combined. It will be on the thick side, so don't worry.

6. Place two sheet pans in the oven, and preheat the oven to 200°F; this will keep the waffles warm as you make them.

7. Heat a waffle iron until hot and spray lightly with nonstick spray.

8. Pour in just enough batter to nearly fill the iron, but do not overload it.

9. Cook the waffles until done, about 5 minutes.

10. As the waffles finish cooking, place them in the oven, uncovered, on the warm sheet pans. To keep the waffles from getting soggy, do not stack them.

11. Serve with honey butter (see recipe in the sidebar) and maple syrup.

**HONEY BUTTER:**

**1 stick unsalted butter (8 tablespoons), softened**

**¼ cup honey, preferably orange blossom**

Mix the butter and honey in a small bowl until thoroughly combined.

**VINAIGRETTE:**

1 tablespoon red wine vinegar

3 tablespoons extra-virgin olive oil

**SALAD:**

3 pears, cored and thinly sliced lengthwise (preferably Bosc, D'Anjou, or Bartlett)

1 bunch watercress, rinsed and dried

1 cup toasted, salted walnuts (see recipe on page 42)

½ cup crumbled mild blue cheese

Freshly ground black pepper, to taste

# PEAR SALAD
## WITH WATERCRESS AND BLUE CHEESE

Looking for the salad that has it all? Look to this salad. Every bite is sweet, salty, creamy, and peppery, and packs a crunch to boot. What more do you need? Well, other than seconds, of course.

1. In a small container with a tight fitting lid, combine the vinegar and olive oil, close the lid tightly, and shake well to combine. Or, whisk to combine the ingredients in a small bowl.

2. In a large bowl, drizzle the pear slices with half the vinaigrette, season to taste with pepper, and gently fold the slices to coat evenly.

3. Divide the pears evenly among four plates, topping with equal portions of the watercress, walnuts and blue cheese. Drizzle over the remaining dressing to taste and serve.

## ARUGULA SALAD
### WITH SHAVED PARMIGIANO

**YIELD: 4 TO 6 SERVINGS**

3 tablespoons extra-virgin olive oil

1 tablespoon freshly squeezed
lemon juice

5 ounces arugula, rinsed and dried

Kosher salt, to taste

Freshly ground black pepper, to taste

Parmigiano-Reggiano cheese,
not pre-grated, for serving

I'll be honest, this is my go-to salad. Okay, okay. I realize that the phrase "go-to salad" seems so passé, but it's true. It's great on its own and also pairs wonderfully with soup or sandwich. Or, try my favorite: set atop a juicy steak grilled medium rare. You only need great ingredients: fresh arugula, fruity extra-virgin olive oil, and top-quality cheese. Simple, pure, and balanced, this salad will never go out of style.

1.  In a small container with a tight fitting lid, combine the olive oil and lemon juice, close the lid tightly, and shake well to combine. Or, whisk to combine the ingredients in a small bowl.

2.  Toss the arugula with half of the dressing in a large bowl. Season to taste with salt, pepper, and additional dressing as desired.

3.  Divide the salad evenly on salad plates and, using a vegetable peeler, top with some fresh shavings of Parmigiano-Reggiano.

YIELD: 4 SERVINGS

1 large apple, unpeeled (preferably Braeburn, Fuji, or Honeycrisp)

1 large fennel bulb

1 medium shallot, peeled and diced small (3 tablespoons)

¼ cup black currants

1 tablespoon white wine vinegar

1 tablespoon freshly squeezed lemon juice

⅓ cup toasted, salted walnut pieces (see recipe on page 42)

¼ cup finely chopped Italian flat-leaf parsley

1 tablespoon extra-virgin olive oil, plus more for drizzling

Kosher salt, to taste

Freshly ground black pepper, to taste

Parmigiano-Reggiano cheese, not pre-grated, for serving

# APPLE AND FENNEL SALAD
## WITH SHAVED PARMIGIANO AND BLACK CURRANTS

I designed this recipe to share with people at the Natural Products Expo West in Anaheim, California. This salad is fast because you can use a Mandoline, which makes quick work of the fennel and apples, alike. Because both fennel and apples are so crispy, you can make this salad hours before you're going to serve it. Even after making countless servings at the Expo, I ran out. So, my advice is to make extra, because whether your party is for 4 or 40,000, this salad is sure to be a hit.

1. Slice the apple and fennel bulb into French-fry strips on a mandoline, for approximately 2 cups apple and 2 cups fennel.

2. Toss together the apple, fennel, shallot, currants, vinegar, lemon juice, walnuts, and parsley in a medium bowl. Drizzle in 1 tablespoon of olive oil, and gently fold to combine. Season to taste with salt and pepper.

3. To serve, divide the salad among 4 large plates and drizzle extra-virgin olive oil over each salad. Lastly, using a vegetable peeler, top each serving with shavings of Parmigiano-Reggiano.

YIELD: 4 TO 5 SERVINGS

CARPACCIO:

1 pound beef tenderloin from the tip end, very cold

2 ounces arugula, rinsed and dried

Kosher salt, to taste

Freshly ground black pepper, to taste

¼ cup fresh flat-leaf Italian parsley leaves

Parmigiano-Reggiano cheese, not pre-grated, for serving

Extra-virgin olive oil, for drizzling

# BEEF CARPACCIO
## WITH SHAVED PARMIGIANO AND LEMON CAPER CITRONETTE

For the past fourteen years, I've been fortunate enough to have been invited to a sort of "orphan" Thanksgiving among friends who are unable to be with their own families on the holiday. It's an event I have always cherished. This past year, the masses converged at my buddy David Poynter's house. David is a long-time keeper of the Thanksgiving flame. He and his family always have amazing wine, fun conversation, and great food.

For the big feast, I planned on making a slow roasted beef tenderloin. Unfortunately, I was unable to prepare it in advance and as the day progressed, I found myself running short on time. However, with hope (and raw tenderloin) in hand, I rushed off to David's, thinking I might still have enough time to prepare my dish. Fat chance, Lyon. So I did what any lover of grass-fed beef tenderloin would do in a pinch. I grabbed a sharp knife, some plastic wrap and a heavy pan. Moments later, I had pounded thin medallions of beef tenderloin into tender, airy slices and topped them with arugula, a lemon-caper vinaigrette, and freshly shaved Parmigiano-Reggiano. My best friend Scott, also a regular Thanksgiving guest of David's, loved the dish so much that he insisted that it be in the cookbook. In the spirit of Thanksgiving, I present it here as an homage to everyone who has so graciously invited me into their homes over the last 14 years to share their meals. To each and every one of you, thank you.

1. Using a very sharp knife, cut the tenderloin into very thin slices; if possible, not thicker than ¼-inch each.

2. Lay a piece of tenderloin between two pieces of plastic wrap on a cutting board. Using a meat mallet or the back of a pan, gently but evenly pound the beef until very thin. Repeat with the remaining slices of tenderloin.

**CITRONETTE:**

1 medium shallot, peeled and diced finely
(3 tablespoons)

2 tablespoons capers, rinsed and drained

3 tablespoons freshly squeezed lemon juice
(juice of 1 lemon)

⅓ cup extra-virgin olive oil

Kosher salt, to taste

Freshly ground black pepper, to taste

3. In a medium container with a tight fitting lid, combine the citronette ingredients, close the lid tightly, and shake well to combine. Or, whisk to combine the ingredients in a medium bowl. Season to taste with salt and pepper.

4. Divide the pounded tenderloin slices among four (if you really love beef carpaccio) or five plates and season lightly with salt and pepper.

5. Top each plate with a small handful of arugula.

6. Using a spoon, drizzle over a tablespoon of the citronette.

7. Sprinkle on some parsley leaves, then using a vegetable peeler, top each serving with some shavings of Parmigiano-Reggiano. Finish with a drizzle of extra-virgin olive oil. Serve.

*"The only time to eat diet food is while you're waiting for the steak to cook."* — JULIA CHILD

# SPICY LEMON QUINOA SALAD
## WITH TOASTED PINE NUTS AND FETA

1. In a small container with a tight fitting lid, combine the citronette ingredients, close the lid tightly, and shake well to combine. Or, whisk to combine the ingredients in a small bowl.

2. Place the quinoa in a colander and rinse well.

3. Add the rinsed quinoa and water to a medium saucepan. Cover, turn the heat to high, bring to a boil, then reduce the heat to low and simmer for 10 to 15 minutes, or until the water is absorbed and the quinoa is translucent.

4. Once cooked, remove the quinoa from the heat and spread it out on a parchment lined sheet pan to cool for 5 minutes.

5. Transfer the quinoa to a medium-sized bowl. Add the chile flakes, salt, pepper, parsley, pine nuts, feta, and olives. Drizzle the vinaigrette over the salad. Fold to mix everything together. Season to taste with additional salt, pepper, and lemon juice. Serve immediately.

YIELD: 5 TO 6 SERVINGS

CITRONETTE:

¼ cup extra-virgin olive oil

¼ cup freshly squeezed lemon juice, plus more to taste

1 medium shallot, peeled and diced finely (3 tablespoons)

SALAD:

1 cup uncooked quinoa

2 cups water

¼ teaspoon crushed red chile pepper (chile flakes), or to taste

1 teaspoon kosher salt, plus more to taste

Freshly ground black pepper, to taste

¾ cup finely chopped fresh flat-leaf Italian parsley

¼ cup toasted pine nuts (recipe on page 42)

1 cup crumbled feta cheese

1 (15-ounce) can of garbanzo beans (chickpeas), rinsed and drained

½ cup roughly chopped kalamata olives, pits removed (optional)

Note: Quinoa is a complete protein source, which means that if you're not down with eating animal protein, quinoa's one of the best culinary options for your dietary needs.

1 large Italian eggplant, peeled and diced medium diced (approximately 7 to 8 cups)

8 tablespoons extra-virgin olive oil, divided, plus more for drizzling

2 large yellow onions, peeled and diced small (3 cups)

Kosher salt, to taste

Freshly ground black pepper, to taste

6 large garlic cloves, peeled and chopped roughly (2 tablespoons)

1 teaspoon ground cumin

½ teaspoon ground coriander

1½ teaspoons ground cinnamon

2 large tomatoes, cored and roughly chopped (2 cups), or 1 (15-ounce) can tomatoes, undrained, fire-roasted if possible

1½ tablespoons freshly squeezed lemon juice (juice of half a lemon), plus more to taste

1 (15-ounce) can garbanzo beans (chickpeas), rinsed and drained

¼ cup roughly chopped flat-leaf Italian parsley, divided

2 tablespoons finely chopped fresh mint, divided

Homemade Crostini (recipe on page 40) or Baked Pita Crisps (recipe on page 212)

# M'SAKA: ROASTED EGGPLANT
## WITH SPICED TOMATOES, CHICKPEAS, AND GARLIC

Gather 'round, eggplant skeptics. This dish will make believers out of you. Want proof? All right: I recently made this appetizer for a big double birthday bash in Hollywood for my friends Tracie and Ahmed. People kept walking into the kitchen and asking me the same question: "What was that amazing dish you just served? The one with mushrooms, right?" "Nope. It's roasted eggplant." "Whoa... but I don't like eggplant." "Well, now you do." "Yeah. I guess I do." Eggplant: 1, Skeptics: 0.

1. Adjust two oven racks to the middle position, then preheat the oven to 450°F.

2. Toss the eggplant with 3 tablespoons olive oil in a large mixing bowl; season well with salt and pepper.

3. Spread out the eggplant in one layer onto two parchment paper-lined sheet pans. Roast, uncovered, in the oven for 15 minutes. Remove the sheet pans from the oven, stir the eggplant, then place the sheet pans back in the oven, this time on opposite racks. Bake 15 minutes more, until the eggplants are lightly colored and cooked through.

4. Set 3 tablespoons olive oil and the onions in a small pot over medium heat; season lightly with salt and pepper.

5. Cook for approximately 8 to 10 minutes until the onions are soft and translucent.

6. Reduce the heat to medium-low, stir in the garlic, cumin, coriander, and cinnamon, and cook for 1 minute or until fragrant.

7. Stir in the tomatoes and garbanzo beans. Continue to cook, stirring occasionally, until approximately half of the liquid is reduced.

8. Stir in the roast eggplant, and continue to cook until most of the liquid is reduced.

9. Stir in the lemon juice, half the fresh parsley and mint, and another 2 tablespoons of olive oil. Season to taste with salt, pepper, and lemon juice.

10. Serve in a bowl, topped with the remaining parsley and mint, a drizzle of olive oil, and a side bowl of crostini or baked pita crisps.

1. M'SAKA: ROASTED EGGPLANT
2. FRESH DATES STUFFED
3. FRESH MINT TEA
4. TABBOULEH

20 large fresh mint leaves, bruised with your fingers

6 cups cool water

1 tablespoon granulated sugar

# Fresh Mint Tea

1. Combine the mint, sugar, and water in a medium saucepan.

2. Place over medium heat, bring to a low simmer, and cook for 5 minutes.

3. Turn off the heat and allow to steep for five minutes. Strain and serve.

Note: For an extra kick of flavor, try adding some slices of fresh ginger.

---

2 (15-ounce) cans white kidney beans (cannellini beans), rinsed and drained

3 tablespoons sesame tahini (roasted sesame seed paste)

3 large garlic cloves, peeled and chopped roughly (1 tablespoon)

6 tablespoons freshly squeezed lemon juice (juice of 2 lemons), plus more to taste

5 tablespoons extra-virgin olive oil

1 teaspoon kosher salt, plus more to taste

¼ teaspoon freshly ground black pepper, plus more to taste

1 tablespoon finely chopped fresh flat-leaf Italian parsley

# White Bean Garlic Hummus

1. Combine the beans, tahini, garlic, lemon juice, olive oil, salt, and pepper in a food processor, and process until smooth.

2. Adjust for taste by adding more lemon juice, salt, and/or pepper. For a slightly thinner consistency, add 1 tablespoon of water. Process one last time.

3. Serve in a bowl with a drizzle of olive oil and chopped parsley.

4. Serve with Baked Pita Crisps (recipe on page 212) or freshly cut vegetables such as carrots, celery, bell peppers, and cucumbers.

# TABBOULEH:
## BULGUR WHEAT SALAD WITH CHOPPED PARSLEY AND LEMON

It's no secret that I am a huge fan of flat-leaf Italian parsley, and after trying this dish, I promise, you will be too. Listen, if your relationship with parsley thus far has been mostly as an on and off "cheap date" garnish, well, then your relationship is about to change big time—and for the better. I can't think of a lot of dishes that aren't made all the more tasty with the addition of flat-leaf Italian parsley. In fact, I'll prove it to you with this dish. How difficult is it to make, you might ask? Well, if you own a knife and can boil water, you can make this dish. Seriously. Tabbouleh: it's not puppy love, it's the real thing.

1. In a medium saucepan, boil the water.

2. In a medium bowl, pour the boiling water over the bulgur; cover the bowl. Let sit for 1 hour, then drain well.

3. While the bulgur is soaking, mix together the remaining ingredients.

4. Mix the drained bulgur into the vegetables. Season to taste with pepper and additional salt or lemon juice.

**YIELD: 5 TO 7 SERVINGS**

2½ cups water

1 cup bulgur wheat

1 small red onion, peeled and diced small (⅔ cup)

3 medium tomatoes, cored, seeded and diced small

3 small Japanese cucumbers, unpeeled, seeded and diced small (1½ cup)

1 large red, yellow, or orange bell pepper, cored, seeded, and diced small (1¼ cup)

2 large garlic cloves, peeled and minced (2 teaspoons)

2 cups finely chopped fresh Italian flat-leaf parsley (it's a lot, I know!)

⅓ cup roughly chopped fresh mint

2 teaspoons kosher salt, plus more to taste

¼ cup freshly squeezed lemon juice, plus more to taste

¼ cup extra-virgin olive oil

Freshly ground black pepper, to taste

3 medium Italian eggplants, unpeeled (approximately 1 pound each)

2 large yellow onions, peeled and diced small (3 cups)

2 tablespoons extra-virgin olive oil, plus more for drizzling

Kosher salt, to taste

Freshly ground black pepper, to taste

3 large garlic cloves, peeled and minced (1 tablespoon)

¼ teaspoon ground cumin

2 tablespoons tahini (roasted sesame seed paste), plus more to taste

1½ tablespoons freshly squeezed lemon juice (juice of half a lemon), plus more to taste

1 tablespoon finely chopped fresh flat-leaf Italian parsley, for garnish

1 tablespoon finely chopped fresh mint, for garnish

Paprika, for garnish


Note: For extra texture, try adding a few fresh pomegranate seeds when serving.

# BABA GHANOUSH:
## ROASTED EGGPLANT PURÉE WITH TAHINI, LEMON, AND PAPRIKA

1. Adjust two oven racks to the middle position, then preheat the oven to 350°F.

2. Using a fork, pierce each eggplant several times and arrange them on a sheet pan lined with parchment paper or aluminum foil.

3. Bake, uncovered, for approximately 1 hour, until soft when poked, or until the eggplant has collapsed. Remove the eggplants from the oven and allow to cool.

4. While the eggplants are baking, combine the onions with 2 tablespoons olive oil in a medium saucepan over medium heat. Add a pinch of salt, a few generous grinds of pepper, and cook, stirring occasionally, for 8 to 10 minutes, until the onions are soft and translucent.

5. Reduce the heat to medium low, then add the garlic and cumin, and cook, uncovered, for 1 minute or until fragrant. Turn off the heat.

6. Once the eggplants are cool enough to handle, cut them in half lengthwise and scoop out the flesh into the work bowl of a food processor. Discard the skins. If the eggplant meat seems watery, spoon it into a fine mesh strainer to drain for a few minutes, then move it back to the food processor.

7. Add the onion-garlic mixture, tahini, and lemon juice, and process until smooth. Season to taste with salt, pepper, adding more tahini, and lemon juice to taste.

8. Serve topped with chopped parsley and mint, a drizzle of olive oil, a dusting of paprika, and Baked Pita Crisps (recipe is on page 212).

1. TRADITIONAL GARLIC HUMMUS    2. BABA GHANOUSH    3. WHITE BEAN GARLIC HUMMUS    4. BAKED PITA CRISPS    5. TZATZIKI

## BAKED PITA CRISPS

YIELD: 48 CRISPS

6 whole wheat pita rounds

Extra-virgin olive oil, for drizzling

Kosher salt, to taste

Freshly ground black pepper, to taste

1. Adjust two oven racks to the middle position, then preheat the oven to 350°F.

2. Slice each pita into 8 equal wedges.

3. Transfer the wedges to a baking sheet and drizzle or brush the side facing up with the olive oil. Season with salt and pepper.

4. Bake, uncovered, for approximately 10 to 12 minutes, until lightly colored and crisp. Remove and serve while still warm.

## TZATZIKI:
### CHILLED CUCUMBER YOGURT DIP

YIELD: 4 TO 6 SERVINGS

1 (16-ounce) carton plain Greek-style yogurt

3 small cucumbers (English, Japanese, or Persian), peeled, seeded, and diced small, (1½ cups)

1 medium garlic clove, peeled and minced (½ teaspoon)

2 tablespoons finely chopped fresh dill or fresh mint, plus more for garnish

1 tablespoon extra-virgin olive oil

½ tablespoon red wine vinegar

Kosher salt, to taste

Freshly ground black pepper, to taste

Looking for a really simple dipping sauce for fresh vegetables or to pair with crispy pita bread? How about something for your spicy burger to take off that fiery edge? No sweat. Tzatziki is just the thing.

1. Mix the yogurt and cucumber in a medium bowl.

2. Stir in the garlic, dill or mint, olive oil, and vinegar to combine. Season to taste with salt and pepper. Refrigerate before serving, or dive in right away!

3. Serve garnished with dill and/or mint.

Note: Tzatziki works great with grilled meat, Baked Pita Crisps (recipe above), or freshly cut vegetables such as carrots, celery, bell peppers, and cucumbers.

# Fresh Dates
## Stuffed with Toasted Almonds

1. Remove the pits of the dates by pushing them out through the date with a chopstick or straw.

2. Stuff each date with an almond. Go nuts.

YIELD: 5 SERVINGS

½ pound fresh dates (approximately 30)

30 toasted, salted whole almonds (recipe on page 42)

---

# Traditional Garlic Hummus

1. Combine the larger portion of garbanzo beans, tahini, garlic, lemon juice, olive oil, salt, and pepper in the work bowl of a food processor, and process until smooth.

2. Adjust for taste by adding more lemon juice, salt, and/or pepper. For a slightly thinner consistency, add 1 tablespoon of water.

3. Serve in a bowl. Using a spoon, spread the hummus to create a divot. Fill the divot with the reserved beans, and drizzle olive oil over the dip. Garnish with chopped parsley and paprika.

Note: Hummus is delicious with Baked Pita Crisps (recipe on previous page) or freshly cut vegetables such as carrots, celery, bell peppers and/or cucumbers.

YIELD: 4 TO 6 SERVINGS

2 (15-ounce) cans garbanzo beans (chickpeas), rinsed and drained, ¼ cup beans reserved

3 tablespoons sesame tahini (roasted sesame seed paste)

3 large garlic cloves, peeled and chopped roughly (1 tablespoon)

6 tablespoons freshly squeezed lemon juice (2 lemons), plus more to taste

5 tablespoons extra-virgin olive oil, plus more for drizzling

1 teaspoon kosher salt, plus more to taste

¼ teaspoon freshly ground black pepper, plus more to taste

½ tablespoon finely chopped fresh flat-leaf Italian parsley

Paprika, for garnish

## SAUTÉED SPINACH
### WITH GARLIC AND RED PEPPER FLAKES

Looking for great sautéed spinach that isn't soggy? Well, you've come to the right place. Great sautéed spinach is determined by two things: temperature and volume. If the temperature of the pan isn't hot enough, the spinach will steam rather than sauté as water leaches from the spinach. If you add too much spinach at once, it will crowd the pan and lower the temperature, resulting in the same unappetizing green moat. The best chance for successful sautéed spinach is to use a large, very hot sauté pan, and sauté the spinach in two or three increments, rather than all at once. With those two tips in hand, you'll see just how easy sautéed spinach can be. Soggy spinach—who needs it?

1. Heat a large sauté pan over high heat until hot. Working quickly, add 1 teaspoon of olive oil, swirl the pan to distribute the oil, then add ⅓ of the spinach.

2. Using tongs, flip the spinach in the pan every few seconds to cook evenly, keeping the spinach from clumping together, so that the water can evaporate properly.

3. After 30 seconds, season very lightly with salt, a few grinds of pepper, chile flakes, and ⅓ of the chopped garlic. This entire cooking process should take no more than one minute.

4. Transfer the spinach to a parchment-lined sheet pan, spread it out, then cook the remaining 2 portions of spinach in the same manner. Serve immediately.

**YIELD: 2 SERVINGS**

3 teaspoons extra-virgin olive oil, divided

9 ounces fresh spinach, rinsed three times and dried

Kosher salt, to taste

Freshly ground black pepper, to taste

1/16 teaspoon crushed red chile pepper (chile flakes), or to taste

2 large garlic cloves, peeled and minced (2 teaspoons), divided

**DRY RUB:**

2 teaspoons freshly ground black pepper

1 tablespoons dark brown sugar

1 tablespoon paprika

½ teaspoon ground cayenne pepper

¾ teaspoon ground cumin

½ teaspoon ground cinnamon

1¼ tablespoons kosher salt

½ teaspoon garlic powder

**PORK:**

1 (4½ to 5½ pound) pork butt, bone in (pork shoulder), trimmed of excess fat

3 medium yellow onions, peeled and quartered

1 head garlic, cloves peeled

½ cup apple cider vinegar

# PULLED PORK SANDWICH
## WITH HOMEMADE BARBECUE SAUCE

In my experience, when it comes to pork barbecue, North Carolina is the place to be. Depending on which side of Interstate 95 you live on, you are, like it or not, part of an age-old debate as to what's better: Western North Carolina (tomato-based) barbecue sauce or the Eastern North Carolina (vinegar-based) barbecue sauce. My oldest brother Craig and his family live in the eastern part of North Carolina, as does my grandmother, Big Ma. Maybe I'm biased, but I like the vinegar sauce and its spicy finish to pair with the whole, slow-cooked hog. At the same time, the sweeter tomato sauce works great with the fattier pork shoulders used further west. What's a chef to do? Well, I've put together my own pork recipe using a slow cooker, dry rub, and homemade barbecue sauce that embraces both sides of I-95: vinegar and tomato. In truth, the only real debate in North Carolina should be whether you want the coleslaw or hush puppies with your order, because when it's all said and done, when it comes to great slow-cooked pork, we all win.

1. To make the dry rub, combine the ingredients together in a small bowl and mix well.

2. Place the onions and garlic into a slow cooker.

3. Pat the pork butt dry. Once dry, rub the dry rub mixture evenly over the pork butt; discard any excess.

4. Place the pork butt in the slow cooker on top of the onions and garlic.

5. Pour the apple cider around the pork butt and cover with the lid.

6. Allow the pork butt to sit undisturbed at room temperature for 1 hour.

7. Set the slow cooker on low and cook for 8½ hours.

**BARBECUE SAUCE:**

1 cup organic ketchup

2 tablespoons unsulfured dark molasses

1 teaspoon Worcestershire sauce

¼ cup plus 2 tablespoons cider vinegar

1 tablespoon whole-grain Dijon mustard

½ teaspoon hot pepper sauce (preferably adobo sauce), optional

8. Carefully transfer the hot pork to a large bowl and let cool for 20 minutes. It will most likely fall apart; this is a good thing.

9. Strain the liquid from the cooker into a medium bowl, discarding the vegetables, and skimming off any fat on the top of the liquid.

10. While the pork cools, combine the ingredients for the barbecue sauce in a small bowl. Easy, right?

11. After 20 minutes' rest, gently shred the pork with two forks. Hold one side of the pork with the first fork and pull the pork with the other fork. You may also chop the pork as they do in North Carolina or tear the pork into strips with your hands. Discard the bone and any sinew or gristle from the meat.

12. Drizzle ¼ cup of the skimmed braising liquid and half of the barbecue sauce over the pork and gently stir until combined, adding more barbecue sauce to taste. Discard any remaining braising liquid.

13. Serve on toasted buns, topped with coleslaw (recipe on the next page) and extra barbecue sauce, and watch the family go wild.

Note: When shopping for pork butt (pork shoulder), look for a lot of white streaks of fat in the meat. As a rule of thumb, the more fat in the pork butt, the more flavor it will have.

# APPLE AND CARROT COLESLAW

I've never been a fan of the traditional (read: old-school) mayonnaise-based coleslaw. It always tastes gloppy and heavy. When I prepare fresh coleslaw, I want to taste the ingredients, not the glop. Therefore, this coleslaw calls for red wine and apple cider vinegars rather than mayonnaise. The carrots stay crisp, the apples stay sweet, and the cabbage stays fresh. In addition, the brightness and acidity from the vinegar cut through the fat of pulled pork, baby back ribs, or even grilled chicken. Move over, mayonnaise, there's a new coleslaw in town!

1. Combine the cabbage, carrots, apples, and parsley in a large bowl.

2. In a small container with a tight fitting lid, combine the vinaigrette ingredients, close the lid tightly, and shake well to combine. Or, whisk to combine the ingredients in a small bowl.

3. Add approximately two-thirds of the vinaigrette to the cabbage mixture, toss to coat, and season to taste with salt and pepper, adding more vinaigrette if needed. Taste again (yes, again).

4. Serve with Pulled Pork (recipe on page 216), or as a side dish. Store any remaining coleslaw in the refrigerator for up to 2 days.

**YIELD: 6 SERVINGS**

**COLESLAW:**

1 small head red cabbage, core discarded, quartered and sliced thinly (⅛-inch thick) on a mandoline (6 cups)

4 medium carrots, peeled and grated (2 cups)

2 medium apples (Pink Lady, Gala, Empire, or Fuji) unpeeled, sliced into French fry strips on a mandoline (3 cups)

½ cup roughly chopped fresh flat-leaf Italian parsley

Kosher salt, to taste

Freshly ground black pepper, to taste

**VINAIGRETTE:**

¼ cup extra-virgin olive oil

2½ tablespoons red wine vinegar

2½ tablespoons apple cider vinegar

YIELD: 6 TO 8 SERVINGS

1 tablespoon extra-virgin olive oil

3 slices applewood-smoked bacon, halved lengthwise and cut crosswise into ¼-inch slices (¾ cup)

2 large yellow onions, peeled and diced small (3 cups)

Freshly ground black pepper, to taste

3 large garlic cloves, peeled and minced (1 tablespoon)

½ teaspoon ground paprika

¹⁄₁₆ teaspoon ground cayenne

⅛ teaspoon mustard powder

2 tablespoons tomato paste

2 tablespoons dark brown sugar

2 tablespoons unsulfured dark molasses

1¼ cups water

1 small dried bay leaf

2 (15-ounce) cans white kidney beans (cannellini beans) or Great Northern beans, rinsed and drained

2 teaspoons apple cider vinegar

Kosher salt, to taste

# BARBECUE KETTLE BEANS

It always makes me happy when someone from Boston compliments me on my barbecue kettle beans. Perhaps it's because they are smoky and sweet (but not too sweet), with a touch of heat at the end. Or it could be because they are cooked slowly on the stove top, leaving space in the oven for other things, like my slow-cooked baby back ribs. Now, my barbecue kettle beans may not be as authentic as those served in Boston, but for those of us who live outside the great state of Massachusetts, I can safely say that mine are wicked good.

1. Add 1 tablespoon of olive oil and the bacon to a medium saucepan over medium-low heat. Cook for approximately 5 to 6 minutes, stirring occasionally, until much of the fat has rendered off and the bacon is just beginning to get nice and crispy.

2. Add the onions and a few good grinds of pepper, stir occasionally, and continue to cook until soft and translucent, 6 to 7 minutes.

3. Stir in the garlic, paprika, cayenne, mustard powder, and tomato paste. Cook, stirring occasionally, for 3 minutes.

4. Add the brown sugar, molasses, water, bay leaf, and beans. Stir well to combine and cover.

5. Increase the heat to high, bring to a boil, then reduce the heat to very low, to just barely a simmer.

6. Continue to cook for 1 hour, stirring every 10 to 15 minutes to prevent scorching.

7. Discard the bay leaf and stir in the apple cider vinegar. Season to taste with salt and pepper. Serve.

# GRILLED CHICKEN SALAD
## WITH APPLE AND TOASTED WALNUTS

1. In a large bowl, combine the chicken, salad greens, apple, celery, cranberries, walnuts, and cheese.

2. In a medium container with a tight fitting lid, combine the dressing ingredients, close the lid tightly, and shake well to combine. Or, whisk to combine the ingredients in a medium bowl.

3. Dress the salad with approximately ¾ of the vinaigrette, adding more to taste. Season to taste with salt and pepper. Divide evenly among the plates and serve immediately.

Note: If the idea of a curried chicken salad sounds good to you, add 1 teaspoon of yellow curry powder to the dressing.

**GRILLED CHICKEN:**

1 grilled whole chicken (recipe on page 224), meat removed (3 cups, chopped)

**SALAD:**

6 ounces salad greens (arugula, frisée, radicchio)

2 medium apples, unpeeled, cored and diced small (preferably Gala, Fuji, Pink Lady, or Winesap) (3 cups)

3 stalks celery, diced small (1½ cups)

¾ cup dried cranberries

¾ cup toasted salted walnuts, chopped roughly (recipe on page 42)

¾ cup crumbled mild blue cheese

Kosher salt, to taste

Freshly ground black pepper, to taste

**DRESSING:**

1 tablespoon whole-grain Dijon mustard

1 small shallot, peeled and diced finely (1½ tablespoons)

1½ tablespoons red wine vinegar

1½ tablespoons freshly squeezed lemon juice (juice of half a lemon)

¼ cup extra-virgin olive oil

2 tablespoons mayonnaise

# SHRIMP
## WITH CHEDDAR GRITS AND CHORIZO

1. Bring the stock and butter to a boil in a medium saucepan over high heat.

2. Reduce the heat to low to achieve a simmer, then, stirring continuously with a whisk, slowly stream in the polenta. Cook for 5 to 8 minutes, or until the polenta is thick and shiny.

3. Remove from the heat, then mix in half the cheese, season to taste with salt and pepper, and cover with a lid.

4. Meanwhile, add the bacon, plus 1 tablespoon of olive oil to a large sauté pan over medium-low heat. Cook approximately 5 to 6 minutes, stirring occasionally, until much of the fat has rendered off, and the bacon is just beginning to get nice and crispy.

5. Stir in the onion or shallot and sausage and continue to cook for approximately 5 minutes, breaking up the sausage into small pieces with the back of a wooden spoon as it cooks.

6. Add the wine, tomato, and lemon juice and continue cooking for 1 minute.

7. Stir in the raw shrimp. Cook approximately 5 minutes until pink and just cooked through. Be careful not to overcook.

8. Remove sauté pan from heat. Season to taste with salt, pepper, and additional lemon juice. Stir in the chives.

4. To serve, divide the polenta among 4 bowls. Top each with a portion of the sausage, shrimp, and remaining cheese. Finish each bowl with a few good grinds of black pepper.

**YIELD: 4 TO 6 SERVINGS**

3 cups chicken or vegetable stock (recipes on page 37 & 38)

1 tablespoon unsalted butter

1 cup quick-cooking corn grits or polenta, preferably Bob's Red Mill brand

1 cup grated aged sharp Cheddar cheese, not pre-grated

Kosher salt, to taste

Freshly ground black pepper, to taste

1 tablespoon extra-virgin olive oil

5 pieces hickory smoked bacon, halved lengthwise and cut crosswise into ¼-inch slices (1¼ cups)

1 medium yellow onion, peeled and diced small (1 cup)

½ pound fresh chorizo sausage, removed from casing, approximately 2 to 3 links

¼ cup dry white wine, such as Sauvignon Blanc

3 medium tomatoes, cored, seeded, and diced small (1½ cups)

1½ tablespoons freshly squeezed lemon juice (juice of half a lemon), plus more to taste

½ pound medium shrimp (16 to 20 shrimp), shelled, tail on, and deveined

¼ cup roughly chopped fresh chives

YIELD: 4 TO 6 SERVINGS

2 whole chickens (3 pounds each)

2½ teaspoons kosher salt

Freshly ground black pepper, for seasoning

1 lemon, halved, cut side rubbed with olive oil

For bonus material relating to this recipe, visit chefnathanlyon.com

# GRILLED WHOLE CHICKEN

1. Working with one chicken at a time, remove the spine by propping the chicken up so that it is sitting on the cutting board, facing away from you. Holding the neck bone with your left hand, while holding your chef's knife in your right, cut straight down the left side of the spine, top to bottom. (If you are left-handed, reverse the sides.) Repeat by cutting down the right side of the spine, and either save it for stock (yay) or discard (boo).

2. Place the chickens, breast side up, on a cutting board. Using both hands, one on top of the other, press down firmly between the chicken breasts to flatten. Pat both sides of the chicken dry.

3. Season the inside of each chicken (non skin side) with ¾ teaspoon salt and a generous amount of pepper. Flip the chickens and season the skin side of each chicken with ½ teaspoon of salt and some generous grinds of pepper. Allow to sit at room temperature for 30 minutes.

4. Heat the grill to medium. Once hot, clean the grill, then, using tongs, lightly dip a cloth in olive oil and wipe to coat the grill rack. Pat the chickens dry, and place them on the grill, skin side down, and close the lid.

5. Grill for 10 minutes until the skin is nicely colored, even perhaps very lightly charred, but not burnt. Using tongs, flip the chickens, skin side up, and continue cooking with the lid closed for an additional 20 minutes until the juice runs clear from the thigh when pierced with a knife. Trust me—if your chickens are 3 pounds, they're done.

6. Grill the lemon halves until soft, with grill marks, then remove.

7. Remove the chickens from the grill, place on a clean cutting board. Rest for 15 minutes before squeezing over the juice of the grilled lemons and serve.

Note: An option to removing the spine of the chicken yourself is to ask your butcher to do it for you. They'll be more than happy to help out. After all, butchers are awesome people. Also, did you say you wanted barbecued chicken? Slather on some of my barbecue sauce (recipe on page 176) during the last 10 minutes of cooking.

2 boneless, skinless chicken breast halves (9 ounces each)

½ teaspoon kosher salt, divided, plus more to taste

Freshly ground black pepper, to taste

½ cup plus 1 teaspoon unbleached all-purpose flour, divided

2 tablespoons plus 1 teaspoon unsalted butter, divided

2 tablespoons extra-virgin olive oil, divided

8 ounces fresh button or cremini mushrooms, sliced ¼-inch thick

2 medium shallots, peeled and diced small (6 tablespoons)

½ cup sweet Marsala wine

1½ cups chicken stock (recipe on page 38)

1 tablespoon roughly chopped fresh flat-leaf Italian parsley

1 teaspoon freshly squeezed lemon juice, plus more to taste

# CHICKEN MARSALA
## WITH MUSHROOM RAGOÛT AND BUTTERED NOODLES

1. Pat the chicken dry and sandwich each chicken breast between two pieces of plastic wrap.

2. Using a mallet, rolling pin, or the back of a saucepan, pound each chicken breast until it is ¼-inch thick.

3. Season each side of each chicken breast with ⅛ teaspoon salt (for a total of ½ teaspoon) and a few good grinds of pepper.

4. In a small bowl, combine 1 teaspoon of the flour with 1 teaspoon of the butter and mix well.

5. Add the remaining flour to a shallow bowl; dredge the seasoned chicken breasts in the flour, shaking each piece to remove any excess.

6. Heat 1 tablespoon olive oil plus 1 tablespoon butter in a large sauté pan over medium-high heat until the butter turns a light golden brown.

7. Add the chicken breasts and cook for approximately 3 minutes per side, until golden brown.

8. Transfer the chicken from the pan to a large plate.

9. Begin preparing the Buttered Egg Noodles (recipe on the next page), so grab a small pot and start boiling some water.

10. With the pan still on the burner at medium-high heat, add the remaining tablespoon of olive oil and the remaining 1 tablespoon butter to the same sauté pan.

11. Add the mushrooms and shallots. Cook, stirring occasionally, until the mushrooms are golden-brown around the edges, 5 to 7 minutes.

12. Add the Marsala wine and chicken stock to the sauté pan. Increase the heat to high and bring to a boil.

13. Stir in the kneaded butter/flour mixture. Cook on high heat for 4 minutes, or until the sauce has thickened slightly.

14. Reduce the heat to medium, then return the breasts to the pan. Continue to cook for 2 minutes, flipping after 1 minute, or until they are warmed through and the sauce has thickened.

15. Add the lemon juice and season to taste with salt, pepper, and additional lemon juice.

16. Transfer the chicken breasts to a cutting board and cut into bite-size pieces.

17. Serve the sliced chicken over the buttered noodles, swirl the chopped parsley and lemon juice into the sauce, then spoon over the chicken. Enjoy.

## BUTTERED EGG NOODLES

1. Bring a small pot of water to a rolling boil, then add the salt.

2. Add the pasta to the boiling water and cook, stirring occasionally, until just tender.

3. Reserve 2 tablespoons of the cooking water, and then drain, but do not rinse the noodles. Return the drained noodles to the same pot.

4. Add the butter and the reserved cooking water. Mix together and cover to keep warm.

**BUTTERED EGG NOODLES:**

2 tablespoons kosher salt

5 ounces egg noodles

2 tablespoons unsalted butter

**KETCHUP GLAZE:**

1 cup organic ketchup

2 tablespoons unsulfured dark molasses

1 tablespoon Worcestershire sauce

Mix the ketchup, molasses, and Worcestershire together in a small bowl.

**MEATLOAF:**

1 small yellow onion, peeled and cut into 8 pieces

3 large garlic cloves, peeled and minced (1 tablespoon)

1 large egg

1 teaspoon ground chile powder

1½ teaspoons ground fennel seed

1½ teaspoons finely chopped fresh oregano

1¼ teaspoons kosher salt

½ teaspoon plus ⅛ teaspoon freshly ground black pepper, divided

1 tablespoon Worcestershire sauce

2 tablespoons ketchup glaze, (recipe above)

2 cups breadcrumbs (recipe on page 44), homemade or panko (Japanese breadcrumbs)

2½ pounds ground beef, 85% lean

# MEATLOAF
## WITH A KETCHUP GLAZE

Growing up, my brothers and I could hardly wait for the days when our mom would make us meatloaf. So good! Mom was a big fan too, because it's simple and effortless to prepare. Oh, and let us not forget that the real reward of making meatloaf comes the following days: cold meatloaf sandwiches slathered with ketchup! It's that type of happiness that you never outgrow.

1. Adjust two oven racks to the middle position, then preheat the oven to 325°F.

2. In a small food processor, process together the onion and garlic until extremely finely chopped—almost liquefied. Transfer to a large bowl.

3. Add the egg, chile powder, fennel seed, oregano, salt, pepper, Worcestershire sauce, and 2 tablespoons of the ketchup glaze. Mix together thoroughly.

4. Sprinkle the bread crumbs and the ground beef over the mixture. Gently mix until just combined. Avoid squeezing the meat.

5. Press the meat into a 9" x 5" loaf pan, pressing the top to make it level. Turn the raw meatloaf out onto a parchment paper-lined sheet pan. If it doesn't want to come out, bang it onto the sheet pan—go for it.

6. Put it into the oven, and bake, uncovered, for 30 minutes.

7. After 30 minutes, remove the sheet pan from the oven and spread 3 tablespoons of the glaze over the loaf, then insert a digital thermometer probe (being sure to not allow the tip of the probe to contact the pan) at a 45-degree angle from above, into the middle of the loaf. Set the temperature alarm for 155°F.

8. Return the meatloaf to the oven, and continue cooking until the temperature alarm sounds, approximately an hour total cooking time. Insert the thermometer in a second location in the meatloaf, just to be sure it's at 155°F.

6. Remove the sheet pan from the oven and let the meatloaf rest for 10 minutes. Slice and serve.

3 slices smoked and cured bacon, halved lengthwise and then cut crosswise into ¼-inch slices (¾ cup)

3 tablespoons extra-virgin olive oil, divided, plus more for drizzling

2 large yellow onions, peeled and diced small (3 cups)

½ pound fresh hot Italian sausage (pork or turkey), removed from casing, approximately 2 to 3 links

7 medium carrots, peeled and chopped roughly (3½ cups)

1 medium fennel bulb, diced small (2 cups)

¼ teaspoon crushed red chile pepper (chile flakes), or to taste

Freshly ground black pepper, to taste

1 tablespoon tomato paste

7 large garlic cloves, peeled and chopped roughly (2 tablespoons plus 1 teaspoon)

1 (28-ounce) can diced tomatoes, undrained, fire-roasted, if possible

4 cups chicken stock (recipe on page 38)

1 (16-ounce) can white beans (great northern beans), drained and rinsed

Kosher salt, to taste

Ingredients continued on next page »

# RIBOLLITA:
## HEARTY TUSCAN VEGETABLE STEW

This Italian dish is classically a re-purposed minestrone soup made new by adding some additional ingredients: bread, veggies, and beans, to name a few. Why, though, should you waste your time waiting for a minestrone soup to come waltzing along when you can enjoy the smoky flavor of bacon, the sweetness of fennel, the heartiness of beans and kale, and that little kick of heat that ribollita has to offer right now? Sure, good things come to those who wait, but why wait if you don't have to?

1. Add the bacon and 1 tablespoon of olive oil to a small pot over medium-low heat. Cook for approximately 5 to 6 minutes, stirring occasionally, until much of the fat has rendered off, and the bacon is just beginning to get nice and crispy.

2. Add onions, stir occasionally, and continue to cook until soft and translucent, 6 to 7 minutes.

3. Add the sausage, carrots, fennel, chili flakes, and a few good grinds of pepper and continue to cook for approximately 10 minutes, stirring occasionally, breaking up the sausage into small pieces with the back of a wooden spoon as it cooks.

4. Add 2 tablespoons olive oil, stir in the tomato paste and garlic, and cook for 3 more minutes.

5. Stir in the tomatoes, chicken stock, beans, ¾ teaspoon salt, and kale.

6. Increase the heat to high until the soup starts to simmer. Reduce the heat to low and simmer for 30 minutes. Season to taste with salt and pepper.

7. At this point, either go classic by adding the crostini to the soup, continuing to cook for 5 minutes, or simply serve the soup with the crostini on top so that the soup begins to soften the bread. Or, do as I do and serve the soup separately with the crostini on the side.

8. Serve in soup bowls and, using a vegetable peeler, top each serving with shavings of Parmigiano-Reggiano, plus a drizzle of olive oil to finish.

Note: This soup is classically served on the thick side. If you prefer your soups to be a touch thinner, add more stock to your liking.

1 bunch cavolo nero kale (also called dinosaur kale or black kale) or curly kale, leaves stripped and thick stems discarded, rinsed and chopped finely (5 packed cups)

Homemade Crostini (recipe on page 40)

Parmigiano-Reggiano cheese, not pre-grated, for serving

**PORK CHOPS:**

1 teaspoon extra-virgin olive oil

2 bone-in pork chops, 1-inch thick (just over 1 pound)

¼ teaspoon kosher salt

Freshly ground black pepper, for seasoning

# PAN-FRIED BONE-IN PORK CHOP
## WITH SPICY ORANGE-MANGO SALSA

If you happen to be one of those people who gave up long ago on cooking a juicy pork chop, then please—come back. We miss you. By "we," I mean me, Karen and Nathan McCall. Karen and Nathan are talented chefs, butchers, and co-owners of McCall's Meat & Fish Company in Los Angeles. I learned this fool-proof cooking method from them, written on the wall of their shop—literally on the wall. Let me tell you, this recipe is a doozie.

Speaking of amazing recipes, at McCall's they also have a maple-glazed pork chop recipe that's to die for. I'm willing to bet if you stop by and ask, they'd be happy to share it with you, because the time has come, America. The writing's on the wall. You deserve a juicy, flavorful pork chop. So, please, come back; you'll be glad you did.

1. Pat the pork chops dry. On a piece of parchment paper or aluminum foil, season both sides of both chops equally with salt and a few grinds of pepper.

2. Allow to sit at room temperature, undisturbed, for 30 minutes. You have your digital timer at the ready, right? Here we go.

3. Heat a large sauté pan over medium-high heat until hot. Add 1 teaspoon extra-virgin olive oil, and swirl the pan to coat evenly. The oil will likely begin to smoke; that's a good thing.

4. Add both chops to the pan, and cook for exactly 1 minute. Using tongs, turn the chops a quarter turn and put them back in the sauté pan in a slightly different spot from where you lifted them.

5. Cook for exactly 1 minute. Flip the chops, and cook for 1 minute.

6. Turn the chops a quarter turn again and put them back in the sauté pan in a slightly different spot from where you lifted them.

7. Cook 1 minute. Flip the chops once more, and cook for 1 minute. Flip the chops one last time, and cook for 1 minute, for a total cooking time of 6 minutes.

8. Transfer the chops from the sauté pan to a cutting board and tent loosely with foil. Let rest for 10 minutes before serving.

9. Arrange the pork chops on a plate with a scoop of salsa over top, or showcase that amazing crust, and serve the salsa in a side ramekin. When you slice into the pork chop, it should be juicy and slightly pink in color. Voilà! Juicy pork chops.

## SPICY ORANGE-MANGO SALSA

1. Combine all the ingredients in a medium bowl and season with salt and pepper to taste.

2. Spoon over the pork, serve on the side, or eat straight from the bowl. Don't say I didn't warn you; this stuff is really good.

**SPICY ORANGE-MANGO SALSA:**

1 mango, peeled, seeded, and diced small

2 small oranges, peel and pith cut off, then segmented and seeded, juice reserved

½ small red onion, peeled and diced small (⅓ cup)

1½ teaspoons minced red jalapeno pepper, seeded and deveined, or to taste

2 teaspoons finely chopped fresh cilantro

1 tablespoon freshly squeezed lime juice (juice of half a lime)

½ teaspoon red wine vinegar

2 tablespoons extra-virgin olive oil

¼ teaspoon kosher salt, plus more to taste

Freshly ground black pepper, to taste

# Herb-Roasted Turkey Breast
## with Turkey Jus

I admit, I find it hard waiting for that one special day of the year, Thanksgiving, to have a turkey feast. I mean, when is it NOT a good time for a tasty roast turkey sandwich with fresh vanilla cranberry sauce? A warm turkey pot pie? A curried turkey salad? Whoa! I can't go without those dishes for a whole year! To satisfy my year-round turkey cravings, I often roast a small turkey breast with butter and fresh herbs. Turkey breast + 90 minutes = delicious turkey dishes, any week of the year. Problem solved.

1. To make the herb butter, place the softened butter, garlic, thyme, sage, salt and pepper in a small bowl and mash to form a paste.

2. Pat the turkey dry. Loosen the skin from the turkey breast, but do not remove it.

3. Spread the herb butter evenly under the skin onto the meat. Flip the turkey breast over, and season evenly with ¼ teaspoon salt and a few good grinds of pepper.

4. Flip the breast once again, skin side up, season the skin lightly with salt and pepper, and let it sit for 1 hour at room temperature.

5. Adjust two oven racks to the middle position, then preheat the oven to 325°F.

6. Mix together the onions, carrots, celery, thyme, garlic, and bay leaf in a small bowl.

7. Make a small bed with the vegetables in the center of the roasting pan. This will keep the turkey slightly elevated and out of the liquid that will accumulate.

YIELD: 4 TO 6 SERVINGS

HERB BUTTER:

2 tablespoons unsalted butter, softened

2 large garlic cloves, peeled and minced (2 teaspoons)

1 teaspoon finely chopped fresh thyme

1 teaspoon finely chopped fresh sage

2 teaspoons kosher salt

¼ teaspoon freshly ground black pepper


TURKEY:

1 whole bone-in turkey breast (2¼ to 3¼ pounds)

¼ teaspoon Kosher salt, plus more for seasoning

Freshly ground black pepper, for seasoning

## VEGETABLE BED:

2 large yellow onions, peeled and diced medium (3 cups)

3 medium carrots, peeled and chopped roughly (1½ cups)

3 celery stalks, roughly chopped (1½ cups)

5 sprigs fresh thyme

3 large garlic cloves, peeled

1 dried bay leaf

1 cup dry white wine, such as Sauvignon Blanc

1½ cups chicken stock (recipe on page 38)

1 tablespoon unsalted butter

Kosher salt, to taste

Freshly ground black pepper, to taste

8. Gently drape the turkey breast over the vegetable bed, skin side up.

9. Pour the wine and stock into the roasting pan.

10. Insert an oven-safe digital thermometer probe into the thickest part of the turkey breast without the end of the probe touching any of the bone, as the temperate reading would be inaccurate. Set the thermometer alarm to sound at 155°F.

11. Transfer the roasting pan with the turkey to the oven and roast, uncovered, for approximately 60 to 90 minutes (depending on the size of the turkey breast), rotating the pan after 30 minutes, until an internal temperature of 155°F is achieved. Check the temperature in at least two places, just to be sure.

12. Transfer the turkey breast from the oven to a cutting board and cover loosely with aluminum foil for 20 minutes prior to serving. Before serving, slice thinly crosswise (across the grain) at an angle.

13. Meanwhile, pour the contents of the roasting pan into a medium saucepan. Simmer over medium heat until approximately 1 cup of the juices remain.

14. Strain out and discard the vegetables, returning the liquid to the saucepan.

15. Return the saucepan to the heat, and swirl in the butter until it melts. Season to taste with salt and pepper. You just made turkey jus—well done. Remove the jus from the heat and cover until you're ready to eat.

16. Serve the slices of turkey breast with the jus on the side.

# VANILLA-ORANGE CRANBERRY SAUCE

Need a sauce that works wonders on a savory cheese plate, or slathered on roast turkey, chicken, or pork? Look no further. I've got just the thing.

1. Stir the apple cider, honey, cranberries, orange zest, chopped oranges and their juice, cinnamon stick, ginger, and vanilla bean seeds and pod in a medium saucepan over medium heat.

2. Cover the saucepan and simmer for 15 minutes, stirring occasionally until the cranberries burst.

3. Remove the saucepan from the heat and allow to cool slightly. Remove the cinnamon stick and vanilla bean pod.

4. Pour into a serving bowl. Any remaining sauce can be stored in the refrigerator for up to a week. Chances are there isn't going to be any left, because this stuff goes fast.

Note: This recipe also works great with frozen cranberries.

**YIELD: 4 TO 6 SERVINGS**

1 cup freshly pressed apple cider

⅓ cup honey, preferably orange blossom

1 (12-ounce) bag fresh cranberries

2 tablespoons orange zest (zest from 2 large oranges), grated on a Microplane

1 small orange, peeled, seeded, and chopped roughly, juice reserved

1 cinnamon stick

½ teaspoon fresh ginger, peeled and grated on a Microplane before measuring

½ vanilla bean, seeds and pod: slice down the length of the pod, spread open, and scrape out the flesh by pressing with a butter knife

**YIELD: 3 TO 4 SERVINGS**

7 medium apples, unpeeled, cored and quartered (preferably Pink Lady, Rome, or McIntosh)

1½ cups freshly pressed apple cider

2 tablespoons dark brown sugar

1 tablespoon fresh ginger, peeled and grated on a Microplane

1½ teaspoons ground cinnamon

¹⁄₁₆ teaspoon kosher salt

Note: If you don't like apple skins in your apple sauce, feel free to peel them first.

# CINNAMON-SPICED APPLESAUCE

One late fall afternoon, during my junior year of college, my dachshund, Heineken, and I were cruising down I-81 on my black Yamaha Virago 750 motorcycle. Tucked inside my old photographer's bag resting on my lap, Heiny was the best wingman a guy could ever ask for, always game for an adventure. Riding through the crisp autumn air, the pastel leaves blanketing the Shenandoah Valley, we had our sights on one target that day: tracking down crisp, juicy apples at a local apple orchard, and Heiny's nose, peering out from my bag, seemed to know the way.

Once there, like a cold, wet canine compass, Heiny's nose led us directly to the best trees. It was quite a sight. Walking behind his tiny legs, I quickly gathered a small bucket of the most delicious apples a man (and dog) could ever hope for. To others, maybe Heineken was just a dog, but I'll tell you one thing: when it came to finding mouth-watering apples, Heiny had a gift. Heiny, this one's for you.

1. Combine the apples, apple cider, brown sugar, ginger, cinnamon, and salt in a large saucepan over medium heat. Just dump it all in.

2. Cover and bring to a boil, then reduce the heat to low and simmer for approximately 15 to 20 minutes, stirring occasionally.

3. Uncover and take a peek. It's going to look a bit like apple soup—not to worry.

4. Mash or whip with a potato masher or sturdy whisk until the desired texture is achieved. Personally, I like more texture in my applesauce. If you prefer a smooth texture, simply process with an immersion blender, the same way as if you were making a soup.

# FLOURLESS CARROT ALMOND TORTE
## WITH LEMON-VANILLA CREAM CHEESE FROSTING

I designed this recipe with two of my close friends in mind: Marni and Finnley. They're both allergic to gluten and can't eat flour, but, hey, they still want to enjoy a delectable dessert every now and again. I mean, who doesn't? Enter the flourless carrot torte: light, simple to prepare, and darn tasty, too! With desserts like this, pffffft! Who needs flour?

1.  Mix the butter and confectioners' sugar together until it forms a paste. Spread the butter/sugar paste evenly along the sides and bottom of a 9-inch spring-form pan and transfer into the refrigerator to cool.

2.  Adjust two oven racks to the middle position, then preheat the oven to 325°F.

3.  Process the almonds, brown sugar, pumpkin pie spice, and salt in a food processor until a very fine, meal-like consistency is achieved.

4.  Pour this into a large bowl, then using a spatula, fold in the grated carrots, egg yolks, ginger, orange zest, and maple syrup. The mixture will be on the thicker side so take your time and mix thoroughly.

5.  Using an electric mixer, whisk the 6 egg whites until just foamy in a large, clean, dry bowl.

6.  Add 1 tablespoon granulated sugar, and continue whipping until medium-firm peaks form.

7.  Using a spatula, fold one-third of the whipped egg whites into the almond/carrot mixture until very few white streaks remain.

8.  Fold in the next third as before, and finally the remaining third.

YIELD: 10 TO 12 SERVINGS

TORTE:

1½ teaspoons unsalted butter

1 tablespoon confectioners' sugar

2 cups whole toasted almonds (recipe on page 42)

1 cup dark brown sugar

2 tablespoons pumpkin pie spice (recipe on page 44)

¼ teaspoon kosher salt

4 medium carrots, peeled and grated (2 cups)

6 large eggs, separated

1 heaping tablespoon fresh ginger, peeled and grated on a Microplane

1 tablespoon orange zest (zest of 1 large orange), grated on a Microplane

2 tablespoons pure maple syrup, preferably Grade B

1 tablespoon granulated sugar

9. Pour the batter into the prepared spring-form pan, transfer to the oven and bake, uncovered, for 55 minutes to 1 hour, until the torte puffs up slightly, firms up, and the top looks nice and brown.

10. Remove from the oven and allow the cake to cool completely.

11. Release the side spring of the pan, then remove the side.

12. Top the cake with a piece of parchment paper, invert the cake onto a plate, and invert the cake again onto a serving plate.

13. Top with the lemon-vanilla cream cheese frosting and optional chopped walnuts, giggle with joy, and serve.

**LEMON-VANILLA CREAM CHEESE FROSTING:**

1 (8-ounce) package cream cheese, softened

4 tablespoons unsalted butter, softened

1½ cups confectioners' sugar

1 teaspoon pure vanilla extract

1 teaspoon freshly squeezed lemon juice

## LEMON-VANILLA CREAM CHEESE FROSTING

1. In a mixer with a paddle attachment (or with a hand mixer), blend the cream cheese with the butter until well combined.

2. With the mixer on low, slowly add the confectioners' sugar, and continue to mix until fully combined.

3. Add the vanilla extract and lemon juice.

4. Mix, scrape the bowl with a spatula, and continue mixing until smooth.

YIELD: 6 SERVINGS

2 cups half-and-half

½ cup pure maple syrup, preferably Grade B, divided

2 tablespoons fresh ginger, peeled and grated on a Microplane before measuring

5 egg yolks

1 cup crystallized ginger, chopped roughly

# DOUBLE GINGER MAPLE ICE CREAM

If you've never tapped a maple tree during the late winter months, you should give it a try. Seriously. At least that's what my buddy Dusty and I attempted to do late February, 1988, in our hometown of Arlington, Virginia. Together, we drilled into a handful of sugar maple trees, inserted some plastic drinking straws, hung covered buckets for the watery sap to drip into and then, we waited. Drip. Drip. Drip. "This is going to take a while, Dusty." Days later we had successfully gathered a few gallons of maple sap that we proceeded to boil down in my mom's pasta pot until we ended up with two cups worth of sweet, golden maple syrup—totally worth our efforts.

Of course, you don't have to boil down your own maple sap to make this recipe, but if the chance to bundle up, head outdoors, and tap a few maple trees ever comes your way, go for it! I highly recommend it.

1. Heat the half-and-half, ¼ cup maple syrup, and grated ginger in a medium saucepan over medium heat.

2. Using a spatula (making sure to scrape the bottom of the saucepan occasionally) stir continuously until you see a few wisps of steam. Remove from the heat and cover.

3. In a medium bowl, using an electric mixer, whip the egg yolks and remaining ¼ cup of maple syrup on high speed until the mixture is canary yellow in color, thick, and doubled in volume.

4. Reduce the speed to low and slowly add a thin stream of the hot, sweetened half-and-half mixture to the whisked egg yolks, stirring continuously so the temperature of the egg mixture rises slowly. This keeps the eggs from cooking.

5.  Pour the mixture into the original medium saucepan. Pressing a spatula gently against the bottom of the pan, stir slowly and continuously and cook over medium-low heat until the custard thickens slightly, but do not let the mixture simmer or boil. Take your time.

6.  After seeing a few wisps of steam, immediately remove from the heat and strain through a fine mesh colander into a wide medium bowl.

7.  Place this bowl into a slightly larger bowl that is filled one-third of the way up with ice and water. Slowly stir the ginger mixture until it is cool to the touch. Cover the bowl with plastic wrap, then refrigerate for 8 hours. Cooling the mix before churning will give a smoother texture.

8.  Pour the chilled mixture into the ice cream machine and churn until a soft-serve consistency is achieved.

9.  Transfer to a large container, stir in the crystallized ginger.

10. Cover with plastic wrap, pressing the plastic wrap to the surface of the ice cream, and freeze until very firm, at least 5 hours.

YIELD: 1 (9-INCH) PIE

Nonstick spray or unsalted butter, to prepare the pie pan

¼ cup plus 2 tablespoons unbleached all-purpose flour, plus more for dusting

¼ cup dark brown sugar

½ teaspoon ground cinnamon

⅛ teaspoon kosher salt

2 teaspoons unsweetened cocoa powder (for the dessert version)

1 tablespoon orange zest (zest of a large orange), grated on a Microplane (for the dessert version)

½ teaspoon baking powder

1 cup roughly chopped dates, pits removed (approximately 30 dates)

2 tablespoons 2% or whole milk

1 cup raw pecan halves, chopped roughly

3 large eggs

# FRESH DATE PECAN BREAD
## TWO WAYS

This date pie recipe serves double duty as either an appetizer served at room temperature along side a selection of cheeses, fresh fruit, and breads, or served warm as a dessert, paired with a scoop of ice cream by simply adding orange zest and cocoa powder. Either way, because it has a full cup of chopped dates, it's naturally sweet, but not overly so. Appetizer or dessert: no matter how you slice it, you just can't go wrong.

1. Adjust two oven racks to the middle position, then preheat the oven to 350°F.

2. Spray or butter a 9-inch pie pan, then dust with flour, tapping out any excess.

3. Mix together the flour, brown sugar, cinnamon, salt, zest and cocoa (if making the dessert version), and baking powder in a medium-sized bowl.

4. Add the dates, milk, eggs, and nuts, and mix very well. Get in there with some elbow grease, and really stir until well combined. It'll be thick and chunky, but that's a good thing.

5. Pour the date batter into the prepared pie pan and give it a little shake to distribute the ingredients evenly, or use the back of a spatula to level off the batter.

6. Place the pie pan on a sheet pan and transfer to the oven.

7. Bake, uncovered, 40 to 45 minutes, until the top is light to golden brown and the center springs back when pressed.

8. Remove from the oven and allow to cool in the pan. Once cool, remove from the pie pan, slice, and serve.

# WINTER

| | |
|---|---|
| APPLES | PARSLEY |
| AVOCADOS | PARSNIPS |
| BEETS | POTATOES |
| BROCCOLI | RADICCHIO |
| BRUSSELS SPROUTS | ROSEMARY |
| CABBAGE | SHALLOTS |
| CELERY | SWEET POTATOES |
| DATES | SWISS CHARD |
| FENNEL | THYME |
| GARLIC | TURNIPS |
| GINGER | WINTER SQUASH |
| GRAPEFRUIT | |
| KALE | |
| KUMQUATS | |
| LEMONS | |
| LIMES | |
| ONIONS | |
| ORANGES | |
| OREGANO | |

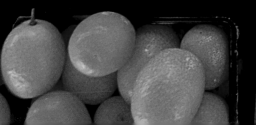
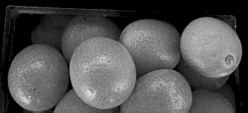

4 tablespoons unsalted butter

½ cup pure maple syrup, preferably grade B

2 teaspoons pure vanilla extract

3 cups uncooked old-fashioned oats (not instant)

¾ cup whole raw almonds

½ cup pumpkin seeds (pepitas)

½ cup sunflower seeds

2 teaspoons ground cinnamon

⅛ teaspoon ground nutmeg

⅛ teaspoon ground cloves

½ tablespoon orange zest (zest of 1 small orange), grated on a Microplane

¼ teaspoon kosher salt

2 cups of any combination of the following:

dried blueberries

dried cranberries

dried sweet cherries

black currants or raisins

# Vanilla-Maple Spiced Granola

All right, the word "granola" may conjure up images of drum circles and hippies for some of us. Those images are so 1960's, though. Skip ahead half a century or so, and gourmet granola is big business. More times than not, those high-end granolas cost a pretty penny or eight hundred. Well, not if you make it at home.

Here's my recipe. Give it a shot; I think you'll really like it. It has plenty of flavor, lots of crunch, and is sweetened with pure maple syrup. So grab the morning paper, pour yourself some coffee, and pull up a chair. All you need is a spoon and a dream—bandana and sideburns optional.

1. Adjust an oven rack to the middle position, then preheat the oven to 325°F.

2. Melt the butter with the maple syrup in a medium saucepan over low heat.

3. Remove from the heat and add the vanilla.

4. Combine the oats, almonds, pumpkin seeds, sunflower seeds, cinnamon, nutmeg, cloves, zest, and salt in a large mixing bowl.

5. Add the melted maple-butter love to the granola-seed mixture and stir until everything is evenly coated.

6. Pour the granola mixture onto a parchment paper-lined sheet pan and place it in the oven. Cook, uncovered, for 30 minutes, stirring once after 15 minutes, until the granola is a toasty light brown color.

7. Remove from the oven and cool to room temperature.

8. Combine the dried fruit and the cooled granola in the same large bowl and gently mix together. Store in a large airtight container for up to three weeks—that is, if there's any left.

**SALAD:**

1 bunch curly kale

¼ cup pine nuts

¼ cup toasted walnuts, chopped roughly
(recipe on page 42)

¼ cup toasted almonds, chopped roughly
(recipe on page 42)

¼ cup pumpkin seeds (pepitas)

½ cup dried cranberries, preferably
unsweetened

3 large oranges

½ cup crumbled feta cheese

Kosher salt, to taste

Freshly ground black pepper, to taste

**VINAIGRETTE:**

1 medium shallot, peeled and diced finely
(3 tablespoons)

1 tablespoon red wine vinegar

3 tablespoons freshly squeezed orange juice
(from the oranges)

⅓ cup extra-virgin olive oil

For bonus material relating to this recipe,
visit chefnathanlyon.com

# RAW KALE SALAD
## WITH FETA, PINE NUTS, AND CRANBERRIES

From Manhattan, to Washington DC, to Los Angeles, to Seattle, I've watched people pay a lot of money for a raw kale salad. Why pay the big bucks when you can make this salad at home? This is the quintessential raw kale salad. It's easy to prepare, refreshingly good, and you feel better after eating it. Bonus round? It's also inexpensive to make. Now that's a great deal, no matter where you live.

1.  Strip the tender leaves from the tough stems of the kale; discard the stems. Rinse and dry the leaves, then roll them up and slice into thin strips. You should have approximately 5 packed cups of kale ribbons.

2.  Cut the peel and pith off the oranges, then segment them by cutting between the dividers. Discard any seeds, but reserve the juice for the vinaigrette.

3.  In a medium container with a tight fitting lid, combine the vinaigrette ingredients, close the lid tightly, and shake well to combine. Or, whisk to combine the ingredients in a medium-sized bowl.

4.  Add the kale, nuts, seeds, cranberries, orange segments, and crumbled feta to a large serving bowl. Drizzle half the vinaigrette over the salad and toss to combine. Season to taste with salt and pepper, adding more vinaigrette if needed.

5.  Wonder aloud why you didn't make this salad sooner, then serve.

Note: Other optional ingredients that go wonderfully in this salad are sunflower seeds, diced avocado, and diced apples.

**TOMATO SOUP:**

7 tablespoons extra-virgin olive oil, divided, plus more for drizzling

2 medium yellow onions, peeled and diced medium (2 cups)

5 large garlic cloves, peeled and chopped roughly (1 tablespoon plus 2 teaspoons)

1 (28-ounce) can diced tomatoes, undrained, preferably fire-roasted

2 cups vegetable stock (recipe on page 37)

5 sprigs fresh thyme

2 dried bay leaves

⅛ teaspoon crushed red chile pepper (chile flakes), or to taste

2 roasted red bell peppers, from a jar, drained and chopped

Kosher salt, to taste

Freshly ground black pepper, to taste

Freshly squeezed lemon juice, to taste

Fresh flat-leaf Italian parsley, roughly chopped, for serving

Gruyère cheese croutons (recipe on page 256)

# SPICY TOMATO SOUP
## WITH GRUYÈRE CROUTONS

1. Heat 4 tablespoons of olive oil and the onions in a large saucepan over medium heat. Cook for 8 to 10 minutes, stirring occasionally, until the onions are soft, translucent, and lightly caramelized.

2. Add the garlic, thyme, and chile flakes, stir and cook until fragrant, 1 minute.

3. Stir in the tomatoes, stock, bay leaves, roasted red bell pepper, a good pinch of salt, and a few good grinds of pepper.

4. Increase the heat to high and bring to a boil, then reduce the heat to low and simmer for 25 minutes.

5. Remove from the heat and discard the bay leaves and thyme sprigs. Using an immersion blender, blend the soup until smooth.

6. Blend in the remaining olive oil and season to taste with lemon juice, salt, and pepper.

7. Serve in soup bowls with a drizzle of olive oil, a sprinkle of chopped parsley, and a few Gruyère cheese croutons. Grab a spoon and enjoy.

**GRUYÈRE CHEESE CROUTONS:**

**YIELD: APPROXIMATELY 4 CUPS**

1 small round loaf of sourdough bread

Extra-virgin olive oil, for drizzling

Kosher salt, to taste

Freshly ground black pepper, to taste

½ cup grated Gruyère cheese, not pre-grated

## GRUYÈRE CHEESE CROUTONS

1. Adjust an oven rack to the middle position, then preheat the oven to 400°F.

2. Remove the crust from the bread using a serrated bread knife. Tear the remaining loaf into 1-inch pieces.

3. Combine the bread pieces, a good drizzle of olive oil, salt, and pepper in a medium bowl and toss to coat.

4. Spread the pieces evenly on a sheet pan lined with a piece of aluminum foil or parchment paper. Bake, uncovered, until lightly toasted but not totally dry, 12 to 15 minutes, stirring every three to four minutes for even cooking.

5. Remove from the oven and sprinkle with the cheese. Return to the oven until the cheese is melted.

6. Remove from the oven and snack. I mean, serve.

# Parmesan Cheese Soufflé

1. Adjust an oven rack to the middle position, then preheat the oven to 350°F.

2. Lightly butter a quart-sized ramekin.

3. In a medium saucepan, over medium-low heat, melt the butter.

4. Whisk in the flour. It might bubble up a bit but keep on whisking. After 2 minutes of cooking/whisking, slowly pour in the milk and continue whisking 2 more minutes. It will thicken and resemble a paste.

5. Remove from the heat, and whisk or stir in the cheese until melted. Using a spatula, transfer the contents into a medium bowl.

6. In a separate clean, dry medium bowl, use your electric mixer to whip the egg whites to medium-firm peaks.

5. At this point the milky cheesy mixture should have cooled down enough to briskly whisk in the egg yolks without scrambling them. Whisk in the yolks, then add the thyme, salt, pepper, and cayenne.

6. Now, using a spatula, slowly and gently fold in one-third of the whites. This is called sacrificing, and is done to cool down the soufflé base so that the remaining two-thirds of the whites won't deflate. Fold in half the remaining egg whites, and then the remaining whites just until no white streaks can be seen. This is your soufflé batter. So pretty!

7. Fill the prepared ramekin with the soufflé batter. Place the ramekin on a sheet pan, then transfer the sheet pan (with the prepared ramekin) to the oven.

8. Bake, uncovered, until the top is golden brown and the soufflé looks all puffed up, beautiful and airy, approximately 30 minutes.

9. Using a large spoon, carefully divide the soufflé onto 4 plates and serve.

**YIELD: 4 SERVINGS**

4 tablespoons unsalted butter, plus more for preparing the ramekin

2½ tablespoons unbleached all-purpose flour

¾ cup 2% or whole milk

3 large eggs, separated

⅓ packed cup grated Parmigiano-Reggiano cheese, not pre-grated

¼ teaspoon kosher salt

⅛ teaspoon freshly ground black pepper

¼ teaspoon finely chopped fresh thyme

1/16 teaspoon ground cayenne pepper

**WILD RICE:**

4 cups water or vegetable stock (recipe on page 37)

1 cup wild rice, rinsed with cold water and drained

**SALAD:**

2 small oranges

2 large apples, such as Braeburn, Fuji, or Honeycrisp, unpeeled, cored and diced small (4 cups)

2 cups toasted pecan halves, chopped roughly (recipe on page 42)

1 cup dried black currants or dried cranberries

3 stalks celery, diced small (1½ cups)

⅓ cup thinly sliced green onions (green part only)

Kosher salt, to taste

Freshly ground black pepper, to taste

**VINAIGRETTE:**

6 tablespoons extra-virgin olive oil

4 tablespoons freshly squeezed orange juice (from the oranges)

6 tablespoons freshly squeezed lemon juice (2 lemons)

1 tablespoon white wine vinegar

# WILD RICE SALAD
## WITH DICED APPLES, ORANGES, AND TOASTED PECANS

1. In a large saucepan, bring the water or vegetable stock to a boil. Add the wild rice, stir, and cover. Reduce the heat to low and simmer, stirring occasionally, until the wild rice pops open and is tender to the bite, 45 minutes. Transfer to a colander, rinse with cold water to cool, and drain well.

2. Cut the peel and pith off the oranges, then segment them by cutting between the dividers. Discard any seeds, but reserve the juice for the vinaigrette.

3. In a medium container with a tight fitting lid, combine the vinaigrette ingredients, close the lid tightly, and shake well to combine. Or, whisk to combine the ingredients in a medium-sized bowl.

4. Add the diced apple, orange segments, drained wild rice, pecans, cranberries, and green onions. Season to taste with salt and pepper and serve.

For bonus material relating to this recipe, visit chefnathanlyon.com

**YIELD: 2 SERVINGS**

Reserved beet greens from 3 pounds of beets, rinsed and dried, 1 pound

1 tablespoon extra-virgin olive oil, plus more for drizzling

½ tablespoon unsalted butter

1 small shallot, peeled and diced small (1½ tablespoons)

1 medium garlic clove, peeled and minced (½ teaspoon)

1 teaspoon roughly chopped fresh thyme

Kosher salt, to taste

Freshly ground black pepper, to taste

1 tablespoon red wine vinegar

# Sautéed Beet Greens

1. Tear the beet greens from their thick stems; discard the stems.

2. Add the olive oil and butter to a large sauté pan over medium-high heat. Heat until the butter just begins to turn brown.

3. Add the shallot and garlic, stir, and cook until fragrant, 1 minute.

4. Add the beet greens and thyme, and season very lightly with salt and pepper. Cook until the leaves are just wilted, then remove from the heat.

5. Immediately sprinkle with the vinegar and mix together. Season to taste with salt and pepper. Add a drizzle of olive oil and serve.

# ROASTED GOLDEN BEET SALAD
## WITH FRISÉE, GOAT CHEESE, AND CANDIED WALNUTS

My first experience with beets was in the 1970s; they came from a glass jar. The deep violet water gently bathed the pre-sliced, pre-cooked beets in a sort of suspended animation. Even though it looked like a science experiment, I became quite fond of those violet vegetables. It wasn't until about a decade later, while assisting my mom shop at our local co-op, that I realized that beets come in different colors. Whoa. Cool! Plus, beets have greens! Now you're telling me that beets can be roasted instead of boiled to intensify the sweet flavors they have on offer? What? Since when?

My relationship with beets has evolved quite a bit since the 1970s, true, but my love for them has always remained the same.

1. Adjust an oven rack to the middle position, then preheat the oven to 350°F.

2. Cut off the greens half an inch above the beets and reserve for sautéed beet greens (recipe on opposite page). Scrub the beets.

3. Cut the peel and pith off the oranges, then segment them by cutting between the dividers. Discard any seeds, but reserve the juice for the vinaigrette.

4. In a roasting pan large enough to hold the beets in one layer, add the beets, then drizzle with 1½ tablespoons of olive oil, the salt, and water. Cover tightly with aluminum foil, place on a sheet pan and roast in the oven for approximately 50 minutes to an hour, or until the beets are easily pierced with the tip of a knife. Remove from the oven, remove the foil, and allow to cool.

5. When the beets are cool enough to handle, using a not-so-important hand

beet greens (recipe on opposite page)

**YIELD: 6 TO 8 SERVINGS**

**BEETS:**

3 pounds golden beets

3½ tablespoons extra-virgin olive oil, divided

¼ teaspoon kosher salt, plus more to taste

⅓ cup water

1 tablespoon freshly squeezed lemon juice

Freshly ground black pepper, to taste

**SALAD:**

1 large head frisée, rinsed, dried, and chopped or torn into bite-size pieces

3 medium oranges

4 ounces goat cheese (chèvre) (about ½ cup)

Candied Spiced Walnuts (recipe on page 43), for serving

cloth, wipe the beet skins off and discard them. Know this, though: even in your sweetest of dreams, you will most likely never wash the red stains out of that hand cloth.

6. Cut the beets into wedges, place them in a bowl, then combine 2 tablespoons of olive oil and 1 tablespoon lemon juice in a cup and drizzle over the beets. Fold to combine. Season to taste with salt and pepper.

7. In a medium container with a tight fitting lid, combine the vinaigrette ingredients, close the lid tightly, and shake well to combine. Or, whisk to combine the ingredients in a medium-sized bowl.

8. Gently toss the frisée and orange segments with your hands, then dress with half the vinaigrette. Season to taste with salt and pepper and additional vinaigrette to taste.

9. Divide the salad among 4 plates, then garnish with the beets, candied walnuts, and goat cheese, divided equally.

**VINAIGRETTE:**

2 tablespoons red wine vinegar

4 tablespoons extra-virgin olive oil

3 tablespoons freshly squeezed orange juice (from the oranges)

1 medium shallot peeled and diced small (3 tablespoons)

Kosher salt, to taste

Freshly ground black pepper, to taste

*"Food is our common ground, a universal experience."*

— JAMES BEARD

½ gallon freshly pressed apple cider

3 sticks cinnamon, plus more sticks
for garnish

1 medium orange, unpeeled, sliced thinly

2 whole cloves

½ vanilla bean, seeds and pod: slice down
the length of the pod, spread open,
and scrape out the flesh by pressing with
a butter knife

1 tablespoon honey, preferably orange
blossom

⅓ cup brandy, optional

# HOT MULLED CIDER

You wanna talk cold, huh? Back in my college days, I would ride my motorcycle from James Madison University, located in the Shenandoah Valley, back home to Arlington, Virginia during the winter holiday break. More often than not, it was freezing outside. Sometimes it would sleet, or worse, it would snow. By the time I made it home safely, two hours later, my fingers and toes would be chilled to the bone. Thankfully, only moments after entering my house, I was greeted with a mug of my mom's fresh spiced cider, kept warm on our wood burning stove in the living room, an immediate respite from the chill of the elements outside.

Now I live in Los Angeles and have long since sold my motorcycle, but when it does eventually get down into the 30's, you'd better believe I'm making a pot of my hot mulled cider. You just never know when a good friend might need to thaw out from winter's chill. With a warm cup of my hot mulled cider, one thing's for sure, that chill doesn't stand a chance.

In a large saucepan or small pot over low heat, add all of the ingredients, and mix together. Stir occasionally until very warm. Serve in mugs with slices of orange.

Note: If the mulled cider will be sitting for an exceptionally long time, remove the cloves when the flavor is to your liking. Also, if you are a big fan of spice, combine 3 star anise and 1 inch of peeled, roughly chopped fresh ginger and put them into a tea strainer or mesh bag to steep along with the other ingredients. Much like steeping tea, remove the tea strainer or mesh bag of ginger and star anise when the desired flavor is achieved.

# Black Olive Tapenade

**YIELD: 1 CUP**

1¼ cup Kalamata olives, drained and pits removed

1 large garlic clove, peeled and chopped roughly (1 teaspoon)

2 small olive oil-packed anchovy fillets, rinsed

2 tablespoons capers, rinsed and drained

3 tablespoons toasted pine nuts (recipe on page 42)

¼ cup extra-virgin olive oil

2 teaspoons freshly squeezed lemon juice

2 teaspoons balsamic vinegar

¼ teaspoon kosher salt

When I get a slathering of tapenade on a vegetable panini, I am one happy camper. Paired with some roasted bell peppers, grilled tomatoes, and goat cheese? Yes, please. How about spread thinly over a pan roast rack of lamb? Double please!

Tapenade is also super easy to make: simply gather the ingredients together and process them in a food processor. Then, serve your fresh tapenade on a cheese plate with crostini, with grilled chicken and vegetables, with roast pork tenderloin, or even added to a fresh heirloom tomato salad with grilled eggplant and mozzarella! With so many amazing options, the question isn't if you should make the tapenade—it's when.

In a food processor, combine the ingredients and process until the desired consistency is achieved.

**YIELD: 4 TO 5 SERVINGS**

3 medium sweet potatoes (2 pounds), peeled and diced into 2-inch cubes

3 tablespoons unsalted butter

3 tablespoons of pure maple syrup, preferably Grade B

3 tablespoons freshly squeezed orange juice

1 tablespoon fresh ginger, peeled and grated on a Microplane

Kosher salt, to taste

Freshly ground black pepper, to taste

# MAPLE SYRUP SWEET POTATO PURÉE

1. Place the potatoes in a small pot filled halfway with cool water.

2. Bring the water to a boil over high heat. Reduce the heat to low and simmer until the potatoes are easily pierced with the tip of a knife, then drain well.

3. Add the drained potatoes to a food processor with a metal blade attachment (for a super smooth texture) or large bowl (for a more rustic texture).

4. Process in the food processor or mash with a potato masher, then add the remaining ingredients and continue processing or mashing. Season to taste with salt and pepper.

5. Cover with aluminum foil until ready to serve, or stand right there in your kitchen, spoon in hand, and enjoy the maple syrup sweet potato purée right then and there. I won't tell.

Note: If desired, ground cinnamon is a nice touch to this dish as well. Your call.

# HORSERADISH WHIPPED POTATOES

What can I say? It's a bowl of warm horseradish whipped potatoes, for goodness' sake! What's not to love? It pairs wonderfully with a steak, meatloaf, or a spoon.

1. Put the potatoes in a small pot, add 1 tablespoon salt, and fill with enough cold water to cover the potatoes by almost 2 inches. Bring to a boil, cover with a lid, reduce the heat to low and simmer until the potatoes crumble when poked with a fork. Drain the potatoes in a colander, then return the drained potatoes to the original pot to allow some of the steam to evaporate off.

2. Meanwhile, heat the milk in a saucepan over medium-low heat until hot, then pour over the potatoes.

3. Mash with a potato masher until well combined. It won't take long.

4. Whisk in the butter and horseradish with a sturdy whisk. Season to taste with salt, pepper, and additional horseradish. Cover with a lid to keep warm until you can't wait any longer.

**YIELD: 4 SERVINGS**

3 large russet potatoes, peeled, cut into 16 equal pieces (2 pounds)

1 cup whole milk, warmed

6 tablespoons cold unsalted butter, cut into 12 pieces

1 tablespoon prepared white horseradish, plus more to taste

Kosher salt, to taste

Freshly ground black pepper, to taste

4 medium Yukon gold potatoes, peeled

¼ cup extra-virgin olive oil, plus more for preparing the potatoes

Kosher salt, to taste

Freshly ground black pepper, to taste

2 tablespoon finely chopped fresh flat-leaf Italian parsley

# OLIVE OIL SMASHED POTATOES

1.  Adjust an oven rack to the middle position, then preheat the oven to 350°F.

2.  Rub each potato lightly with olive oil, then wrap individually in aluminum foil and bake for approximately 50 minutes, or until easily pierced with a knife.

3.  Remove from the oven, remove the foil, and mash the potatoes with the back of a fork into a small bowl.

4.  Stir in the olive oil and season to taste with salt and pepper.

5.  Stir in the chopped parsley and cover with foil until you're ready to eat.

# GINGER GLAZED CARROTS

1. Add the carrots, butter, ginger, maple syrup, salt, a few healthy grinds of pepper, and the water in a medium-sized sauté pan over high heat. Bring to a boil and cook, stirring occasionally, until the liquid has thickened slightly (like a glaze) and almost completely evaporated. The carrots will be just cooked through in 8 to 10 minutes.

2. Remove from the heat and stir in the chopped parsley.

3. Season to taste with additional salt and pepper. Serve immediately.

**YIELD: 2 TO 3 SERVINGS**

1 pound carrots, peeled and cut diagonally into ¼-inch slices

1½ tablespoons unsalted butter

1 teaspoon fresh ginger, peeled and grated on a Microplane

2 tablespoons pure maple syrup, preferably Grade B

⅛ teaspoon kosher salt, plus more to taste

Freshly ground black pepper, to taste

¾ cup water

2 tablespoons finely chopped fresh flat-leaf Italian parsley

4 medium carrots, peeled and cut into bite-size pieces

2 medium turnips, peeled and cut into bite-size pieces

1 large rutabaga, peeled and cut into bite-size pieces

2 large Yukon Gold potatoes, peeled and cut into bite-size pieces

5 small parsnips, peeled and cut into bite-size pieces

1 head garlic, separated into cloves, unpeeled

5 medium shallots, peeled and halved

3 tablespoons extra-virgin olive oil

1 teaspoon kosher salt, plus more to taste

¼ teaspoon freshly ground black pepper, plus more to taste

2 tablespoons roughly chopped fresh thyme

1 tablespoon finely chopped fresh rosemary

For bonus material relating to this recipe, visit chefnathanlyon.com

# THYME-ROASTED ROOT VEGETABLES

1. Adjust an oven rack to the middle position, then preheat the oven to 400°F.

2. Put the vegetables in a large bowl, then add the olive oil to coat and stir well to combine.

3. Add the salt and pepper and stir.

4. Now taste one of the carrots to see if you need more salt or pepper, adding more to taste.

5. Sprinkle with the thyme and rosemary and stir well.

6. Distribute the vegetables evenly over a parchment paper-lined sheet pan. Roast, uncovered, for 50 to 60 minutes, until lightly caramelized, stirring once after 35 minutes for even cooking.

7. Remove the sheet pan from the oven, return the vegetables to the bowl, lightly coat the vegetables with olive oil, and season to taste with salt and pepper. Try not to spoil your appetite by snacking on them.

**BRUSSELS SPROUTS #1**

1 pound Brussels sprouts

1 teaspoon kosher salt, plus more to taste

1 tablespoon extra-virgin olive oil, plus more for drizzling

3 slices applewood-smoked bacon, halved lengthwise and then cut crosswise into ¼-inch slices (¾ cup)

1 medium shallot, peeled and diced small (3 tablespoons)

½ teaspoon finely chopped fresh thyme

Freshly ground black pepper, to taste

1 tablespoon balsamic vinegar

2 tablespoons finely chopped fresh flat-leaf Italian parsley

½ cup toasted salted pecan halves (recipe on page 42)

½ cup grated Parmigiano-Reggiano cheese, not pre-grated

# PAN ROASTED BRUSSELS SPROUTS
## TWO WAYS

"Mon petit chou" is a French term of endearment which translates into "my little cabbage." Sounds romantic, no? Something you might say to your beloved or your… Brussels sprout? If you grew up in the 1970s on the East Coast, where seemingly every parent would boil them within an inch of their little lives, chances are you're thinking, "a term of endearment? More like little balls of cabbage stink, right?" There is another way, two ways, in fact, to transform Brussels sprouts into, dare I say it, culinary gems. I have no doubt, when prepared just right, these "little cabbages" will become very dear to you, too.

## BRUSSELS SPROUTS #1

1. Bring a medium saucepan of water to a rolling boil. While waiting for the water to boil, trim the ends off of the sprouts, and remove any yellow leaves. Quarter the very large sprouts and halve the medium sprouts.

2. Add the sprouts and 1 teaspoon of salt to the boiling water and cook for 3 minutes. Remove from the water and drain well in a colander.

3. Add the bacon and 1 tablespoon of olive oil, to a large sauté pan. Turn the heat to medium-low. Cook for approximately 5 to 6 minutes, stirring occasionally, until much of the fat has rendered off, and the bacon is just beginning to get nice and crispy. Pour off half of the bacon fat, reserve for another use (give it to my best friend Scott!), or discard.

4. Increase the heat to medium-high and add the diced shallots, thyme, a crank of black pepper, plus the drained Brussels sprouts. Cook, stirring occasionally, until the Brussels sprouts are lightly colored, approximately 5 to 6 minutes.

## BRUSSELS SPROUTS #2

1 tablespoon extra-virgin olive oil, plus more for drizzling

3 slices applewood smoked bacon, halved lengthwise and then cut crosswise into ¼-inch slices (¾ cup)

2 large yellow onions, peeled and diced small (3 cups)

1 teaspoon finely chopped fresh thyme

1 pound Brussels sprouts

3 large garlic cloves, peeled and minced (1 tablespoon)

½ cup half-and-half

Kosher salt, to taste

Freshly ground black pepper, to taste

2 tablespoons finely chopped fresh Italian flat-leaf parsley

Parmigiano-Reggiano cheese, not pre-grated, for serving

5. Drizzle with the vinegar, stir to combine, and remove from the heat.

6. Transfer the contents of the sauté pan to a medium bowl and stir in the chopped parsley, pecans, and Parmigiano-Reggiano. Season to taste with salt and pepper and serve with a drizzle of olive oil.

## BRUSSELS SPROUTS #2

1. Add the bacon and 1 tablespoon of olive oil to a large sauté pan, then place over medium-low heat and cook for approximately 5 to 6 minutes, stirring occasionally, until much of the fat has rendered off and the bacon is just beginning to get nice and crispy.

2. Pour off half the bacon fat, reserve for another use, or discard. Add the onions and thyme to the sauté pan and cook for 6 to 7 minutes until the onions are soft and translucent.

3. While the onions are cooking, trim the ends off of the sprouts, and remove any yellow leaves. Quarter the large sprouts and halve the medium and small sprouts.

4. Once the onions are lightly colored, increase the heat to medium. Add the sprouts to the sauté pan, stirring to combine, and cook for approximately 8 to 10 minutes until the sprouts are lightly colored.

5. Toss the garlic in the sauté pan, stir, and cook until fragrant, 1 minute.

6. Pour the half-and-half over the Brussels sprouts, stir, cover, and cook for 3 minutes.

7. Turn off the heat, uncover the sauté pan, and season to taste with salt and pepper.

8. Stir in the parsley, then serve with some grated Parmigiano-Reggiano and a drizzle of olive oil.

# LENTIL STEW
## WITH SPICY SAUSAGE AND KALE

I'm glad to see more people introducing lentils to their kitchens. "Lentils, this is my kitchen. Kitchen, say hello to lentils." I mean, what's not to like? Unlike dried beans, lentils require no pre-soaking, which makes them super easy to prepare; just cook them until they're done. Also, lentils tell great jokes (true story) and they're highly nutritious, play well with other flavors, and—wait for it—lentils are inexpensive. A healthy, low maintenance, cheap date with great taste and a good sense of humor? Whoa! Now there's something you want to bring home to introduce to the entire family.

1. Strip the tender leaves from the tough stems of the kale; discard the stems. Rinse the leaves, then chop roughly. You should have approximately 6 packed cups of kale.

2. Add ¼ cup olive oil, the onions, carrots, and celery to a small pot set over medium-high heat. Season lightly with salt and pepper, and cook for 10 to 15 minutes, stirring occasionally, until the celery begins to soften.

3. Add the garlic, curry, and sausage. Cook, breaking up the sausage into small pieces with the back of a spoon, until the sausage is mostly cooked through, 5 minutes. At this point your kitchen should smell insanely good.

4. Add the tomatoes, bay leaves, thyme, lentils, kale, and the stock. The stock should just barely cover the kale. Stir it all together.

**YIELD: 6 TO 8 SERVINGS**

1 bunch curly kale

¼ cup extra-virgin olive oil

2 large yellow onions, peeled and diced small (3 cups)

5 medium carrots, peeled and chopped roughly (2½ cups)

4 stalks celery, chopped roughly (2 cups)

6 large garlic cloves, peeled and minced (2 tablespoons)

1 tablespoon yellow curry powder

½ pound fresh spicy Italian or fennel sausage (pork or turkey), removed from casing, approximately 2 to 3 links

1 (24-ounce) can diced tomatoes, undrained, preferably fire-roasted

3 small dried bay leaves

3 sprigs fresh thyme

1⅓ cups green (Puy) lentils, rinsed and picked over for small pebbles

8 cups chicken or vegetable stock (recipes on page 37 & 38)

1 tablespoon sherry vinegar

¾ teaspoon kosher salt, plus more to taste

Freshly ground black pepper, to taste

Parmigiano-Reggiano cheese, not pre-grated, for serving

Note: If your sausage is on the spicy side, add a dollop of crème fraîche (recipe on page 45) to take the edge off the heat.

5. Cover with a lid, bring to a boil, then reduce the heat to low and simmer for 35 to 40 minutes, until the lentils are just tender. The consistency should be like a thick soup, so add a bit of water to thin it out if the lentils are not quite cooked at this point.

6. Once the lentils are tender, remove from the heat and stir in the salt, pepper, and vinegar. Discard the bay leaves and thyme sprigs. Adjust the seasoning with salt and pepper.

7. Serve in soup bowls, and shave some Parmigiano-Reggiano on top with a vegetable peeler. Grab a spoon and go crazy.

*"As the days grow short, some faces grow long. But not mine. Every autumn, when the wind turns cold and darkness comes early, I am suddenly happy. It's time to start making soup again."* — LESLIE NEWMAN

YIELD: 6 TO 8 SERVINGS

7 medium carrots, peeled and chopped roughly (3½ cups)

2 medium sweet potatoes, peeled and chopped roughly (3 cups)

1 large apple, peeled, cored, and chopped roughly (2 cups)

4 cups chicken or vegetable stock (recipes on page 37 & 38)

2 teaspoons fresh ginger, peeled and grated on a Microplane

¼ teaspoon ground cinnamon, plus more to taste

1/16 teaspoon ground cayenne pepper, plus more to taste

1 tablespoon honey, preferably orange blossom

2 tablespoons freshly squeezed lemon juice, divided, plus more to taste

3 tablespoons extra-virgin olive oil

Kosher salt, to taste

Freshly ground black pepper, to taste

Candied Spiced Pecans (recipe on page 43), for serving

Fresh flat-leaf Italian parsley, chopped roughly, for serving

# SWEET POTATO-CARROT SOUP
## WITH CANDIED PECANS

1. Combine the carrots, sweet potatoes, apple, and stock in a large saucepan over high heat. Cover and bring to a boil, then reduce the heat to low and simmer for approximately 30 minutes until both the sweet potatoes fall apart and the carrots are soft and can be pierced easily with a fork. Remove from the heat.

2. Blend the mixture to a smooth texture carefully with an immersion blender.

3. Add the grated ginger, cinnamon, cayenne pepper, honey, lemon juice, and olive oil to the saucepan and continue to blend. Season to taste with additional lemon juice, salt, and pepper; add more cayenne pepper for heat and more cinnamon for sweetness.

4. Serve in soup bowls topped with candied spiced pecans and chopped parsley.

Note: If you prefer a slightly thinner consistency, add a splash of hot water or stock.

1 (4-pound) kabocha squash, peeled, seeded, then cut into 1-inch cubes

1 tablespoon roughly chopped fresh thyme

½ teaspoon kosher salt, plus more to taste

Freshly ground black pepper, to taste

6 tablespoons extra-virgin olive oil, divided, plus more for drizzling

2 large yellow onions, peeled and diced small (3 cups)

2 cups pearled barley

1 medium garlic clove, peeled and minced (½ teaspoon)

⅛ teaspoon crushed red chile pepper (chile flakes), or to taste

½ cup dry white wine, such as Sauvignon Blanc

4 cups vegetable or chicken stock (recipes on page 37 & 38)

3 tablespoons freshly squeezed lemon juice (juice of 1 lemon)

½ cup grated Parmigiano-Reggiano, not pre-grated

Fresh flat-leaf Italian parsley, chopped roughly, for garnish

# BARLEY RISOTTO
## WITH ROASTED WINTER SQUASH AND SHAVED PARMIGIANO

Peel. Cut. Roast.

Peel a butternut squash? Absolutely. Any hard winter squash, for that matter. Granted, sometimes this can be difficult, so do what an eighty-two-year-old grandmother taught me at the Hollywood farmers market. Grab a pot large enough to accommodate the squash, fill it with one inch of water, and bring to a boil. Carefully lower the squash into the steaming pot, cover, then allow the squash to steam for approximately 7 to 9 minutes, or until a wooden skewer or fork easily penetrates the very outer skin. Turn off the heat, carefully remove the squash, and allow to cool. The skin can now be removed easily with a vegetable peeler. Presto. No more sore wrists. If an eighty-two-year-old grandmother can do it, so can you.

1. Adjust an oven rack to the middle position, then preheat the oven to 475°F.

2. Add the squash, thyme, salt, a few good cranks of pepper, and 3 table-spoons of olive oil (enough to fully coat all the squash) to a large bowl and mix well.

3. On a parchment paper-lined sheet pan, spread out the seasoned squash in a single layer and roast, uncovered, for approximately 30 minutes, stirring after 15 minutes until nicely caramelized and cooked through. Remove from the oven and season to taste with salt and pepper.

4. While the squash is roasting, add 3 tablespoons of olive oil and the onions to a small pot over medium-low heat and cook, stirring occasionally, for 8 to 10 minutes, until the onions are soft and translucent.

5. Stir in the barley, garlic, and chile flakes and cook until fragrant, 1 minute.

6. Pour in the wine, stir, and reduce until very little wine remains.

7. Add the stock, stir, cover, and increase the heat to high to bring to a boil. Reduce the heat to low and simmer for approximately 35 minutes, until the barley is pleasantly chewy with a little body remaining.

8. Uncover and cook, stirring occasionally, until about ½ cup of liquid remains.

9. Remove from the heat and fold in the squash and the lemon juice. Season to taste with salt and pepper.

10. Serve topped with Parmigiano-Reggiano, a drizzle of olive oil, and chopped parsley.

*"The trouble with eating Italian food is that five or six days later you're hungry again."*
— GEORGE MILLER

# Rosemary White Bean Soup
## WITH SMOKED BACON AND SHAVED PARMIGIANO

It's a classic. It's a one-pot wonder. It's nothing shy of delicious.

1. Strip the tender leaves from the tough stems of the kale; discard the stems. Rinse the leaves, then chop roughly. You should have approximately 6 packed cups of kale.

2. Add the bacon and 1 tablespoon of olive oil to a small pot. Place over medium-low heat and cook for approximately 5 to 6 minutes, stirring occasionally, until much of the fat has rendered off, and the bacon is just beginning to get nice and crispy.

3. Add the onions, stir occasionally, and continue to cook until soft and translucent, 6 to 7 minutes.

4. Add the garlic and cook until fragrant, 1 minute.

5. Using a piece of butcher's twine, tie together the rosemary, thyme sprigs and bay leaves; toss the herbs in the pot.

6. Stir in the beans, kale, and stock.

7. Cover and increase the heat to high. Bring to a boil, then reduce the heat to low and simmer for 20 minutes, or until the beans are soft and the kale is cooked through.

8. Remove the tied herbs and discard. Add the vinegar and season to taste with salt, pepper, and additional vinegar.

9. Serve in bowls. Shave some Parmigiano-Reggiano over the soup with a vegetable peeler, then top with a drizzle of olive oil and some pepper.

**YIELD: 4 SERVINGS**

1 bunch curly kale

1 tablespoon extra-virgin olive oil, plus more for drizzling

3 slices smoked bacon, halved lengthwise and then cut crosswise into ¼-inch slices (¾ cup)

2 medium yellow onions, peeled and diced small (2 cups)

5 large garlic cloves, peeled and minced (1 tablespoon plus 2 teaspoons)

3 (5-inch) sprigs fresh rosemary, bruised with your fingers

5 sprigs fresh thyme

2 dried bay leaves

2 (16-ounce) cans white kidney beans (cannellini beans), rinsed and drained

6 cups vegetable or chicken stock (recipes on page 37 & 38)

Kosher salt, to taste

Freshly ground black pepper, to taste

¼ teaspoon red wine vinegar, plus more to taste

Parmigiano-Reggiano or Pecorino Romano cheese, not pre-grated, for serving

1 (3½ to 4 pound) butternut squash, peeled, seeded, then cut into 1-inch cubes

½ teaspoon kosher salt, plus more to taste

Freshly ground black pepper, to taste

5 tablespoons extra-virgin olive oil, divided, plus more for drizzling

2 large yellow onions, peeled and diced small (3 cups)

⅛ teaspoon crushed red chile pepper (chile flakes), or to taste

1 teaspoon yellow curry powder

1 teaspoon finely chopped fresh thyme

3 large garlic cloves, peeled and chopped roughly (1 tablespoon)

⅛ teaspoon ground cinnamon

4 cups chicken stock or vegetable stock (recipes on page 37 & 38)

½ cup freshly squeezed orange juice

Fresh flat-leaf Italian parsley, chopped roughly, for serving

Crème fraîche, for serving (recipe on page 45)

Pomegranate seeds, for serving

Homemade Crostini (recipe on page 40), optional

# BUTTERNUT SQUASH SOUP
## WITH SWEET CURRY AND POMEGRANATE SEEDS

As kids, my brothers and I would spend hours on the front steps of our house, eating pomegranates. Little by little, our fingers and shirts would take on the deep red color of the pomegranate as we excavated the juicy seeds from their soft, paper-white layers. However, if stained fingers and clothing aren't your thing, I've found a stain-free way to get the seeds out of a pomegranate: underwater. Not you—the pomegranate. First, fill a medium bowl halfway with cold water. Second, cut a pomegranate in half, horizontally. Third, working with one submerged half at a time, turn the pomegranate inside out, then separate the white pith from the seeds. The seeds will sink, and the white pithy stuff will float to the surface. So long, dry cleaners!

1. Adjust an oven rack to the middle position, then preheat the oven to 475°F.

2. Add the squash, salt, a few good cranks of pepper and a healthy drizzle of olive oil (enough to fully coat all the squash) to a large bowl and mix well.

3. Spread the seasoned squash in a single layer on a parchment paper-lined sheet pan and roast, uncovered, for approximately 30 minutes, stirring after 15 minutes, until nicely caramelized and cooked through. Remove from the oven and season to taste with salt and pepper.

4. Add 3 tablespoons of olive oil, the onions, chile flakes, curry powder, and thyme to a small pot and cook, stirring occasionally, for 8 to 10 minutes, until the onions are soft and translucent.

5. Add the garlic and cook until fragrant, 1 minute.

6.  Add the cinnamon, roasted squash, and stock to the caramelized onions. Cover, increase the heat to high and bring to a boil, then reduce the heat to low and simmer for 5 minutes.

7.  Add the remaining 2 tablespoons olive oil and orange juice and purée with an immersion blender until smooth. Season to taste with salt and pepper.

8.  Spoon the soup into bowls and garnish with chopped parsley, a dollop of crème fraîche, and some pomegranate seeds. Serve with several crostini on the side, if desired.

*"Good soup is one of the prime ingredients of good living. For soup can do more to lift the spirits and stimulate the appetite than any other one dish."*

— LOUIS P. DE GOUY

**BRAISED CHICKEN:**

6 chicken legs, 3 pounds total weight, at room temperature

¾ teaspoon kosher salt, plus more to taste

Freshly ground black pepper, for seasoning, plus more to taste

1 tablespoon extra-virgin olive oil

2 medium yellow onions, peeled and diced small (2 cups)

3 medium carrots, peeled and chopped roughly (1½ cups)

3 large garlic cloves, peeled and chopped roughly (1 tablespoon)

1 dried bay leaf

5 sprigs fresh thyme

2 cinnamon sticks

½ cup roughly chopped dried figs, stems removed or dried apricots, unsulfured if possible

¾ cup dry white wine, such as Sauvignon Blanc

1½ cups chicken stock (recipe on page 38)

2 teaspoons apple cider vinegar

1 tablespoon honey, preferably orange blossom

# BRAISED CHICKEN
## WITH SWEET CURRIED COUSCOUS AND BLACK CURRANTS

1.  Adjust an oven rack to the middle position, then preheat the oven to 375°F.

2.  Trim any excess flaps of skin and fat from the chicken legs. Pat the chicken legs dry.

3.  Season all sides of the chicken liberally with salt and a few generous grinds of pepper. Let sit at room temperature for 30 minutes.

3.  In a medium sauté pan, over medium-high heat, add ½ tablespoon olive oil, swirl the pan to distribute, and heat until the oil begins to smoke.

4.  Add three of the chicken legs, skin side down, and cook undisturbed for about 4 minutes, until golden brown in color.

5.  Using tongs, flip the legs and cook for 2 minutes more until nicely colored.

6.  After the legs are seared, place them skin side up on a plate. Carefully pour out any liquid in the pan and discard.

7.  Repeat this entire process with the next 3 legs, but do not pour out the liquid from the sauté pan the second time around.

8.  Return the pan to the medium-high heat. Add the diced onion and carrots. Cook, stirring occasionally until the vegetables are nicely caramelized, approximately 6 to 7 minutes.

9.  Add the garlic and cook until fragrant, 1 minute.

10. Add the wine and stock, bring the pan to a simmer, then pour the contents into a roasting pan.

11. Add the bay leaves, thyme sprigs, cinnamon sticks, and chopped apricots. Arrange the chicken legs over the vegetables, skin side up, pressing the legs down so that the liquid comes to approximately halfway up the side of the legs.

12. Transfer the roasting pan to the oven and cook, uncovered, for 40 minutes.

13. Remove the chicken from the oven and discard the thyme sprigs, bay leaf, and cinnamon sticks.

14. Stir in the vinegar and honey, then season to taste with salt and pepper.

**COUSCOUS:**

**YIELD: 5 CUPS**

2 tablespoons extra-virgin olive oil

2 large yellow onions, peeled and diced small (3 cups)

5 large garlic cloves, peeled and minced (1 tablespoon plus 2 teaspoons)

1 teaspoon yellow curry powder

2 cups chicken or vegetable stock (recipes on page 37 & 38)

1 (10-ounce) box instant couscous

3 tablespoons roughly chopped fresh flat-leaf Italian parsley

⅓ cup dried black currants

1 teaspoon kosher salt, plus more to taste

Freshly ground black pepper, to taste

## COUSCOUS

1. Add the olive oil, onion, garlic, and curry to a medium saucepan set over medium heat and cook, stirring occasionally, for 8 to 10 minutes, until the onions are soft and translucent.

2. Add the stock, black currants, salt, and a few generous cranks of pepper. Increase the heat to high and bring to a boil. Add the couscous, stir, cover, then remove from the heat. Let sit, undisturbed, for at least 5 minutes.

3. Uncover, then gently fluff the couscous with a fork, stir in the parsley, and season to taste with the salt and pepper. Cover to keep warm until ready to serve.

# PASTA WITH SPICY SAUSAGE, RICOTTA, GOLDEN RAISINS, AND PINE NUTS

This recipe always reminds me of cooking for a great cause: education.

I flew back to the Washington, DC area late last year to cook for three couples who paid for my services as their personal chef. The silent auction where they purchased my time was a fundraiser for my alma mater, Long Branch Elementary School. That night, with the amazing sous chef skills of my mom, we cooked eleven courses over the span of five hours—no joke. This particular recipe stands out to me because during the course of the evening one of the guests, Evan, came back for seconds of this very dish. Keep in mind, we were already eight courses in, but Evan was on a mission for seconds. We loaded him up, and off he went, smiling down at his plate as he returned to his seat. Needless to say, the evening was a complete success: money was raised, bellies were filled, and food coma-induced smiles filled the room.

I'm excited to say that I'll be cooking again for the same cause, because supporting the education of our youth is something that benefits all of us, and together we can make a difference—one delicious plate at a time.

1. Strip the tender leaves from the tough stems of the kale; discard the stems. Rinse the leaves, then chop finely.

2. Combine 4 tablespoons of olive oil and the onions in a small pot over medium-low heat and cook, stirring occasionally for approximately 8 to 10 minutes, until the onions are soft and translucent.

3. Add the garlic, rosemary, and ground fennel, stir to combine, and cook until fragrant, 1 minute.

**YIELD: 4 TO 6 SERVINGS**

2 bunches cavolo nero (also known as black, dinosaur, Lacinato, or Tuscan kale)

6 tablespoons extra-virgin olive oil, divided, plus more for drizzling

2 medium yellow onions, peeled and diced small (2 cups)

6 large garlic cloves, peeled and minced (2 tablespoons)

2 (6-inch) fresh rosemary sprigs, bruised with your fingers

½ teaspoon ground fennel seed

½ pound fresh spicy Italian sausage (pork or turkey), removed from casing, approximately 2 to 3 links

½ cup golden raisins

1 (14-ounce) can diced tomatoes, undrained, preferably fire-roasted, if possible

1¼ cup vegetable or chicken stock (recipes on page 37 & 38)

2 teaspoons freshly squeezed lemon juice

2 teaspoons red wine vinegar

2 tablespoons kosher salt, plus more to taste

Freshly ground black pepper, to taste

12 ounces gemelli or penne pasta

Ingredients continued on next page »

4. Add the sausage to the pot. Cook for approximately 7 to 8 minutes until the sausage has browned, breaking up the sausage into small pieces with the back of a wooden spoon as it cooks.

5. Add the chopped kale, golden raisins, drained diced tomatoes, and stock to the sausage mixture and stir to combine.

6. Turn the heat to high to bring to a simmer, then reduce the heat to low to continue simmering and cover with a lid. Continue simmering until the kale is soft, and less than one-third of the liquid remains, 20 to 25 minutes, stirring occasionally.

7. Remove the rosemary sprigs, stir in the lemon juice and vinegar, and season to taste with salt and pepper. Turn off the heat and cover to keep warm.

8. Meanwhile, bring a small pot of water to a rolling boil. Add 2 tablespoons of salt.

9. Add the pasta to the boiling water and cook, stirring occasionally, until *al dente* (almost done, or "to the tooth").

10. Drain the pasta without rinsing, then immediately return it to the pot. Add 2 tablespoons olive oil to the pasta and stir to coat.

11. Add the pasta to the warm sausage-kale mixture, gently stir together and season to taste with salt and pepper.

12. Serve in shallow pasta bowls, topped with the ricotta salata or Pecorino Romano. If using ricotta salata, shave some Parmigiano-Reggiano over each serving with a vegetable peeler. Top with a drizzle of olive oil and the toasted pine nuts.

2 cups ricotta salata, drained and crumbled, or grated Pecorino Romano, not pre-grated

Parmigiano-Reggiano cheese, not pre-grated, for serving

⅓ cup toasted pine nuts (recipe on page 42), for serving

**TENDERLOIN:**

1 pound pork tenderloin, silver skin removed (see note on opposite page)

½ teaspoon kosher salt

Freshly ground black pepper, for seasoning

1 tablespoon extra-virgin olive oil

# OVEN-ROASTED PORK TENDERLOIN
## WITH APPLE-ROSEMARY-DIJON PAN SAUCE

A classic flavor combination: pork with rosemary, apples, and Dijon. Impressive, quick, and inexpensive—with an easy pan sauce to boot? Let's eat!

1. Season the tenderloin with the salt and a few really generous grinds of pepper. Allow to sit at room temperature for 30 minutes. Pat the tenderloin dry.

2. Adjust an oven rack to the middle position, then preheat the oven to 350°F.

3. Heat a large, oven-safe sauté pan (large enough to accommodate the pork) over high heat until very hot. Add the olive oil, swirl the pan to distribute the oil and heat until shimmering. If it begins to smoke, that's okay.

4. Immediately add the tenderloin and allow to cook for 2 minutes, undisturbed, until nicely seared. Using tongs, rotate the tenderloin ¼ turn and continue to sear, again for 2 minutes. Once seared, rotate again another ¼ turn and sear for another 2 minutes. Upon rotating the tenderloin to the fourth and final side, hold the tenderloin off the pan with your tongs and insert the digital probe of an oven-safe meat thermometer from the end of the tenderloin into the center. The tip of the probe must reach approximately halfway into the tenderloin.

6. Replace the tenderloin in the pan on the fourth and final side, and transfer the sauté pan, uncovered, into the oven. Set the digital thermometer to 145°F.

7. When the thermometer beeps, after about 15 minutes, transfer the tenderloin to a cutting board, cover loosely with foil, and allow the tenderloin to rest for 15 minutes before slicing.

## PAN SAUCE

1. While the tenderloin is resting, place the same sauté pan over medium-high heat.

2. Add the shallot, stir, and cook for 1 minute.

3. Add the apple cider and rosemary sprigs. Reduce until only approximately ½ cup remains. Remove from the heat and discard the rosemary.

4. Add the Dijon and cider vinegar, then stir in the butter until glossy and insanely beautiful looking. Season to taste with salt and pepper.

5. Slice the pork into 1-inch medallions, serve on plates, then spoon the pan reduction sauce over the meat.

Note: Similar to the iridescent color of a pearl, silver skin is the inedible connective tissue that covers a small portion of the thicker end of the tenderloin. Too tough to pull off with your bare hands (unlike a layer of fat), the silver skin can be removed, using your knife of choice, by simply filleting it off. Do this by cutting just under the silver skin with the tip of your knife, angling your knife slightly upwards, then cutting the silver skin off in strips. Alternatively, you can ask your butcher to remove the silver skin.

**PAN SAUCE:**

1 medium shallot, peeled and diced small (3 tablespoons)

1½ cups apple cider

1 tablespoon apple cider vinegar

1 tablespoon whole-grain Dijon mustard

2 (3-inch) sprigs fresh rosemary

2 tablespoons unsalted butter

For bonus material relating to this recipe, visit chefnathanlyon.com

YIELD: 8 TO 10 SERVINGS

TRI-TIP:

1 (2½-pound) tri-tip steak

SPICE RUB:

YIELD: 6 TABLESPOONS (ENOUGH FOR THREE TRI-TIPS)

1 tablespoon whole fennel seeds
(or 1 tablespoon plus 1 teaspoon ground fennel)

1 tablespoon whole coriander seeds
(or 2½ teaspoons ground coriander)

2 teaspoons whole cumin seeds
(or 1 tablespoon ground cumin)

1 teaspoon whole black peppercorns
(or 2 teaspoons ground black pepper)

½ tablespoon garlic powder

½ teaspoon ground chili powder

1½ tablespoons kosher salt

# ROAST SPICED TRI-TIP
## WITH ROSEMARY CANNELLINI BEAN PURÉE

1. If starting with whole spices, combine the fennel seeds, coriander seeds and cumin seeds in a small sauté pan and place over medium-low heat. Toast for approximately 4½ minutes total (stirring often) until you can begin to really smell the spices, and a few wisps of white smoke are seen. After 2½ minutes the spices may begin to pop. Transfer the seeds from the hot pan and allow to cool on a large plate before grinding.

2. Combine the cooled toasted seeds with the black peppercorns in a spice grinder (or dedicated coffee grinder) or mortar and pestle and process until finely ground. Mix the freshly ground spices with the garlic powder, chili powder and salt in a small bowl.

3. Place the tri-tip steak on a cutting board, pat dry, then rub the entire surface of the meat with one-third (2 tablespoons) of the spice mix. Allow to sit for 1 hour at room temperature. Store excess spice mix in a small airtight container with your other spices.

4. Adjust an oven rack to the middle position, then preheat the oven to 375°F.

5. Place the tri-tip, fat side down, on a parchment paper-lined sheet pan. Insert the tip of your digital thermometer probe lengthwise into the middle of the meat and roast, uncovered, for approximately 20 minutes.

6. Turn the tri-tip fat-side up and roast 15 minutes more, for 35 minutes total—or until your thermometer registers 135°F. When it beeps, it's done.

7. Remove the steak from the oven, transfer to a cutting board, cover loosely with foil and allow to rest at least 30 minutes prior to carving very thin slices against the grain.

## ROSEMARY CANNELLINI BEAN PUREE

1. In a large saucepan set over medium-low heat, add the olive oil, rosemary, salt, a few good grinds of pepper, the diced onion, and chile flakes. Cook, stirring occasionally, for 10 to 12 minutes, until the onions are soft and translucent.

2. Add the garlic and cook until fragrant, 1 minute.

3. Stir in the drained beans, the water, and the bay leaf. Cover, bring to a boil, then reduce the heat and simmer until the beans have softened, 15 minutes.

4. Turn off the heat. Remove the rosemary sprigs and bay leaf. Drain the beans, but reserve any of the liquid.

5. Pour the drained bean mixture into the food processor (or blender), season lightly with salt, pepper, and lemon juice, and blend until smooth, adding small amounts of the cooking liquid back into the beans to adjust the texture of the purée. Taste, and adjust the seasoning with additional salt, pepper, and lemon juice. Blend once more and cover to keep warm.

**ROSEMARY CANNELLINI BEAN PUREE:**

⅓ cup extra-virgin olive oil

2 (6-inch) sprigs fresh rosemary, bruised with your fingers

¼ teaspoon kosher salt

Freshly ground black pepper, to taste

2 large yellow onions, peeled and diced small (3 cups)

¹⁄₁₆ teaspoon crushed red chile pepper (chile flakes), or to taste

3 large garlic cloves, peeled and chopped roughly (1 tablespoon)

2 (15-ounce) cans white kidney beans (cannellini beans), rinsed and drained

⅓ cup hot water

1 dried bay leaf

1 teaspoon freshly squeezed lemon juice, plus more to taste

1 (2½- to 3-pound) boneless beef chuck roast

1½ teaspoons kosher salt, plus more to taste

1 teaspoon freshly ground black pepper, plus more to taste

4 tablespoons extra-virgin olive oil, divided

2 large yellow onions, peeled and diced medium (3 cups)

3 celery stalks, chopped roughly (1½ cups)

5 large carrots, peeled and chopped roughly (5 cups)

3 tablespoons tomato paste

3 large garlic cloves, peeled and chopped roughly (1 tablespoon)

2 cups red Zinfandel wine

4 cups chicken stock (recipe on page 38)

2 dried bay leaves

5 sprigs fresh thyme

1 pound small yellow potatoes (7 to 10), scrubbed

6 kumquats, halved and seeded

# POT ROAST
## WITH ROOT VEGETABLES AND KUMQUATS

As American as baseball, apple pie, and… pot roast? Sure! I mean, who doesn't love a good pot roast? It's sooooo easy, sooooo good, and gets better with time! Oh, and the kumquats? Just you wait. They lend the most delightful, subtle heady scent of orange that balances out the dish's richness.

Great food, Americana, and easy cleanup—that's a home run in my book every time.

1. Remove the roast from the refrigerator, pat dry, and season all sides with the salt and pepper. Allow the roast to sit at room temperature for 1 hour.

2. Adjust an oven rack to the middle position, then preheat the oven to 300°F. Open a few windows or turn on the oven hood/fan; it might get a little smoky.

3. Heat a small oven-safe pot over medium-high heat until hot, then add 1 tablespoon oil. It will most likely start to smoke. Immediately add the roast and brown on all sides, 2 minutes per side. Transfer the roast to a large plate and discard the oil.

4. Return the pot to medium-high heat. Add 2 tablespoons olive oil, the onion, celery, and carrots. Cook, stirring occasionally for 5 to 7 minutes until the onions are soft and translucent.

5. Add 1 additional tablespoon of olive oil, the tomato paste, and the garlic. Cook 2 minutes more, stirring often.

6. Add the wine and stir with a wooden spoon, loosening up any brown bits stuck to the bottom of the pan. Cook for 3 minutes more; it will begin to thicken just a bit.

Note: When shopping for your boneless beef chuck, look for a lot of marbling in the meat. Those white streaks are marbling, or fat.

It is the fat, in part, that gives this dish loads of flavor and keeps the meat moist. The total cooking time is just over 1 hour per pound of meat. Thus, a 2½-pound beef chuck roast will take approximately 2¾ hours to cook.

*"And, of course, the funniest food: kumquats."*

— GEORGE CARLIN

7. Stir in the stock, bay leaves, thyme, potatoes, and kumquats. Replace the roast in the pan. Depending on the size of your pot, the roast may be halfway or completely submerged.

8. Bring the pot just barely to a simmer, cover, and carefully place in the oven for 2 hours and 45 minutes. Remove from the oven.

9. Season to taste with salt and pepper. To serve, remove the roast and cut into pieces, or simply pull apart with two forks. Discard the bay leaves and thyme sprigs. Ladle pieces of the roast, vegetables, and broth into soup bowls.

# Ragù alla Bolognese

It's always good to have a recipe for a classic Italian meat sauce up your sleeve. My favorite being Bolognese, or "from Bologna," a sauce made with (among other things) pork, beef, wine, onions, and milk. My version of Bolognese doesn't need six hours to cook down, like others meat sauces out there, or even three hours. In fact, how about we agree to slowly simmer this flavorful Bolognese sauce for exactly one hour and call it a day. *Sì? Splendido!* Now that's *amore*.

1. Add the bacon and 1 tablespoon of olive oil to a small pot, then set over medium-low heat. Cook for approximately 5 to 6 minutes, stirring occasionally, until much of the fat has rendered off, and the bacon is just beginning to get nice and crispy.

2. Increase the heat to medium-high, then add the onions, carrots, and celery, a pinch of salt, and a few good grinds of pepper. Cook, stirring occasionally, for 8 to 10 minutes, until the vegetables begin to soften.

3. Add the garlic and tomato paste, stir, and cook for 2 minutes.

4. Add the meat, oregano and thyme. Cook, breaking the meat up with the back of a wooden spoon, until almost cooked through, 5 minutes.

5. Add the wine to the pot and cook, stirring occasionally, until the liquid begins to thicken slightly, approximately 5 minutes.

6. Stir in the half-and-half, tomatoes, and bay leaves. Increase the heat to high, bring to a simmer, then reduce the heat to low and gently simmer for 1 hour, stirring every 7 to 10 minutes. The finished sauce will still be a little bit thin as to be soaked up by the cooked pasta.

**YIELD: 6 TO 8 SERVINGS**

1 tablespoon extra-virgin olive oil

3 slices applewood smoked bacon, halved lengthwise and then cut crosswise into ¼-inch slices, (¾ cup)

2 medium yellow onions, peeled and diced small (2 cups)

5 medium carrots, peeled and chopped roughly (2½ cups)

3 stalks celery, diced medium (1½ cups)

7 large garlic cloves, peeled and chopped roughly (2 tablespoons plus 1 teaspoon)

¼ cup tomato paste

1 cup red wine (red Zinfandel, Merlot, or Cabernet Sauvignon)

1 pound ground chuck (82% lean)

1 pound fresh spicy Italian sausage (pork or turkey), removed from casing, approximately 5 links

¾ teaspoon finely chopped fresh oregano

5 sprigs fresh thyme

2 tablespoons kosher salt, plus more to taste

Freshly ground black pepper, to taste

1 (28-ounce) can diced tomatoes, undrained, preferably fire-roasted

½ cup half-and-half

Ingredients continued on next page »

2 dried bay leaves

1 (16-ounce) package of tagliatelle, pappardelle, or fettuccine pasta

Parmigiano-Reggiano cheese, not pre-grated, for serving

3 tablespoons finely chopped flat-leaf Italian parsley, for serving

7. Remove the thyme sprigs and bay leaves. Season to taste with salt and pepper.

8. Meanwhile, bring a small pot of water to a rolling boil, then add the salt.

9. Add the pasta to the boiling water and cook, stirring occasionally, until *al dente* (almost done, or "to the tooth").

10. Once done, drain without rinsing, then return the pasta to the pot. Immediately add half of the Bolognese sauce to the pasta and stir until evenly coated.

11. Serve in pasta bowls, topped with a scoop of Bolognese sauce.

12. Shave some Parmigiano-Reggiano onto each bowl with a vegetable peeler, then sprinkle with chopped parsley.

Note: Any leftover Bolognese makes one heck of a sloppy joe or meat sauce for fresh lasagna.

YIELD: APPROXIMATELY 50 MERINGUES

¾ cup egg whites (approximately 5 egg whites)

¾ cup granulated sugar, processed in a food processor until very fine, 1 minute

⅛ teaspoon cornstarch

½ teaspoon pure vanilla extract

For bonus material relating to this recipe, visit chefnathanlyon.com

# CRISPY VANILLA MERINGUES

So maybe you made a few cheesecakes, perhaps even a batch of ice cream or three. Before long you're going to find yourself with a container full of egg whites. What now? Well, you could make one heck of a huge egg white omelet. (Snooze.) Or, if you have a sweet tooth—or a mouthful of sweet teeth for that matter—I recommend you put those egg whites to use and make some crispy vanilla meringues. (Yay!) They're like little pillows of vanilla flavored dreams. Wait, what? Vanilla flavored dreams? That beats an egg white omelet any day.

1. Adjust an oven rack to the middle position, then preheat the oven to 210°F.

2. Combine the cornstarch and vanilla extract in a small bowl to make a slurry.

3. Place the egg whites in a clean and dry medium bowl and whip on medium speed with an electric mixer until just foamy.

4. Turn the mixer back on to medium and gradually add all of the sugar. Continue to beat until soft peaks form.

5. Whip in the slurry mixture. Increase the speed to high and whip until stiff peaks are achieved.

6. Dot the four corners of each of two sheet pans with some of the meringue batter.

7. Line the sheet pans with parchment paper. The dots of meringue batter will help to keep the parchment paper from curling up.

Note: After whipping the meringues, bake them right away or else they may begin to deflate and the texture may be compromised. Also, make meringues on a dry, sunny day, not a wet, rainy one. Too much moisture in the air will result in a sticky or tacky meringue, because sugar attracts moisture.

---

*"Dessert is probably the most important stage of the meal, since it will be the last thing your guests remember before they pass out all over the table."* — WILLIAM POWELL

8.  Using a piping bag with a medium star tip, or a good, old-fashioned tablespoon, pipe or spoon 1-inch to 1½-inch circles of meringue batter onto the parchment paper-lined sheet pans. Unlike cookies, meringues won't spread when baked, so less space is needed between them.

9.  Place the sheet pans in the oven and bake, uncovered, for 2½ hours. After 2½ hours, do not remove the meringues. Rather, turn off the oven and let the meringues cool for 1 hour, just to be sure the meringues are crunchy.

10. Store meringues in an airtight container, layered between sheets of wax or parchment paper.

# DOUBLE APPLE SPICE CAKE

Having made my fair share of spiced cakes over the years, starting in second grade with my dark rum-soaked spiced fruit cake I made as a Christmas present for my teacher, Mrs. Cottrell (she gave me an "A" for the cake), this recipe is my favorite. It has plenty of moisture from the applesauce, a great texture from the diced apple, and a well-rounded flavor from the spices. It tastes great in the morning when paired with a Latte or three, as a light afternoon snack with tea, and even though it isn't too sweet, it is just sweet enough to serve as a dessert. After your first bite, I think you'll agree—this recipe is an A+!

1. Adjust an oven rack to the middle position, then preheat the oven to 325°F.

2. Mix together the confectioners' sugar and 1 tablespoon butter in small bowl until thoroughly combined. Evenly coat the inside surface of a 10-inch fluted tube pan and transfer the prepared pan to the refrigerator to chill.

3. Whisk together the flour, baking powder, baking soda, salt, nutmeg, cinnamon, cloves, and allspice in a medium bowl.

4. Place the remaining 8 tablespoons butter, cut into three equal pieces, and the brown sugar in the bowl of an electric mixer. Using the paddle attachment, beat on medium until light and fluffy, 5 minutes.

5. Scrape down the sides of the bowl, return the mixer to medium, and add the eggs, one at a time to the butter mixture, waiting until each egg is fully incorporated before adding the next egg, and scraping the sides down after the third egg.

**YIELD: 10 TO 12 SERVINGS**

1 tablespoon confectioners' sugar, plus more for serving

9 tablespoons unsalted butter, divided

1½ cups dark brown sugar

5 large eggs

½ cup applesauce (recipe on page 242)

1 tablespoon pure vanilla extract

3 cups unbleached all-purpose flour

1 tablespoon baking powder

1 teaspoon kosher salt

½ teaspoon ground nutmeg

1½ tablespoons ground cinnamon

½ teaspoon ground cloves

1 teaspoon ground allspice

1 cup 2% or whole milk

1 large apple, such as Pink Lady, Rome, or McIntosh, peeled, cored, and diced small (2 cups)

1 cup toasted, salted walnuts, chopped roughly (recipe on page 42)

6. Continue beating and add the applesauce and vanilla. At this point the mixture will look disgusting—just terrible. Keep going. Everything will work out fine.

4. With the mixer set on the lowest setting, and working in three additions, alternately, add the flour mixture and the milk. Mix until just combined; do not overmix. The entire mixing process should only take approximately 1 minute.

5. Remove the bowl from the electric mixer. Using a spatula, gently fold in the diced apples and walnuts. The mixture will be on the thick side.

6. Pour the batter into the prepared fluted tube pan, and bake, uncovered, for exactly 1 hour, rotating the pan half way after 30 minutes. It'll be light brown and firm to the touch.

7. Remove the cake from the oven and allow to sit, undisturbed, for 15 minutes. During this time the cake will shrink slightly, making it easier to un-mold.

8. Turn the cake out onto a cookie rack to cool completely. Once the cake is totally cooled, use a small strainer to sift confectioners' sugar over top, or drizzle with vanilla caramel, slice, and serve.

# CHOCOLATE

1½ cups unbleached all-purpose flour

3 tablespoons natural unsweetened cocoa powder

1¼ teaspoons baking powder

⅛ teaspoon kosher salt

1 stick unsalted butter, cut into 8 pieces

1 cup dark brown sugar

2 large eggs

½ cup buttermilk

1 teaspoon pure vanilla extract

1 cup toasted almonds, chopped roughly

3 ounces dark chocolate (containing 60% to 62% cocoa solids), chopped roughly

1 cup dried cranberries

1½ tablespoons orange zest (zest of 3 small oranges), grated on a Microplane

# DOUBLE CHOCOLATE TOASTED ALMOND ORANGE ZEST CRANBERRY MUFFINS

(Say that five times fast)

This recipe has taken quite the wild ride. It began its journey nine months ago as a fresh vanilla plum cake. However, the resulting cake just wasn't that great. Back to the drawing board. I tried again and again, adding new ingredients each time: lemon zest, rosemary, chopped fruit: the list goes on. After each new attempt, the resulting cakes were good, but never great.

On April 1, 2011, April Fool's Day, I totally changed things up. I dropped the lemon zest and rosemary completely, replacing them with orange zest and cocoa powder. Yeah, baby! Then, I added some texture: chocolate and almonds—a perfect match. Finally, I tossed in some cranberries for that sweet-tart flavor. Voilà! My recipe had finally arrived: balance, texture, and flavor, in the cute shape of a muffin.

You know, sometimes you have to discover different ways that don't work before you find one that does. In this case, I discovered eleven ways that didn't work. That's a lot of baking, but boy, what a ride.

1. Adjust an oven rack to the middle position, then preheat the oven to 425°F. Place 12 (2½-ounce) paper baking cups in a muffin tin.

2. Whisk together the flour, cocoa powder, baking powder, and salt in a small bowl.

3. Combine the butter and brown sugar in a medium mixing bowl, then cream together with an electric mixer, using the paddle attachment, for a full 5 minutes on medium speed until light and fluffy, scraping down the sides as needed.

4.  Add one egg at a time, blending well on medium speed after each addition and scraping down the sides. Note: When adding the eggs, it may look a bit chunky, as if something has gone terribly wrong. Not to worry: that look is only temporary. Keep going! You're doing great.

5.  Reduce the speed to medium-low, add one-third of the flour mixture to the butter/egg mixture, and mix until just combined.

6.  Add half of the buttermilk and the vanilla extract, and mix until just combined.

7.  Add half the remaining flour, mix, then repeat with the remaining buttermilk and the rest of the flour; stir just until no flour is visible.

8.  Remove the bowl from the electric mixer, and fold in the chopped almonds, chopped chocolate, cranberries, and orange zest.

9.  Spoon ⅓ cup of batter into each of the 12 cups. Bake the muffins, uncovered, for 20 minutes, until the tops are rounded, and a toothpick inserted in the center of a muffin comes out clean.

10. Let the muffins cool slightly in the tin before transferring them to a rack, then allow the muffins to cool completely before enjoying them with a delightful expression and perhaps my good friend Latte to keep them company.

# TRIPLE CHOCOLATE BISCOTTI

**YIELD: 20 BISCOTTI**

**(GIVE OR TAKE, DEPENDING ON HOW MANY YOU EAT BEFORE YOU BRUSH THEM WITH CHOCOLATE.)**

I love espresso drinks. In fact, whenever I fly, I pack my cappuccino machine, burr grinder, and fresh beans from Jones Coffee Roasters in Pasadena, California in my carry-on luggage. That way, if my checked bag doesn't make the flight, I may not get my clothes, but at least I'll have Latte to keep me warm, a drink so important that I capitalize it. Now, what better to pair with Latte (oh, how I love thee) than a crunchy triple chocolate biscotti? Honestly, be it on the ground or at 36,000 feet, I can't think of a single thing.

**BISCOTTI:**

2 cups plus 2 tablespoons unbleached all-purpose flour, divided

⅓ cup natural unsweetened cocoa powder

¼ teaspoon kosher salt

½ teaspoon baking powder

½ teaspoon baking soda

1 stick unsalted butter, cut into 8 pieces

1 cup plus 1 tablespoon dark brown sugar, divided

2 large eggs

2 teaspoons pure vanilla extract

½ teaspoon almond extract

2 tablespoons orange zest (zest of 2 large oranges), grated on a Microplane

4 ounces dark chocolate (containing 60% to 72% cocoa solids), chopped roughly

1. Adjust an oven rack to the middle position, then preheat the oven to 300°F.

2. In a medium bowl, whisk together the flour, cocoa, salt, baking powder, and baking soda.

3. Place the butter and the brown sugar in the bowl of an electric mixer and, using the paddle attachment, cream on medium speed for 5 minutes until fluffy. Time it. After 5 minutes, scrape down the sides of the bowl.

4. With the mixer on medium, add the eggs one at a time, being sure the first egg is fully incorporated before adding the second egg. Scrape down the sides of the bowl again.

5. Turn the mixer to low speed and add the vanilla and almond extract.

6. Add the flour mixture and mix until it comes together as a rough dough, scraping down the sides of the bowl as needed.

7. Put in the chopped chocolate and zest and mix for 10 seconds. It will be a bit tacky. Not tacky like acid-washed jeans—those were cool. Rather, tacky, like modeling clay.

8. Flour the counter top and, using your hands, form the dough into a long tube, about 16 inches long by 2 inches in diameter.

9. Place the dough on a parchment paper-lined sheet pan, and bake, uncovered, for 45 minutes. It will spread slightly as it cooks.

10. Transfer the biscotti loaf to a cutting board and allow it to cool completely.

11. Using a serrated bread knife, slice across the loaf into ¾-inch thick pieces.

12. Lay the pieces on the parchment paper, cut side down, and return the sheet pan to the oven.

13. Bake at 300°F, uncovered, for 20 minutes, then turn them over and bake for 25 more minutes, for a total of 45 minutes.

14. Transfer the biscotti to a cookie rack placed over a sheet pan lined with parchment paper. Allow the biscotti to cool completely. Now they're ready for the chocolate bath.

**CHOCOLATE BATH:**

8 ounces roughly chopped dark chocolate (containing 60% to 72% cocoa solids)

1 tablespoon Amaretto liqueur

## CHOCOLATE BATH

1. Melt the chopped chocolate in a heatproof glass or metal bowl set over a saucepan of simmering water, stirring slowly to combine. The simmering water should not touch the bottom of the bowl.

2. Once melted, turn off the heat, and carefully remove the bowl.

3. Whisk in the Amaretto until fully combined.

4. Brush the chocolate onto one end of each biscotti, including the sides, leaving half free of chocolate.

5. Eat the chocolate that dripped down onto the parchment paper-lined tray below the rack.

6. Transfer the biscotti into the refrigerator until the chocolate is firm, then remove from the refrigerator and enjoy. Store layers of biscotti, separated by parchment paper, in an airtight container in the refrigerator.

½ cup granulated sugar

¼ cup natural unsweetened cocoa powder

2½ tablespoons cornstarch

2½ cups whole milk, divided

1 tablespoon unsalted butter

5 ounces dark chocolate (containing 60% to 72% cocoa solids), chopped finely

½ teaspoon pure vanilla extract

⅛ teaspoon kosher salt

# THE REAL DEAL CHOCOLATE PUDDING

My friend Lisa is a chocolate pudding connoisseur. Knowing this, I created this recipe recently for Lisa's birthday as small celebratory gesture before she and her friends went out to tear up the town. It went something like this: three beautiful women, all decked out in their finest attire, quickly entered my apartment. Not to slow their evening's momentum, I immediately presented Lisa with a spoon and my homemade chocolate pudding, topped with a dollop of my freshly made Madagascar vanilla whipped cream. After her first bite, Lisa slowly sat down, gazed directly into the pudding, smiled, and cooed, "Nummy." In Lisa-speak, that is a compliment of the highest regard. Now, if this pudding recipe could slow Lisa's roll during an evening of birthday debauchery, imagine the effect it will have on your family.

1. Combine the sugar, cocoa powder, and cornstarch in a medium saucepan.

2. Slowly whisk in ½ cup of the milk until smooth in texture and turn the heat to medium.

3. Whisking continuously, slowly pour in the remaining 2 cups of milk. Whisk for approximately 7 minutes, until the pudding thickens.

4. Remove the saucepan from the heat and slowly whisk in the butter, chocolate, vanilla extract, and salt until everything is melted and fully incorporated.

5. Using a teaspoon, sample some—just because.

6. Divide into 6 ramekins or dessert dishes and serve warm, or cover with plastic wrap, pressing directly on the surface to prevent a film from forming on the pudding, and refrigerate until chilled.

6 ounces dark chocolate (containing 60% to 72% cocoa solids), chopped roughly

1 (14-ounce) carton soft tofu, drained well and patted dry

1 teaspoon pure vanilla extract

¼ cup natural unsweetened cocoa powder

2 tablespoons honey, preferably orange blossom

Fleur de sel or kosher salt, to taste

# NON-DAIRY DOUBLE CHOCOLATE PUDDING

1. Melt the chopped chocolate in a heatproof glass or metal bowl, set over a saucepan of simmering water, stirring slowly to combine. The simmering water should not touch the bottom of the bowl. Once melted, remove from the heat to cool slightly.

2. Blend the tofu and vanilla extract in a blender on the lowest setting, or in a food processor, and process until smooth.

3. Add the melted chocolate, cocoa and honey and process until smooth.

4. Using a spatula to scrape down the sides, blend until fully mixed.

5. Spoon into dessert dishes and refrigerate until chilled. Before serving, sprinkle a tiny pinch of salt. Now, that's just ridiculously good.

Note: For adults, go ahead and add 1 tablespoon of either Grand Marnier or Amaretto. It's fun being an adult, isn't it?

# CHOCOLATE TRUFFLES FOUR WAYS

**YIELD: 40 TRUFFLES,
10 OF EACH FLAVOR**

1 cup heavy whipping cream

12 ounces dark chocolate (containing 60% to 72% cocoa solids), chopped finely

3 tablespoons unsalted butter, softened

1/16 teaspoon kosher salt

1/2 teaspoon pure vanilla extract

1/4 teaspoon dark rum, almond oil, peppermint oil, and orange oil

1/2 cup each: finely crushed hard mint candies, unsweetened shredded coconut, and finely chopped almonds, in separate bowls

1/4 cup natural unsweetened cocoa powder

Chocolate truffles are one of the most elegant bite-sized desserts out there. They're simple to prepare, make great gifts, and above all else, are fun to make! Ask your kids to give you a hand. Believe me, when they hear the word chocolate, they'll come running. What's more? From a single batch of melted chocolate, you can create a number of different flavors of chocolate truffles. That seems like reason enough to gather the family together and indulge, don't you think? As the saying goes, a family that gets wired on chocolate together, stays awake together. You know that saying, right? Right?

1. Pour the cream into a medium saucepan and stir slowly over medium-low heat to just a simmer, being careful not to let it to boil.

2. Combine the chopped chocolate, butter, and salt in a large bowl. Remove the cream from the heat, and pour it over the chocolate mixture. Cover with plastic wrap.

3. Let the mixture sit undisturbed for 1 minute, then uncover and slowly stir with a spatula until fully incorporated. Stir in the vanilla extract.

4. Divide the melted chocolate evenly among 4 small bowls. Add the dark rum to the first bowl, the orange oil to the second, the almond oil to the third, and the peppermint oil to the fourth. Cover each bowl loosely with plastic wrap and refrigerate until firm, approximately 1 1/2 to 2 hours.

5. Using a melon baller, small ice cream scoop, or teaspoon, scoop the chilled chocolate into one-teaspoon portions. Quickly roll each portion of chocolate between the palms of your hands to achieve a somewhat round ball.

*"As with most fine things, chocolate has its season. There is a simple memory aid that you can use to determine whether it is the correct time to order chocolate dishes: any month whose name contains the letter A, E, or U is the proper time for chocolate."*

— SANDRA BOYNTON

6.  Gently roll each chocolate ball in one of the four separate bowls filled with the cocoa powder, mint candies, shredded coconut, and toasted almonds.

7.  Transfer the coated truffles to a parchment paper-lined plate, cover loosely with plastic wrap and refrigerate until firm, approximately 30 minutes. Remove truffles from the refrigerator 15 minutes before serving.

Note: Enjoy a little heat with your chocolate? Try stirring in some ground cayenne pepper with some melted chocolate. Whoa! Spicy.

# Chocolate Pots de Crème

**YIELD: 9 SERVINGS**

2 cups half-and-half

½ cup whipping cream

4 tablespoons sugar, divided

7 ounces chocolate (containing 60% to 68% cocoa solids), chopped finely

5 large egg yolks

1 whole large egg

⅛ teaspoon kosher salt

1 teaspoon pure vanilla extract

Do not be fooled by the pretty photo. No, no. This dessert is not for the weak at heart, this is for hardcore chocolate lovers only. If you happen to be one of said chocolate lovers and are planning a gathering of fellow chocoholics any time soon, you can prepare these Chocolate Pots de Crème a few days ahead of time, seal them in plastic wrap, and pop them into the refrigerator. Oh, how I pity the person who wanders between a chocolate addict and these creamy chocolate delights. Don't say I didn't warn you.

1. Adjust an oven rack to the middle position, then preheat the oven to 300°F.

2. Pour the half-and-half, cream, and 2 tablespoons sugar into a medium saucepan.

3. Set the pan over medium heat and stir frequently until it comes to just barely a simmer, being careful not to let it boil.

4. Add the finely chopped chocolate and, using a whisk, stir slowly until the chocolate is fully incorporated, then remove from the heat.

5. Whisk together the egg yolks, eggs, the remaining sugar, and salt in a large bowl until the sugar is just incorporated into the eggs.

6. Next, slowly pour the warm creamy chocolate mixture into the eggs, stirring continuously with a whisk, until fully combined, then stir in the vanilla extract. This is your custard. Beautiful, isn't it? Well done.

7. Fill 9 (4-ounce) ramekins (which are 3-inches wide and 1½-inches deep) four-fifths full with the chocolate liquid loveliness and place them in a large roasting pan. Being careful not to spill any hot water inside the ramekins, add very hot tap water to the roasting pan, filling until approximately halfway up the sides of the ramekins.

Note: Try serving your pots de crème with a
nice dollop of freshly whipped cream, a drizzle
of caramel sauce (recipe on page 332), and
a raspberry. Sounds good, right?

8. Rest a sheet of parchment paper over the top of the ramekins and cover
   the entire pan with aluminum foil. Poke several small holes into the foil,
   and very carefully transfer the roasting pan to the oven.

9. Bake for 40 minutes.

10. Remove the pan from the oven, uncover, and transfer the ramekins (care-
    ful—they're hot!) to a cookie rack. Allow to cool completely.

11. Once cool, wrap the ramekins in plastic wrap and refrigerate for at least
    1 hour, until completely chilled. The pots de crème will firm up as they cool.

# Chocolate Toasted Almond-Amaretto Ice Cream

I've seen grown women melt after a few bites of this chocolate ice cream. Okay, not literally melt. Upon first bite, however, my friend Randie's eyes did, in fact, roll back as she braced herself on one arm. Her mouth then dropped open and out poured a barely audible, "Ohhhh myyyyyyy Gawwwwwd." Okay, so maybe she was overacting just a wee bit, but still, melting or not, last I checked, that's a pretty good sign.

1. Heat the half-and-half and ¼ cup sugar in a medium saucepan over medium heat.

2. Using a spatula (making sure to scrape the bottom of the saucepan occasionally), stir continuously until you see a few wisps of steam.

3. Remove the pan from the heat, add the chopped chocolate and cocoa powder, and whisk until fully combined.

4. In a medium bowl, using an electric mixer, whip the egg yolks and remaining ¼ cup sugar on high speed until the mixture is canary yellow in color, thick, and doubled in volume.

5. Reduce the speed to low and slowly add in the melted chocolate until combined.

6. Pour the mixture into the original medium saucepan. Pressing a spatula gently against the bottom of the pan, stir slowly and continuously and cook over medium-low heat until the custard thickens slightly, but do not let the mixture simmer or boil. Take your time.

**YIELD: 4 TO 6 SERVINGS**

2½ cups half-and-half

½ cup granulated sugar, divided

3 ounces dark chocolate (containing 60% to 72% cocoa solids), chopped finely

1 cup natural unsweetened cocoa powder

5 large egg yolks

2 teaspoons pure vanilla extract

⅛ teaspoon kosher salt

1 tablespoon plus 1 teaspoon Amaretto or Grand Marnier

¼ cup toasted almonds (see recipe on page 42), chopped finely

7. After seeing a few wisps of steam, immediately remove from the heat and strain through a fine mesh colander into a wide medium bowl. Stir in the vanilla, salt, and Amaretto or Grand Marnier.

8. Place this bowl into a slightly larger bowl that is filled ⅓ of the way up with ice and water. Slowly stir the chocolate mixture until it is cool to the touch. Cover the bowl with plastic wrap, then refrigerate for 8 hours. Cooling the mix before churning will give a smoother texture.

9. Pour the chilled mixture into the ice cream machine and churn until a soft-serve consistency is achieved.

10. Transfer to a large container, stir in the chopped almonds, cover with plastic wrap, pressing the plastic wrap to the surface of the ice cream, and freeze until very firm, at least 5 hours.

11. Serve in dessert dishes with chopped almonds sprinkled on top, or go old school and scoop some into an ice cream cone.

Note: Don't have an ice cream machine? No problem. Surely you love a creamy, fudgy ice pop, yes? Great. Then grab yourself a plastic ice pop container, fill it up with the ice cream base, pop in the handles, and freeze. I swear you're going to love it.

YIELD: 8 SOUFFLÉS

3 tablespoons unsalted butter, plus more for preparing the ramekins

¼ cup granulated sugar, divided, plus more for preparing the ramekins

¼ cup unbleached all-purpose flour

2 tablespoons natural unsweetened cocoa powder

2 tablespoons honey, preferably orange blossom

1¼ cups whole milk

¼ teaspoon pure vanilla extract

5 large eggs, separated

3 ounces dark chocolate (containing 60% to 72% cocoa solids), chopped finely

Confectioners' sugar, for garnish

# CHOCOLATE SOUFFLÉ

Chocolate soufflés are pure magic. Pop them into the oven, and minutes later, out come puffy columns of chocolate heaven. Yes, that's magic. They're not that difficult to make either—really. For parties, you can make the soufflé base well ahead of time. Then, when you're ready for dessert, simply whip the egg whites, fold them into the base, and put them into the oven. You never know, your guests may just spontaneously applaud your efforts. If that isn't a magical moment, I don't know what is.

1. Using a pastry brush—or your finger—coat the entire inside surface of eight (4-ounce) ramekins (which are 3-inches wide and 1½-inches deep) with a thin layer of softened butter, brushing from the bottom upwards.

2. Add 1 teaspoon granulated sugar to each ramekin. Tilt the ramekin down at a slight angle and rotate the ramekin to allow any excess granulated sugar to spill out. The sugar acts like a stepladder for the soufflé to climb as it bakes.

3. Using your thumb, wipe any excess granulated sugar from the rim of the ramekins. Refrigerate the prepared ramekins until needed.

4. Adjust an oven rack to the middle position, then preheat the oven to 400°F.

5. Melt 3 tablespoons butter in a medium saucepan over very low heat, then add the flour and cocoa.

6. Whisk every few seconds for 2 minutes until completely combined. It will ultimately look like thick peanut butter. This is your roux, which will give your soufflé structure and keep it from deflating so quickly. Remove from the heat.

Note: This is one recipe where you will definitely want to have all of your ingredients prepared, measured, and ready to go before cooking.

7. Combine the honey and the milk in a second small saucepan, and slowly warm until a low simmer is achieved.

8. Whisk the honey and milk mixture into the roux and whisk until smooth. This mixture will get thick like a wet paste; don't panic. Remove it from the heat.

9. Stir in the chopped chocolate and vanilla extract, until it looks... like a thick, smooth chocolate paste. Surprise!

10. Whisk the egg yolks with 2 tablespoons granulated sugar in a large bowl until well-combined and the granulated sugar is dissolved.

11. Whisk the wet chocolate paste mixture into the yolks until smooth. Cover with plastic wrap. This is your base.

12. Whip the egg whites on high speed using an electric mixer (in a very clean and dry metal or glass bowl—no plastic) until just frothy.

13. Add the remaining 2 tablespoons granulated sugar and continue to whip on high speed until medium-firm peaks are achieved.

14. Using a spatula, fold the egg whites slowly into the base, one-third of the total volume at a time, until fully incorporated.

15. Transfer the ramekins from the refrigerator to a sheet pan. Ladle the soufflé batter into the prepared ramekins, level with the rim.

16. Run the side of your thumb around the inside edge of the soufflé dish. The ramekins will resemble very short top hats with center circles slightly higher than the outer edges.

17. Transfer the sheet pan to the oven. Bake, uncovered, for 16 to 17 minutes, until the outside top edges of the soufflés are golden brown.

18. Remove the sheet pan from the oven, and serve immediately with a dusting of confectioners' sugar.

# MOLTEN CHOCOLATE CAKE
## WITH VANILLA CARAMEL SAUCE

Nothing quite compares to the WOW! factor of a molten chocolate cake. I'm still like a kid when I see it on a restaurant menu, grinning widely, and pointing eagerly at the selection. Now, this isn't a chocolate cake like your sister used to make in her toy oven. This is a grown-up dessert, but it's just about as easy to make. In fact, when you realize that something so delicious, found on most dessert menus across the country, can be so easily made at home, you just gotta try it. For ages 8 to adult.

1. Adjust an oven rack to the middle position, then preheat the oven to 375°F.

2. Butter the insides of six (4-ounce) ramekins (which are 3-inches wide and 1½-inches deep), then dust the insides with the cocoa: while tilting the ramekin down at a slight angle, rotate the ramekin to allow any excess cocoa to spill out from the first ramekin into the second ramekin, and so on, until all of the ramekins are dusted evenly with cocoa. Put the prepared ramekins in the refrigerator.

3. Melt together the butter and chocolate in a heatproof glass or metal bowl, set over (not in) simmering water, stirring occasionally until fully combined. Once combined, remove the bowl from the heat to cool slightly.

4. Place the eggs, sugar, and salt in a medium bowl, and using an electric mixer, whisk on high until tripled in size, fluffy and thickened. It will look like a cloud of sweet love.

5. Whisk in the vanilla extract and cayenne pepper.

**YIELD: 6 SERVINGS**

1 stick unsalted butter (8 tablespoons), plus more for preparing the ramekins

2 teaspoons natural unsweetened cocoa powder

7 ounces dark chocolate (containing 60% to 72% cocoa solids), chopped roughly

4 large eggs

¼ cup granulated sugar

1⁄16 teaspoon kosher salt

1 teaspoon pure vanilla extract

⅛ teaspoon ground cayenne pepper

2 tablespoons unbleached all-purpose flour

6.  Using a tiny strainer, sift the flour evenly over the whisked eggs, then whisk in the melted chocolate, on medium-high, until thickened, glossy and well combined, 1 minute. It will be thick, like brownie mix.

7.  Transfer the chilled ramekins onto a baking sheet, distribute the batter evenly into the prepared ramekins (approximately four-fifths of the way full) and bake, uncovered, for 17 minutes. Set your digital timer.

8.  Remove the ramekins from the oven, and let the cakes cool for 1 minute. This allows the cake to shrink just enough to turn out easily onto a plate.

9.  Turn the cakes out onto plates. If necessary, loosen the cakes from the sides using a paring knife, running the knife around the inside rim of the ramekin. Cover each cake with a dessert plate, then carefully (they're hot!) invert each one. The cake should come right out.

10. Serve immediately with a small drizzle of vanilla caramel (see recipe on page 332). When your guests cut into the cake, the center should slowly ooze onto the plate.

11. Lean back. Bask in the glory.

1 cup granulated sugar

3 tablespoons water

¾ cup heavy whipping cream, divided

½ teaspoon pure vanilla extract


For bonus material relating to this recipe,
visit chefnathanlyon.com

# VANILLA CARAMEL SAUCE

Let me share with you the three keys to success for making this insanely good dessert: one, you will need a good-quality pot for even heating and a glass lid, if possible, to monitor the progress of your caramel. Two, do not walk away from the caramel as it is cooking because after about 8 minutes, the caramel will darken somewhat quickly, and will burn if left unattended. Most importantly, number three: once made, grab a spoonful of peanut butter, dip it into the warm vanilla caramel sauce, spread that onto a large slice of crisp apple, then enjoy with a block of chocolate. Easy as one, two, three!

1. Combine the sugar with the water in a heavy saucepan—it will look like wet sand—and cover with a glass lid. Do not stir.

2. Place over medium-low heat. After approximately 8 to 10 minutes you will see the color of the sugar darken slightly to a light golden tan. At this point, swirl the saucepan to ensure that one part of the caramel doesn't cook faster than another part.

3. Reduce the heat to low, remove the lid, and continue to cook until a light brown caramel color is achieved, swirling the pan as necessary.

4. Carefully drizzle the cream over the sugar (the mixture is going to bubble up quite a lot).

5. Stir slowly with a wooden spoon until fully combined.

6. Add the vanilla and stir 1 minute until smooth. Remove from the heat and transfer to a small heat-proof bowl to cool slightly before use. Keep in mind the caramel is very hot, so be careful.

7. Any leftover caramel should be used to make caramel Lattes.

# BIOGRAPHY

Chef Nathan Lyon is known to television viewers across the country for his simple, innovative cuisine featuring fresh, local ingredients. Chef and co-host of *Growing A Greener World* (PBS), Nathan was the creator and host of *A Lyon in the Kitchen* (Discovery Health and Fit TV), among the final four on the second season of *The Next Food Network Star*, and appeared as a guest chef and expert on *Home Made Simple* (TLC) and *Real Simple Real Life* (TLC).

After graduating from James Madison University with a Bachelor of Science in Health Science and a minor in Public Health, Nathan backpacked his way across Europe, learning about local customs, culture, and cuisine. Although every town and country along Nathan's journey provided its own culinary lesson, the watershed moment occurred in an outdoor market just outside of Florence, Italy: an old woman, agog at the massive amount of produce Nathan was stockpiling, eagerly asked, "Why are you buying so much food? Why not just buy fresh every day?" Nathan immediately dumped out half his basket and began pondering those two simple questions. It was in that market, clutching a wheel of cheese, that Nathan discovered his truth: great food starts fresh.

Laden with ideas and information, Nathan headed home, eventually opting for culinary school at Le Cordon Bleu in Los Angeles, where he earned a Culinary Arts degree. Since that time, Nathan has worked in many restaurants, both in and out of the kitchen and, has also worked with local growers in California farmers markets for over a decade. He has cooked for the Inspector General, cooked and spoken at numerous charity functions, is one of Monterey Bay Aquarium's 2011 Sustainable Seafood Ambassadors, and has even written and co-illustrated (with his older brother, Craig) a children's adventure book, *Sam the Clam*.

These days, when Nathan isn't shooting a show or cooking a delicious meal, you can find him shopping at the local farmers market and advising customers how to pick, store, and prepare fresh produce.

# REFERENCES

## FARMS AND FARMERS

Adams Olive Ranch
1200 S. Aster Street
Lindsay, California 93247
559-920-0533
agoliveman@gmail.com
agserviceonline.com

Arata Pumpkin Farm
185 Verde Road
Half Moon Bay, California 94019
650-726-7548
info@aratapumpkinfarm.com
aratapumpkinfarm.com

Bautista Family Organic Date Ranch
93800 Hammond Road
Mecca, California 92254
760-396-2337
7hotdates.com

Bernard Ranches
*(Citrus and Avocados)*
15870 Winters Lane
Riverside, California 92504
951-850-1404

Bill's Bees *(Honey)*
12640 Little Tujunga Canyon
Lake View Terrace, California 91342
billsbees@wildblue.net
818-312-1691

Briar Patch
*(Fresh Fruits and Vegetables)*
Fresno, California
818-667-4752

Clearwater Farms *(Mushrooms)*
California

Gloria's Fresh Fruits and Vegetables
Oxnard, California
tamai@aol.com
805-279-4172

Life's a Choke
*(Artichokes and Asparagus)*
Lompoc, California
805-588-5482

Ken's Top Notch Produce
*(Fresh Fruits)*
Reedley, California
kwlee72@gmail.com

McGrath Family Farms
*(Fresh Fruits and Vegetables)*
1012 West Ventura Blvd.
Camarillo, CA 93010
Markets: 805-983-0333
Office: 805-485-4210
Restaurant Deliveries: 805-983-1211
mcgrathfamilyfarm@gmail.com
mcgrathfamilyfarm.com

Peter Lee
*(Herbs and Vegetable Plants)*
peterblee54@yahoo.com

Roland Tamai
*(Fresh Fruits and Vegetables)*
Camarillo and Oxnard, California
rtamai@aol.com

Salisbury Vineyards
6985 Ontario Road
San Luis Obispo, California 93405
805-595-9463
harvest@salisburyvineyards.com
salisburyvineyards.com

Soledad Goats *(Goat Cheese)*
6501 Backus Road
Mojave, CA 93501
661-824-4514
soledadgoats@wildblue.net
soledadgoats.com

T & D Farms
*(Fresh Fruits and Vegetables)*
12224 San Timoteo Canyon Road
Redlands, California 92473
909-648-6002

Weiser Family Farms
*(Root Vegetables and Melons)*
19247 Highline Rd.
Tehachapi, California 93561
weiserfamilyfarms.com

Windrose Farm
*(Fresh Fruits and Vegetables)*
5750 El Pharo Road
Paso Robles, California 93446
805-239-3757
windrosefarm.org

Yasutomi Farms *(Asian Vegetables)*
Pico Rivera and North Long Beach,
California
562-201-6104
yasutomifarms@gmail.com

## BOOKS

*The Art of Simple Food: Notes, Lessons, and Recipes from a Delicious Revolution,* by Alice Waters. New York: Clarkson Potter/Publishers, 2007.

*The Associated Press Stylebook and Briefing on Media Law,* edited by Darrell Christian, Sally Jacobsen, and David Minthorn. New York: Basic Books, 2011.

*Culinary Artistry,* by Andrew Dornenburg and Karen Page. New Jersey: John Wiley & Sons, Inc., 1996.

*The Elements of Style,* by William Strunk, Jr. and E. B. White. New York: Dover Publications, Inc., 2006.

*The Flavor Bible: The Essential Guide to Culinary Creativity, Based on the Wisdom of America's Most Imaginative Chefs,* by Karen Page and Andrew Dornenburg. New York: Little, Brown and Company, 2008.

*Farmer John's Cookbook: The Real Dirt on Vegetables, Seasonal Recipes and Stories from a Community Supported Farm,* by Farmer John Peterson and Angelic Organics. Utah: Gibbs Smith, 2006.

*Food Lover's Companion: Comprehensive Definitions of Nearly 6,000 Food, Drink, and Culinary Terms,* by Sharon Tyler Herbst. 3rd ed. New York: Barron's Educational Series, Inc., 2001.

*Keys to Good Cooking: A Guide to Making the Best of Foods and Recipes,* by Harold McGee. New York: Penguin Press, 2010.

*Melissa's Great Book of Produce: Everything You Need to Know about Fresh Fruits and Vegetables,* by Cathy Thomas. New Jersey: John Wiley & Sons, Inc., 2006.

*New Good Food: Shopper's Pocket Guide to Organic, Sustainable, and Seasonal Whole Foods,* by Margaret M. Wittenberg. California: Ten Speed Press, 2008.

*On Food and Cooking: The Science and Lore of the Kitchen, Completely Revised and Updated,* by Harold McGee. New York: Scribner, 2004.

*The Produce Bible: Essential Ingredient Information and More than 200 Recipes for Fruits, Vegetables, Herbs & Nuts,* by Leanne Kitchen. New York: Stewart, Tabori & Chang, 2007.

*The Recipe Writer's Handbook: Revised and Expanded,* by Barbara Gibbs Ostmann and Jane L. Baker. New Jersey: John Wiley & Sons, Inc., 2001.

*Sunday Suppers at Lucques: Seasonal Recipes from Market to Table,* by Suzanne Goin. New York: Alfred A. Knopf, 2005.

*The Visual Food Encyclopedia.* Montreal, Quebec: Les Éditions Quebec/Amerique Inc., 1996.

*The Zuni Cafe Cookbook: A Compendium of Recipes & Cooking Lessons from San Francisco's Beloved Restaurants,* by Judy Rogers. New York: W. W. Norton & Company, Inc., 2002.

## BUSINESSES

The Bastion (bastionrestaurant.com)
Bel Gioioso Cheese, Inc. (belgioioso.com)
Calphalon (calphalon.com)
Civia (civiacycles.com)
Fabrik Magazine (fabrikmagazine.com)
Guittard Chocolate Company (guittard.com)
The Icon (iconla.com)
Jones Coffee Roasters (jonescoffee.com)
KCRW (kcrw.com)
Le Creuset (lecreuset.com)
Lucini Italia (lucini.com)
Lucques Restaurant (lucques.com)
McCall's Meat & Fish Co. (mccallsmeatandfish.com)
Microplane (microplane.com)
Miyas Sushi (miyassushi.com)
My Spice Sage (myspicesage.com)
Nueske's (nueskes.com)
Paul Soady (paulsoady.com)

TCHO (tcho.com)
The Village Bakery and Cafe (thevillagebakeryandcafe.com)
Victorinox (victorinox.com)

## MUSICIANS

Fair Market Band (fairmarketband.com)
Hisao Shinagawa (hisaoshinagawa@gmail.com)
Phillip "Professor Pitt" Colas (professorpitt.com)

## WEBSITES

The Cook's Thesaurus
*Cooking Encyclopedia—ingredients and kitchen tools*
foodsubs.com

Local Harvest
*Directory of organic and local food sources in the United States*
localharvest.org

Monterey Bay Aquarium
*Sustainable Seafood Resource*
montereybayaquarium.org

# INDEX

THANKS, LATTE!